HEBREWS

BELIEF

A Theological Commentary on the Bible

GENERAL EDITORS

Amy Plantinga Pauw

William C. Placher†

HEBREWS

D. STEPHEN LONG

First edition
Published by Westminster John Knox Press
Louisville, Kentucky

11 12 13 14 15 16 17 18 19 20—10 9 8 7 6 5 4 3 2 1

Book design by Drew Stevens
Cover design by Lisa Buckley
Cover art: © David Chapman/Design Pics/Corbis

Library of Congress Cataloging-in-Publication Data

Long, D. Stephen
Hebrews / D. Stephen Long. — 1st ed.
p. cm. — (Belief)
Includes bibliographical references (p.) and indexes.
ISBN 978-0-664-23251-1 (alk. paper)
1. Bible. N.T. Hebrews—Commentaries. 2. Bible. N.T. Hebrews—Theology. I. Title.
BS2775.53.L66 2011
227'.8707—dc23

2011023668

PRINTED IN THE UNITED STATES OF AMERICA

♾ The paper used in this publication meets the minimum requirements of the American National Standard for Information Sciences—Permanence of Paper for Printed Library Materials, ANSI Z39.48-1992

Westminster John Knox Press advocates the responsible use of our natural resources. The text paper of this book is made from 30% post-consumer waste.

In gratitude for the sustaining grace
of those other horsemen of the apocalypse,
George Kalantzis, L. Edward Phillips,
and Brent Waters.

The scope of [Hebrews] is to confirm their faith in Christ: and this [the author] does by demonstrating [Christ's] glory. All the parts of it are full of the most earnest and pointed admonitions and exhortations: and they go on in one tenor, the particle *therefore* everywhere connecting the doctrine and the use.

—John Wesley, *Explanatory Notes Upon the New Testament*

Contents

Publisher's Note

William C. Placher worked with Amy Plantinga Pauw as a general editor for this series until his untimely death in November 2008. Bill brought great energy and vision to the series, and was instrumental in defining and articulating its distinctive approach and in securing theologians to write for it. Bill's own commentary for the series was the last thing he wrote, and Westminster John Knox Press dedicates the entire series to his memory with affection and gratitude.

William C. Placher, LaFollette Distinguished Professor in Humanities at Wabash College, spent thirty-four years as one of Wabash College's most popular teachers. A summa cum laude graduate of Wabash in 1970, he earned his master's degree in philosophy in 1974 and his Ph.D. in 1975, both from Yale University. In 2002 the American Academy of Religion honored him with the Excellence in Teaching Award. Placher was also the author of thirteen books, including *A History of Christian Theology, The Triune God, The Domestication of Transcendence, Jesus the Savior, Narratives of a Vulnerable God,* and *Unapologetic Theology.* He also edited the volume *Essentials of Christian Theology,* which was named as one of 2004's most outstanding books by both *The Christian Century* and *Christianity Today* magazines.

Series Introduction

Belief: A Theological Commentary on the Bible is a series from Westminster John Knox Press featuring biblical commentaries written by theologians. The writers of this series share Karl Barth's concern that, insofar as their usefulness to pastors goes, most modern commentaries are "no commentary at all, but merely the first step toward a commentary." Historical-critical approaches to Scripture rule out some readings and commend others, but such methods only begin to help theological reflection and the preaching of the Word. By themselves, they do not convey the powerful sense of God's merciful presence that calls Christians to repentance and praise; they do not bring the church fully forward in the life of discipleship. It is to such tasks that theologians are called.

For several generations, however, professional theologians in North America and Europe have not been writing commentaries on the Christian Scriptures. The specialization of professional disciplines and the expectations of theological academies about the kind of writing that theologians should do, as well as many of the directions in which contemporary theology itself has gone, have contributed to this dearth of theological commentaries. This is a relatively new phenomenon; until the last century or two, the church's great theologians also routinely saw themselves as biblical interpreters. The gap between the fields is a loss for both the church and the discipline of theology itself. By inviting forty contemporary theologians to wrestle deeply with particular texts of Scripture, the editors of this series hope not only to provide new theological resources for the church, but also to encourage all theologians to pay more attention to Scripture and the life of the church in their writings.

We are grateful to the Louisville Institute, which provided funding for a consultation in June 2007. We invited theologians, pastors, and biblical scholars to join us in a conversation about what this series could contribute to the life of the church. The time was provocative and the results were rich. Much of the series' shape owes to the insights of these skilled and faithful interpreters, who sought to describe a way to write a commentary that served the theological needs of the church and its pastors with relevance, historical accuracy, and theological depth. The passion of these participants guided us in creating this series and lives on in the volumes.

As theologians, the authors will be interested much less in the matters of form, authorship, historical setting, social context, and philology—the very issues that are often of primary concern to critical biblical scholars. Instead, this series' authors will seek to explain the theological importance of the texts for the church today, using biblical scholarship as needed for such explication but without any attempt to cover all of the topics of the usual modern biblical commentary. This thirty-six-volume series will provide passage-by-passage commentary on all the books of the Protestant biblical canon, with more extensive attention given to passages of particular theological significance.

The authors' chief dialogue will be with the church's creeds, practices, and hymns; with the history of faithful interpretation and use of the Scriptures; with the categories and concepts of theology; and with contemporary culture in both "high" and popular forms. Each volume will begin with a discussion of *why* the church needs this book and why we need it *now*, in order to ground all of the commentary in contemporary relevance. Throughout each volume, text boxes will highlight the voices of ancient and modern interpreters from the global communities of faith, and occasional essays will allow deeper reflection on the key theological concepts of these biblical books.

The authors of this commentary series are theologians of the church who embrace a variety of confessional and theological perspectives. The group of authors assembled for this series represents more diversity of race, ethnicity, and gender than any other commentary series. They approach the larger Christian tradition with a critical respect, seeking to reclaim its riches and at the same time to acknowledge its shortcomings. The authors also aim to make available to readers a wide range of contemporary theological voices from many parts of the world. While it does recover an older genre of writing, this series is not an attempt to retrieve some idealized past. These commentaries have learned from tradition, but they are most importantly commentaries for today. The authors share the conviction that their work will be more contemporary, more faithful, and more radical, to the extent that it is more biblical, honestly wrestling with the texts of the Scriptures.

William C. Placher
Amy Plantinga Pauw

Acknowledgments

I am grateful to William Placher of blessed memory, Amy Plantinga Pauw, and Donald K. McKim for the opportunity to write this theological commentary. When first asked to do so, I was ambivalent and wondered if another commentary on Hebrews was needed. After having read so many fine commentaries ancient and modern, I continue to wonder. Yet just as the faithful must continue to read and hear this important sermon, so I reckon we should continue to comment on it. If this commentary prompts anyone to pick up Hebrews and read through it carefully, then it will have been worth it.

Writing this commentary has been a duty of delight. I conveyed to Donald McKim that I thought every theologian should do this first in her or his career. Theology will be enriched once theologians are more attentive to Scripture, and biblical scholars to theology. Sometimes we fear doing this because of the disciplinary division of labor in the university and seminary. Sometimes we theologians fear looking too confessional or ecclesial, as if knowing the latest philosophical or political trend matters more than submersion in Scripture. Fortunately, these fears seem to be subsiding, opening up new possibilities. Placher, Pauw, and McKim recognized this and made this endeavor possible, sharing its labor with us. I am in their debt.

I have attempted to listen to a number of voices in writing this commentary, voices from the church and university, voices ancient and contemporary. I am particularly indebted to the Church of the Servant King in Eugene, Oregon, for inviting me to do lectures on Hebrews in spring 2008. Their comments on my initial forays into Hebrews were immensely helpful. My home church, Evanston First

United Methodist Church, also invited me to teach a Sunday school class on Hebrews, for which I remain grateful. Working through Hebrews with such dedicated folk helped me clarify many things. My first doctoral seminar at Marquette University, spring 2008, was on hermeneutics and biblical interpretation in which we tried to get a fix on what theological interpretation is. That seminar mixed graduate students from Garrett-Evangelical, where I formerly taught, with those from Marquette, and doctoral students in Scripture with those in theology. It was a rich and memorable class even if we were often better at figuring out what theological interpretation is not, rather than what it is. I am grateful for the assistance provided by Brad Anderson, Wesley Bidde, Rusty Brian, Jimmy Cooper, Joseph Flipper, Ryan Hansen, Geoff Holsclaw, Matthew Keiser, Jackson Lashier, Catherine Marcy, Rebecca Meier-Rao, Sara Martin, and Jason Roberts in thinking about theological interpretation. My New Testament colleague Rodrigo Morales has been of immense help in thinking about theological interpretation and Hebrews. I am grateful for his conversations, suggested readings, and the "Scripture Project" at Marquette that seeks to break down the disciplinary walls between theology and Scripture. A number of persons read the following manuscript in part or whole. I am much obliged for their assistance. Randy Cooper is a United Methodist pastor who embodies what it means to be a scholar-pastor. He made invaluable comments on my work, especially pointing out to me in all charity where it was dull and insipid. I am in his debt for speaking the truth. David Moffitt, who is currently a visiting professor of New Testament at Duke Divinity School, made copious comments throughout the text. Conversation with him kept me from errors and showed me Hebrews in a new light. We all anxiously await his published work on Hebrews; it will shake things up so that what is unshakable will remain. Nathan Kerr was gracious to read my comments on apocalyptic, and my critique of his work. He helped me clarify where he and I disagree and why. I remain in his debt.

My wife, Ricka, and my children, Lindsey, Rebecca, and Jonathan, provide so much material from everyday life that found its way into this work, but which will and should remain unknown to the reader. I am grateful that God enriched my life with them as we struggle together in figuring out what it means to live together and "let mutual love continue."

Finally I should explain why this text is dedicated to the other horsemen of the apocalypse. I spent nine years working in a mainline Protestant seminary, which to quote Dickens was the worst and best of times. It was truly an apocalyptic experience unlike anything else I have known in my life as students and faculty debated and upended, revised and defended, nearly every aspect of the Christian faith and life. To say the least, there was never a dull moment. One student, frustrated by those of us who defended Christian tradition and demanded students know it through difficult exams, referred to us as "the four horsemen of the apocalypse." The title stuck and was passed down from student to student. I am grateful to the other three horsemen for helping me "hold fast the confession" through their prayers, conversation, and support; for this reason I dedicate the book to them.

Christmas Eve, 2010

Abbreviations

BGBE	Beiträge zur Geschichte der biblischen Exegese
KJV	King James Version
LW	Luther's Works
LXX	Septuagint (Greek OT)
NIV	New International Version
NRSV	New Revised Standard Version
SNTSMS	Society for New Testament Studies Monograph Series

Introduction: Why Hebrews? Why Now?

Hebrews is a fascinating sermon that has guided the church in and out of controversies. Its relevance is found precisely in its irrelevance, its willingness to stand in tension with some of our contemporary sensibilities. It questions whether a world that can be laid out on a technological grid, for all its advantages, is the only one that is. Hebrews matters so much in the present for at least the following three reasons. First, it presents a sermon integrating doctrine, ethics, and politics, helping the faithful negotiate troubled times. Second, its metaphysical assumptions invite us into a robust world that is not as "flat" as many metaphysical assumptions that have held sway since the dominance of science. To hear it well we will need, at least temporarily, to suspend belief in our own modern metaphysics. Hebrews lets us do this without losing the significant gains the modern era brought; for it encourages neither speculative mythology nor superstition. Christ's humanity matters too much for that. Related to these first two is an important third reason for Hebrews' contemporary significance: it teaches us how to read Scripture after Christ's odd triumph.

Negotiating Troubled Times

Hebrews has guided the church through some of its most significant controversies. Sometimes it did so as the solution to a problem, sometimes as a problem that still seeks solution. Its words helped resolve the Trinitarian and christological controversies during the fourth and fifth centuries. Its explanatory power demonstrated its canonical legitimacy. When the ecumenical council gave definitive answers to those controversies, it also taught us to read Hebrews. This was easy to do since Hebrews lends itself so well to that reading; it was often the council's source.

The council fathers never imagined they were reading into Hebrews their own theological commitments; those commitments had been forged by engaging, debating, and coming to terms with what Hebrews taught in light of ongoing theological developments. But Hebrews has not always been the solution to controversy; it has also been its source, as it was in theological controversies in the sixteenth century. Calvin used Hebrews to argue against the Catholic doctrine of the repetition of the sacrifice in the Mass, its theology of priesthood, and its doctrine of faith. The Heidelberg Catechism took this argument so far as to reject the Catholic understanding of the Mass in its question 80. It was "a denial of the one sacrifice and suffering of Jesus Christ," and therefore "a condemnable idolatry." This was not originally in the catechism, but may have been added by Calvin's protégé, Caspar Olevianus, in response to the Roman Catholic Council of Trent's condemnation of the Protestant doctrine of justification by faith.[1] Significant progress has been made in overcoming these Protestant and Catholic condemnations of each other. In 1998 the Christian Reformed Church undertook a serious investigation of question 80 and in 2006 revised it accordingly, acknowledging that although differences remained, question 80 misrepresented Catholic teaching. Likewise in 1999 the "Joint Declaration" between Catholics and Lutherans clarified and found convergence between their teachings on justification and its dependence on Christ's one, final, and sufficient sacrifice, which divided them since Trent. Progress has been made, but these controversies remain unsettled, and our churches cannot yet "meet together" (Heb. 10:25); we still lack full communion. Nonetheless on the matter of Christology, Catholics and Protestants now read Hebrews in communion. These old controversies have been resolved, but new

1. See the Christian Reformed Church in North America document, "The Lord's Supper and the Roman Catholic Mass," at www.crcna.org/site_uploads/uploads/Lord'sSupper%26RCMass.pdf, p. 7. I am indebted to Amy Plantinga Pauw for pointing this out to me.

> **Rhetorical-Word Outline**
>
> **Using Aristotle's rhetorical elements, the structure would look like this:**
>
> ***Exordium* and *Narratio* (1:1–4:3) providing an introduction and narration of the key themes to be presented and defended.**
>
> ***Probatio* (4:14–10:31) that sets forth the argument.**
>
> ***Peroratio* (10:32–13:25) that summarizes and amplifies the main argument.**

ones, less ecclesially defined, have also emerged. Hebrews' language of Christ's atonement as "sacrifice" stirs up such controversy. Hebrews still gives insight and counsel to this and other controversies that may, through God's reconciling grace, bring forth unity.

How we structure Hebrews, and whether we find its central message to be Jesus' high priestly work or the rhetorical effectiveness of the Word, still depend in part on whether we read it as Catholics or Protestants. Does Hebrews draw on Aristotle's rhetoric and present its word in terms of a tripartite structure? If so, then the essential structure is divided into three parts that emphasize speaking. Such a structure fits well a Protestant emphasis on the Word.[2]

The Jesuit priest Albert Vanhoye does not deny Hebrews' use of rhetoric, but rather than finding a linear structure building on the word, he finds a circular structure emphasizing Christ as priest who offers sacrifice. Hebrews has an elaborate structure based on "inclusions,"[3] which are terms or concepts that form the beginning and ending of a section. Vanhoye sees a well-crafted, balanced, five-part structure that intentionally places the key theme in the middle of these inclusions, reaching its crescendo in the "main point" in 8:1. The inclusions end with a statement about the theme to be developed in the next section. Some of these inclusions contain inclusions within them. Below is his five-part structure with the key terms

2. See James W. Thompson, *Hebrews,* Paideia Commentaries on the New Testament (Grand Rapids: Baker Academic, 2008), 16–19. David deSilva, who has done extensive work on the rhetorical analysis of Hebrews, is less convinced this structure nicely fits Hebrews: "Hebrews certainly defies divisions into *exordium, narratio, propositio, probatio,* and *peroratio.* Nevertheless, the classical discussions of what exordia are expected to accomplish help us understand what the author is doing in Hebrews 1:1–2:4. Hebrews 13:1–25, similarly, accomplishes some of the typical functions of perorations" (*Perseverance in Gratitude: A Socio-Rhetorical Commentary on the Epistle "to the Hebrews"* [Grand Rapids: Eerdmans, 2000], 46).

3. Albert Vanhoye, *Structure and Message of the Epistle to the Hebrews,* trans. James Swetnam, S.J. (Rome: Editrice Pontifico Instituto Biblico, 1989), 20–40.

Vanhoye's Sacramental Outline

1. 1:1–4 Exordium
2. 1:5–2:16: Jesus greater than the "angels," then 2:17–18 announces the theme for the next section: "Jesus, merciful and faithful high priest"
   a. 3:1–4:14: Jesus as high priest who is "worthy of faith"
   b. 4:15–5:10: Jesus as "merciful" or "compassionate" high priest, who is in the order of Melchizedek, which leads into the next section
3. "Preliminary exhortations": 5:11–6:20
   a. 7:1–28: Jesus as priest who perfects "according to the order of Melchizedek"
   b. 8:1–9:28: Jesus as priest who saves bringing to "perfection" or completion
   c. 10:1–18: Jesus as the cause of salvation
   "Final exhortation": 10:19–39
4. a. 11:1–40: "Faith" of forebears
   b. 12:1–13: "endurance"
5. 12:14–13:18: "Make paths straight"
   Peroration: 13:20–21

he finds in the inclusions. Vanhoye finds the center of Hebrews to be 9:11–12. The emphasis is on Christ's priesthood and sacrifice.

The differences between Vanhoye and the threefold structure should not be overstated, but they do reflect, to some degree, the different emphases Protestants and Catholics find in Hebrews. For Vanhoye it is the priest and the sacrifice that are at the center. For Thompson this overstates the case: "Vanhoye's approach, despite its helpful insights, is not totally satisfactory. The focal point of the argument is not the high priesthood of Christ but the climactic exhortation at the latter part of the homily." It is "exhortation" that most matters, not sacrifice. Although Hebrews does explicitly state that the "main point" is that we have a "high priest" (8:1), it also explicitly asks its readers to bear with his "word of exhortation" at the end of the letter (13:22). So does Hebrews build to a "climactic exhortation" or does it circle around Christ as high priest who offers sacrifice? Any answer to this question will depend on how the Greek word *Kephalion* in 8:1 gets interpreted. For Vanhoye, it is the "main point" of the letter. We get the central theme in the center. For a Protestant such as F. F. Bruce, it is more of a summary and restatement of the argument thus far, pointing in the direction of the next linear development.[4] Of course, Vanhoye would not deny the importance of Hebrews as a "word of admonition," any more than Thompson or Bruce denies the central role of Christ as high priest who offers sacrifice. Catholics and Protestants may read Hebrews differently, but they share a canon that makes the content normative for both traditions. Nonetheless, these differences in interpretation have a long history, dating back to Calvin's commentary in the sixteenth century. That should at least cause us to ask if the ecclesial setting within which we hear Hebrews might not also contribute to the divisions by which the structure and main point are heard.

Like Christians who lived in the fourth, fifth, and sixteenth centuries, Christians living today face great internal controversy. Despite efforts toward unity and the glimmer of hope that briefly emerged from Vatican II, Christian churches seem increasingly divided by doctrinal, moral, and structural issues. Protestant theologians and church leaders subjected nearly every Christian doctrine to revision during the modern era. Traditional teaching on the "attributes" of God, the Trinity, incarnation, crucifixion, and resurrection have been denied, revised, and defended. Along with doctrinal revision come moral revisions and developments. Attitudes to war and peace, capital punishment, economics, patriarchy, sex, and reproduction differ so decisively among Christians that they seem to hold little in common. Likewise significant structural shifts in the church's practice have arisen, such as remarriage after divorce, artificial contraception, women's ordination, gay marriage, and ordination. The church of the twentieth and twenty-first centuries is living through momentous shifts. Our time is not unique; as Hebrews itself shows, such shifts are constantly set before the faith community. In response, Hebrews offers two pieces of counsel, which might appear contradictory: hold fast the confession you received, and be willing to wander, moving toward that which you have not yet received. To "hold fast" does not always fit well with "wandering." How can we adhere to both? We are encouraged and exhorted to "hold fast the confession," and also to be unsettled, to recognize that we do not yet have a

4. F. F. Bruce, *The Epistle to the Hebrews,* rev. ed., New International Commentary on the New Testament (Grand Rapids: Eerdmans, 1990), 80.

city where we should find ourselves at home. We are still God's wandering people, called to go "outside the gates," outside the city. How can we "hold fast" and wander at the same time? Answers to that apparent contradiction will emerge as we work through Hebrews' call to faithfulness.

Metaphysics of Hebrews

The Epistle to the Hebrews always seems to find trouble, not only because of its role in Christianity's controversies, but also because its author, setting, intent, audience, sources, and even name are contested. But Hebrews should also trouble us, like an uncomfortable guest invited into our home. Against the background of modern sensibilities, it cannot but be odd. A second important reason to read Hebrews today is because it offers us such an untimely metaphysics.

The world is flat. So Thomas Friedman, three times Pulitzer Prize winner, tells us. He intends the statement provocatively. After all, Columbus set sail in part to prove the world was not flat, and he was successful. No person of serious intellect believes in a flat world any longer. We have even seen images of the sphere-shaped earth we inhabit. Of course, Friedman does not deny this. The flat world of which he speaks is not the earth, but the shape of those things that are basic to our everyday lives, especially how we earn our daily bread. For Friedman, economic globalization flattened, is flattening, and will continue to flatten our world, homogenizing our relations to one another and to the earth for better and worse. "What the flattening of the world means," he states, "is that we are now connecting all the knowledge centers on the planet together into a single global network."[5] *Network* is the key term here. A network is a large grid, a flat space of intersecting lines each bearing some relation to the others. Like the GPS that knows when I am lost even before I do, nearly every facet of our lives can now be laid out on a network, a grid that links us to one another and to the world, and gives us basic information about where and who we are. This might appear to be

5. Thomas L. Friedman, *The World Is Flat: A Brief History of the Twenty-first Century* (New York: Farrar, Straus and Giroux, 2005), 8.

the end of *meta*physics, for nothing is "beyond" the grid. But it is actually a working out of a specific metaphysics that culminated in "technology" as our supposed only access to the "real." Virtuality is our reality. We prefer television to conversation, digitized music to learning an instrument.

Friedman, however, is correct only in part. Although much of our ordinary life bears out his claim, he overstates the inevitability of the flattening process. Take as an example our ability to travel. In the course of two years I made three trips from my home in Indiana to California. The first was by bicycle. It took twenty-one days, numerous jars of peanut butter, and a great deal of effort, especially through the mountains. Bicycling over Loveland Pass in the Rocky Mountains was an achievement I will never forget. The second was by automobile. Three of us took turns driving and made the trip in less than forty-eight hours. The third was by plane. I sat in a seat in Indianapolis, took off, flew above the clouds, and four hours later landed on a very similar-looking tarmac in a similar-looking airport with the same fast-food restaurants, shops, and hotels as were back in Indianapolis. Each of those trips had some similarities in their mode of transportation. Bicycles, automobiles, and planes all have wheels, without which they would not work. They share a common ancestry in the technological revolution the wheel produced, and no reasonable person would want to undo that revolution. It brings great advances to us. But it also changes our perspective, our ability to see the world in which we live. When you drive or fly across the country, the world is most certainly flat. It does not seem to take any more energy on our part to drive a car uphill than downhill. When you bicycle, however, you realize the world is anything but flat. The world has a depth and richness to it that can easily be lost when you sit comfortably (or uncomfortably as the case may be) and are transported by means of energy others produced to connect us quickly across space and time without the need for an adventure or journey to get us from one place to the next.

Perhaps one reason we have a difficult time hearing the testimony of the book of Hebrews is because of our cultural context that Friedman names. We live in a flat world, but the world of Hebrews is anything but flat. It is a world of various tabernacles earthly and heavenly, ideals, types and figures, ministering angels, sacrifices, theophanies, strange characters without genealogy like Melchizedek, and levels of participation in earthly and spiritual realities. Hebrews asks us to see a reality that does not readily appear on the surface; it asks us to go off the grid. This is troubling because it is dangerous. Perhaps no book in the New Testament other than Revelation is as dangerous as Hebrews. It cannot be bridled, domesticated, turned into an inoffensive treatise. Its apocalypticism could lead, and has led, to resentment, Gnosticism, or political indifference, even while it is also free of these unsavory consequences.

Hebrews is difficult for us to hear because everyday life in our flat world has radically different metaphysical assumptions in comparison to those of this mysterious letter. The term *metaphysics* quickly conjures up bad memories of Greek philosophy with abstract and obtuse discussions of being, existence, essence, and so on. This is unfortunate. At its core metaphysics summons us to see in the particulars of everyday life something more, an excess of meaning that requires we use language like *truth, goodness*, and *beauty* to explain them. Our modern metaphysical assumption is that everything is *contextual.* Everything could be identified on the grid at a specific point in time and receive its meaning from its location. Hebrews assumes that material reality can participate in something more, in eternity itself, without absorbing eternity into its temporal matrices. Jesus enters into the eternal holy of holies and offers his own materiality, his own blood, as a full and sufficient sacrifice. Friedman's flat world has little place for this. In the flat world everything that matters can be plotted on a binary code of 1 or 0. Everything is what it is because it can be given a value and exchanged. This is part of what Max Weber termed the "disenchantment"[6] of our world.

We live in a disenchanted world with very little place for mystery because we live in a secular age. As Charles Taylor has noted, a secular age does not necessarily mean an age that is hostile to faith; it just means that faith becomes one option among many.[7] Religion,

6. Max Weber, "Science as a Vocation," in *From Max Weber: Essays in Sociology*, trans. and ed. H. H. Gerth and C. Wright Mills (1946; repr. New York: Oxford University Press, 1958), 139.
7. Charles Taylor, *A Secular Age* (Cambridge, MA: The Belknap Press of Harvard University, 2007), 3.

mystery, may be one way to make sense of one's life, but it is not the only way. Other compelling ways are always present for us, and will be into the foreseeable future. Christianity may have, in part, assisted this process by purifying the world of religious mythology. But it would be a mistake to think Christianity has no place for mystery, or that secularism was an inevitable consequence of Christianity's demythologization of the ancient world. Indeed, Christianity has a theological depth that cannot fit well within the metaphysics of our flat world. Take, for instance, the statement about angels in Hebrews 1. Having already proclaimed that Jesus bears a name greater than the angels, the author then quotes a number of psalms referring to angels, including a quote from the Septuagint (the Greek version) of Psalm 104:4: "Of the angels he says, 'He makes his angels winds, and his servants flames of fire'" (Heb. 1:7). This stands in a tradition of Judaism and Christianity where angels are ministering spirits. Hebrews draws on the Jewish tradition that had the angels assist in the giving of the Torah. But what are we to do with this passage, as well as other passages that depict graphic images of a mysterious enchanted world filled with temples, priests, strangers, and a character like Melchizedek? Is it possible for any of us to enter into that world other than ironically?

Looking chronologically at various interpretations of Hebrews' use of Psalm 104:4 reveals our growing disenchantment. In the fourth century, John Chrysostom interprets this verse as setting forth the angels' subservient status to Christ akin to our own: "So that it is an angelical work, to do all for the salvation of the brethren: or rather it is the work of Christ Himself, for He indeed saves as Lord, but they as servants. And we, though servants are yet Angels' fellow-servants. Why gaze ye so earnestly on the Angels (saith he)? They are servants of the Son of God, and are sent many ways for our sakes, and minister to our salvation. And so they are partners in service with us."[8] Chrysostom does not doubt the role of angels in Christ's work. The question is their status. Do they serve us as Christ's ministers, or do they serve Christ as fellow servants with

8. John Chrysostom, "Homilies on the Epistle to the Hebrews," in *Christian Classics Ethereal Library,* http://www.ccel.org/ccel/schaff/npnf114.iii.html 377.

us? His answer, following the argument of Hebrews, is the latter. The angels are not to be "gazed" upon, for they are creatures as are we. Yet Chrysostom, like Hebrews, does not doubt their existence. This is not an option. Angels are not explained as a metaphor for some other kind of empirical reality.

Nor does Aquinas raise doubts about their existence some nine centuries later when he comments on this passage and finds in it an important distinction among angels between "legates" and "ministers." Legates are angels who "enlighten," whereas ministers are "mediators of divine works."[9] Aquinas finds in Hebrews' use of Psalm 104 evidence not only that the angels assist in the divine economy, but also of specific tasks they perform.

By the time we get to Calvin in the sixteenth century we find a growing divide between the work of the angels and the work of human creatures. He does not deny their existence in the heavenly realm, but he finds other ways to interpret Hebrews' use of Psalm 104 than did Chrysostom and Aquinas. Calvin reads the reference to the angels "metaphorically," and therefore this passage refers to the winds that obey God's commands. He eschews "allegorical" readings about the role of angels.

> He shows how quick and speedy His messengers are to obey his orders. None of this has anything to do with angels. Some take refuge in allegory as though the apostle were expounding the clear and literal meaning (as they say) allegorically with reference to angels. It seems more satisfactory to me to adduce this evidence as referring to angels metaphorically in this way, that David compares the winds to angels as performing in this world the duty which the angels perform in heaven; for the winds are a sort of visible spirits.[10]

Like Chrysostom and Aquinas, Calvin does not deny the existence of angels. His world too has a mysterious depth that allows for metaphysical entities that cannot be graphed on to the grid of

9. Thomas Aquinas, *Commentary on the Epistle to the Hebrews*, trans. Chrysostom Baer, O. Praem. (South Bend, IN: St. Augustine's Press, 2006), 29–30.

10. John Calvin, *The Epistle of Paul the Apostle to the Hebrews*, trans. William B. Johnston, Calvin's New Testament Commentaries (Grand Rapids: Eerdmans, 1963), 13.

a flat network. There is still something beyond (*meta*) the physical realm. However, with Calvin we begin to see the reinterpretation of the "angels" as natural forces like wind, which can be readily graphed onto that emerging world. The angels work in heaven. Natural forces work on earth. The odd world of Hebrews is being demythologized, disenchanted.

Calvin's reading finds allies in modern interpreters. Harold Attridge lends support by citing the original Hebrew. He writes, "In the Hebrew original the psalmist praises God, 'who makes the winds thy messengers and the flames of fire thy servants.' In rendering the Hebrew so that the predication is reversed and angels are explicitly introduced, the translator of the LXX may have had in mind theophanies in which meteorological phenomena were taken to be transformed angels."[11] Such a scientific explanation goes one step further than Calvin. It lends itself to the suggestion that what the LXX (Septuagint) and the book of Hebrews take to be the role of angels can be explained by scientific facts. Meteorology replaces angelology.

Who among us moderns does not find the meteorological interpretation more compelling than that of Chrysostom, Aquinas, or even Calvin? Hebrews presents several vivid theophanies. Could we not translate these as the power of nature itself, as the forces of wind and fire before which we often stand in awe? Perhaps Kant's concluding words in his second critique would be the best interpretation of such a passage: "Two things fill the mind with ever new and increasing wonder and awe, the oftener and the more steadily we reflect on them: the starry heavens above me and the moral law within me."[12] Whatever mystery is left to us is the kind of mystery consistent with that flat, scientific world. We need no *meta*.

We might have a place for a god in a flat world, perhaps for a god who is first cause among causes or moral governor, but the lavish God of Hebrews surrounded with a heavenly entourage of angelic beings does not easily fit. When we live in a flat world, translating the odd metaphysics of Hebrews into something more tangible is a great

11. Harold W. Attridge, *The Epistle to the Hebrews*, Hermeneia (Philadelphia: Fortress Press, 1989), 58.
12. Immanuel Kant, *Critique of Practical Reason*, trans. Lewis White Beck, 3rd ed. (New York: Macmillan, 1993), 169.

temptation. But if we succumb, it will prevent us from hearing well the witness of Hebrews. Rather than forcing it into what its author would surely find as the strange metaphysics of our flat world, perhaps we will make more headway if we suspend our own metaphysical commitments to the latter and for a moment open ourselves to those of Hebrews. Perhaps creation has a depth that goes beyond the flatness to which we have become so familiar? After all, if we confess faith in God, then we have already posited a rich metaphysical world where not everything can be reduced to immanence.[13] Why should we begin with disbelief, with failing to recognize the existence of other incorporeal entities—angels, heaven, an ideal temple, a cosmic liturgy? If we are to invite readers into the odd world of Hebrews, we will first need to invite them to suspend their belief in the metaphysics of the flat world, to begin to think that there might be something more than causes and effects that can always potentially be calibrated once we get the right instruments. We should be open even to the possibility of entertaining angels unaware. This might be the first step in hearing its message. How might we do this?

Reading Hebrews Reading Scripture

Rudolf Bultmann, who certainly accepted the flat metaphysics of the modern era, famously wrote, "We cannot use electric lights and radios and, in the event of illness, avail ourselves of modern medical and clinical means and at the same time believe in the spirit and wonder world of the New Testament."[14] Bultmann overstated the technological rupture with the past that modernity brought, but he was on to something with his assertion. Living in a world we create ourselves, where the rhythms of the day no longer matter, where 24/7 is possible, readily lends itself to the illusion that the world is our own creation. Bultmann intended his statement to show the need to demythologize the Bible, rid it of its enchantments, and

13. Theologians who claim to be post-metaphysical, or who deny metaphysics, can ultimately only underwrite modern atheism.

14. Rudolf Bultmann, *New Testament and Mythology and Other Basic Writings*, trans. and ed. Schubert M. Ogden (Philadelphia: Fortress Press, 1984), 4.

make it palatable to life on the grid. Hebrews challenges this intent by asking us which is the "real" world. Is it the flat metaphysics of the grid, or is it the illusion that requires a disciplined act of inattentiveness to see it as real?

After the Wachowski brothers' film *The Matrix,* Bultmann's famous statement appears naive. Is the "grid" more like the "Matrix"? When Morpheus reveals the Matrix to Neo he tells him that it represents the "world . . . pulled over your eyes to blind you from the truth." It is an interesting expression. Could what seems most real be the actual illusion, the world masquerading as wool, and what now is dismissed as illusory be that which is most real? Neo responds, "What truth?" Morpheus tells him, "That you are a slave . . . born into . . . a prison for your mind." Then he gives him the choice. He can take the blue pill and remain in the Matrix without any consciousness of its illusory power, or he can take the red pill and discover what really is. But the reality he is to discover will take him further into "Wonderland." The red pill that shows reality also shows "how deep the rabbit hole goes." Living in the Matrix does not reenchant; it narcotizes. By opting for the red pill Neo opts for reality and reenchantment at the same time.

Morpheus's Statement to Neo

The Matrix is everywhere. It is all around us, even now in this very room. You can see it when you look out your window or when you turn on your television. You can feel it when you go to work, when you go to church, when you pay your taxes. It is the world that has been pulled over your eyes to blind you from the truth.

http://en.wikiquote.org/wiki/The_Matrix

Perhaps we should think of Hebrews' message as analogous to the red pill. Reading and being open to its message is like falling deep into the rabbit hole. But we will need to relinquish even temporarily the world we create for ourselves and comfortably live within to take that plunge. The first step in reading Hebrews well requires some kind of fast to see reality beyond the grid. Athanasius suggested such an approach when he reminded his readers:

> But for the searching and right understanding of the Scriptures there is need of a good life and a pure soul, and for Christian virtue to guide the mind to grasp, so far as human nature

> can, the truth concerning God the Word. One cannot possibly understand the teaching of the saints unless one has a pure mind and is trying to imitate their life. Anyone who wants to look at sunlight naturally wipes his eye clear first, in order to make, at any rate, some approximation to the purity of that on which he looks; and a person wishing to see a city or country goes to the place in order to do so. Similarly, anyone who wishes to understand the mind of the sacred writers must first cleanse his own life, and approach the saints by copying their deeds.[15]

Perhaps an analogous fast will be necessary for us to hear Hebrews well. Perhaps reading Scripture well is less a matter of finding the proper method to engage the text and more the embodiment of certain ways of living, of a "philosophy" in the ancient sense, that will allow us to see more clearly? We might fast from the use of motor oil for a brief time by riding a bicycle or walking to work in order to rid ourselves of the illusion that we live in a flat world of our own making. Or spend a few days living with the homeless, seeking angels unaware. Then we might notice the world's depth. Perhaps we should contemplate the Eucharist, gaze upon an icon, or abstain from using the Internet. Hebrews' message assumes the ability to see something beyond the ordinary in the ordinary. We should approach it as it approaches us. Can Hebrews be heard only by those who have been divested of some property (10:34), pursue peace with everyone (12:14), show hospitality to strangers (13:2), attend to prisoners (13:3), or honor marriage (13:4)?

Listening to Hebrews as Holy Scripture we not only learn essential content of the Christian faith, but we are also invited into a sacred world and taught how to read Scripture after Christ's odd and not readily apparent triumph. In many respects, Hebrews resists conceding its meaning in terms of a strict scientific study of texts, especially biblical texts, through the modern historical-critical method. As Luke Timothy Johnson notes, "Hebrews challenges the capacity of the historical-critical approach to do what it does best." This is largely because it "proposes as real a world that most of us consider

15. Athanasius, *On the Incarnation* (Crestwood, NY: St. Vladimir's Seminary Press,1996), 96.

imaginary."[16] This is not to deny the gains of a historical-critical approach. In fact, "history" and "critical" are not new approaches to biblical interpretation. They are, have been, and will be essential. Take for instance Augustine's counsel concerning all that the biblical interpreter should know. Interpreters should memorize the Scriptures, then learn languages, the significance of numbers, the importance of music, reject superstition, learn human institutions that help understand Scripture—including nonecclesial history, biology, and the role of philosophy. The interpreter should understand rules of valid inference, propositions, science of definition, division, and partition.[17] Of course, Augustine, like Origen before him, also thought Scripture had a meaning that exceeded any literal, empirical referent. Our reading of Scripture must always be historical and critical, but that a singular method is necessary to produce meaning reflects a shift in interpretation, a shift that could not have occurred without a change to our modern metaphysics.

For all of its benefits, the historical-critical method shares two assumptions with the metaphysics of the grid that can keep us from reading Hebrews well. The first assumption is that meaning emerges through a method of immanent causality where everything is put in its proper place. The second is that meaning emerges when the technician placing everything in its proper place remains detached from the object under consideration. The extent to which this constitutes the historical-critical method will be disputed, but take as an example the important work of James Dunn. He is willing to suspend belief in the traditional dogmas of Christianity, in order to discover the author's original intention. Suspending belief is not itself unique. Anselm did something similar as a hypothetical exercise in his *Cur Deus Homo?* It became known as *remoto Christo* (removing Christ). But for Dunn, such detachment is not hypothetical—it is intrinsic to the method. Whereas Anselm was willing to argue *remoto Christo* with the assumption that faith will seek understanding even when the "faith" is hypothetically bracketed, Dunn finds the

16. Luke Timothy Johnson, *Hebrews: A Commentary*, New Testament Library (Louisville: Westminster John Knox Press, 2006), 1, 2.

17. Augustine, *On Christian Doctrine*, trans. D. W. Robertson Jr. (New York: Macmillan, 1958), 55, 63, 65, 75.

tradition of faith a hindrance to the method he employs. Tradition provides layers of interpretation with which we are so familiar that we readily interpret something like Hebrews 1 as suggesting Jesus' preexistence, which provides evidence for the doctrines of incarnation and Trinity. To discover the original meaning in its historical context, however, we "must attempt the exceedingly difficult task of shutting out the voices of early Fathers, Councils and dogmaticians down the centuries."[18] This will "let context rather than developed dogmas . . . determine our exegesis."[19] Then the "New Testament evidence" will "speak in its own terms and dictate its own patterns."[20] But which context allows for an undeveloped dogmatic approach to reading Scripture? What neutral grid exists on which we can map these texts?

Dunn then attempts to determine when the doctrine of the incarnation, including Jesus' preexistence, emerges through a punctiliar account of meaning that puts specific questions to the text, questions that assume meaning arises solely from an immanent causality. Where and when can we locate it at a specific time and place? What sources gave rise to it? For Dunn to answer these questions means to place the "text" in its "historical context" by explicating the "original intention" behind "subsequent interpretation."[21] Dunn's method suggests that if we are to arrive at meaning we will need to know the author's original intention in this neutral, nondogmatic context. We will need some important information in order to locate the origin of meaning properly. We need to ask what is the original intention of the author. We need chronology—what is the time in which he or she wrote? We need geography—where is the place from which the author wrote and where is his or her audience located? We need to know the circumstances that elicited the writing. What is the main issue the letter/sermon addresses? We need to know the sources upon which the author drew. Then through a reconstruction of these elements, bracketing out the dogmatic tradition as unreliable, we can begin to suggest what the text meant in its original historical

18. James Dunn, *Christology in the Making: A New Testament Inquiry into the Origins of the Doctrine of the Incarnation*, 2nd ed. (Grand Rapids: Eerdmans, 1996), 13.

19. Ibid., xviii.

20. Ibid., 9.

21. Ibid., xiv.

setting. Once these "facts" are firmly in place, then we venture on to the hermeneutic task by saying what the text might mean for us today in our very different circumstances. Most commentators go in search of answers to these questions; for without them "meaning" cannot emerge. They are important to ask even if answers are not readily forthcoming. Nonetheless, if these questions locate meaning, then Johnson is correct. Hebrews challenges the capacity of this method to do its work; it escapes being located by these questions.

We do not know who wrote Hebrews. Traditionally Paul was thought to be the author, and this tradition was supposedly given canonical status at the Council of Nicaea (although it cannot be found in its canons, and Hebrews was not regarded as canonical in the West until around 350).[22] Aquinas was well aware that prior to Nicaea the authorship of Paul was in question, but for him after Nicaea it became dogma. Yet for Aquinas two questions remained outstanding about Pauline authorship. First, why is the Greek more "elegant" here than in other Pauline letters? Second, why did Paul not sign his name like he did with his other letters? Aquinas follows a long tradition that suggests Luke translated Paul's letter, which explains the more elegant style. Origen suggested this as one of two ways to explain the letter, the other that Clement of Alexandria composed it. (Tertullian thought Barnabas wrote it.) But Origen was much less certain than Aquinas that Paul wrote it: "But who wrote the epistle, in truth God knows."[23] He was not preoccupied with the question. This seems the best position. All others are more speculative than the airiest metaphysical claims.

Aquinas, convinced by the authority of Nicaea, is less circumspect. For him, Paul wrote it. He gives a threefold reason why Paul did not sign his name, echoing answers given in tradition. First, Paul's calling was not to the Jews but to the Gentiles. Thus he did not presume an "apostolate, except to the Gentiles." Second, his name was "odious to the Jews since he said that the observances of the Law were not to be kept." He remains silent so as not to provoke them and keep them from salvation. Third, Paul was a Jew. "And the

22. Rowan A. Greer, *The Captain of Our Salvation: A Study in the Patristic Exegesis of Hebrews*, BGBE 15 (Tübingen: Mohr [Siebeck], 1973), 7.
23. Attridge, *Hebrews*, 1.

members of one's household do not suffer well the excellence of one of their own."[24] So out of a sense of humility about his apostolate, concern for Jewish salvation, and a desire not to provoke envy, Paul did not sign his name. Aquinas's reasons for this are not unique to him. They can be found in other commentators, who before and after Nicaea assume Pauline authorship.

Even if Pauline authorship has the dogmatic authority of Nicaea, it no longer has the consent of the faithful. Pauline authorship has about as much authority today as does the canon of Nicaea that any bishop who takes interest on his money should be deposed. Of course it is a critical, historical judgment that Paul did not write Hebrews. It is also a judgment against the dogmatic tradition. Therefore, it is on the basis of a critical use of history that most theologians now recognize, contra the dogmatic tradition, that Paul did not write Hebrews, and this conclusion challenges the use of the historical-critical method. There is an interesting irony here. A historical-critical reading, which is always necessary, challenges the ability of a modern method to locate meaning by identifying the author and his original intention.

We do not know who wrote Hebrews. Nor do we know from where it was written and to whom it was written. We do not know the author and thus have no way of discovering his original intention. Nor do we know when Hebrews was written. Most guess it was written somewhere between AD 60 and 100 based on whether the Jerusalem temple was still standing and sacrifices were being offered. If Hebrews describes extant temple worship, then it would have been written prior to the destruction of the temple in 70. We do know that Clement of Rome quotes portions of text identical to Hebrews at the turn of the century, so it was most likely not later than that, although some scholars even argue that they could have both used a common text.

Barring some future (unlikely) archaeological discovery, we have no way of adjudicating these scholarly debates. Any answer to them is at most an educated guess. We know neither to whom the author was writing nor from where. The cryptic reference at the end of

24. Aquinas, *Hebrews*, 7.

Hebrews—"Those from Italy send you greetings"—does not give us enough to ascertain its geographical location. We do not know the exact reason that elicited the sermon. Was it a fear of "judaizing" or encouragement in the face of persecution? No single reason for the sermon has been persuasively set forth. Nor do we know the sources upon which Hebrews draws. Were they gnostic, Jewish apocalyptic, Platonic, wisdom, or a combination of these? All these and others have been suggested. While allusions in Hebrews can be found that might be referring to all these sources, Hebrews offers no footnotes or citations that allow us to fit the author's work into any of these sources without remainder. These questions are important, and answers can be ventured. But if meaning emerges through a method that allows a text to be mapped on a grid by answers to these questions, then Hebrews escapes the grid. Its immanent causality cannot render it intelligible. Is the result that Hebrews is meaningless or that it has whatever meaning we seek to find in it?

Obviously the book was, is, and remains meaningful. People still read it, hear it, and respond. This is an empirical fact. Its meaning is found neither in an act of power that imposes meaning from an authoritarian structure nor in a scholarly consensus that answers questions raised by such a method. No such consensus exists, and yet who would deny Hebrews has been, is, and will continue to be meaningful? Its meaning resides in both its content and the ability of its hearers to receive and embody that content. In order to make sense of this, we will have to examine that content and its reception. We discover that it already reads Scripture within a developed, and developing, dogmatic tradition. What else is Holy Scripture? Hebrews finds Jesus bearing the identity, activity, and name of the God of Israel. But Jesus does this through his own unique mission to become all that humanity is (without sin) and bring it to its proper glory within God's presence. For this reason, Hebrews admonishes its readers to hold fast to this confession. To read Hebrews well requires such a steadfast act; to bracket it out and keep this confession at arm's length begins by rejecting Hebrews' main point.

1:1–2:18
God Speaks

If Hebrews were a symphony it would begin with the crescendo. Before we have time to prepare ourselves to listen well, Hebrews sounds forth its central themes. We get no introductory information or words of greeting. Instead we are immediately confronted with the subject—God—and what this subject does—speak. Hebrews begins by making a startling claim about language. God uses it to communicate to God's people; this communication creates communion. Hebrews' first sentence makes four claims about God and human language. First, God was speaking in the past in diverse ways. Second, God has now spoken decisively in the Son. Two more claims about language follow from this. Third, the Son in whom God speaks is the one who bears all things by his word. Finally, because of how he speaks, the Son inherits a more excellent "name." All these claims are found in the *exordium*, which is the first four verses, a single sentence in the Greek text.

This insistence on God's speaking, and its relation to the Son, continues in the *catena* that follows the exordium in 1:5–14. In these verses God's former speaking long ago and God's definitive speaking "in these last days" come together in the "today" still present when Hebrews' listeners, including us, hear. God's definitive speech in the Son was present even in the diverse manners God spoke in the prophets and ancestors. Hebrews sets forth God's definitive speech "today" by "recontextualizing" seven OT passages. They show how God spoke long ago in the prophets and to the fathers, but now decisively speaks in the Son. Why all this matters is then set forth in 2:1–18, which begins by setting out the first of many exhortations to those who would hear Hebrews' message: "Therefore we must pay greater attention to what we have heard, so that we do not drift away from it" (2:1). What they heard was "spoken" not merely by angels, but by the Lord himself and conveyed to them (2:2–3). In this exhortation to pay attention, Hebrews returns to the same verb used in the exordium, *lalēsai,* to speak. Speaking matters. Having heard God speak, their proper response is to be attentive, to hear well. That requires yet another speaking, and the author provides it by writing and sending Hebrews to be read to his hearers. The listeners' task is to hear in such a way that they hold fast the confession; this is what it means to "pay attention." If they do, then unlike what happened to those who refused to listen to Joshua, they will inherit what God promises: the true glory intended for creatures.

In order then to make sense of Hebrews' content and its effect on its readers, we must begin with these four sections:

1. Exordium and the Name of Christ (1:1–4)
2. The Catena: God Spoke of Christ in the Old Testament (1:5–14)
3. Exhorting the Hearers (2:1–4)
4. The Glory of Creatures (2:5–18)

Each of these sections will be discussed in turn, but with cross-references, in an attempt not to lose sight of the connections Hebrews makes throughout the sermon.

1:1–4

Exordium and the Name of Christ

"Long ago God spoke to our ancestors in many and various ways by the prophets, but in these last days he has spoken. . . ." The ellipsis here matters, for we must not end the opening line of Hebrews at this point, even if we must pause and consider the theological significance of what has already taken place. We cannot end here, for the first four verses of Hebrews are so tightly interwoven that they must all be heard together, not only in content but also in form.

The form these verses take is not only beautiful but also theologically rich. The first few words of Hebrews emphasize, through alliteration in the Greek text, the diverse ways God previously spoke, but they do so by a repetition of sound that unifies those diverse ways of speaking. Verse 1 begins like this in the Greek: *polymerōs kai polytropōs* (in many and various ways).[1] Already we find an intriguing use of language. By repeating the same prefix—*poly*—Hebrews emphasizes the diverse ways God spoke in the past. This diversity was understood to be so vast by some of the early church fathers that it included not only the OT prophets, but even ancient philosophers outside the Jewish faith.[2] This alliteration continues when the author tells us God spoke *palai* (long ago) to the *patrasin* (forebears, literally the "fathers")—and God spoke by the *prophētais* (prophets).

When you hear all those *p* words together in the first stanza of Hebrews, its lyrical quality leads the listener to be attentive to what follows. For this opening has a powerful purpose. The emphasis on the diversity of God's former speaking by means of a common alliterative repetition gives way to a final and definitive Word that breaks off altogether from the alliteration. Where before we had diversity in terms of the repetition of sameness—*p-p-p-p-p*—now we have a sameness that repeats itself differently. God has now decisively spoken in the Son, but this speech will be repeated in diverse ways, as Hebrews itself repeats it.

God's definitive speech in the Son opens up into a threefold manner of speaking that, even though it is final and definitive, leads us into the major themes not only of Hebrews but also of the Christian life. It is the reason the sermon cannot end with verse 4 but must explain with more words what this definitive Word is. Hebrews expresses this speaking through three usages of personal pronouns, each referring to the Son in a different case. The last usage, where the Son is the subject, expands the Son's speech into five activities. The effect is an all-encompassing, yet confusing, sense of agency between God and the Son/Lord in whom God has now spoken. This can be laid

1. Attridge suggests that the first term implies "God's speech of old was disjointed," while the second "suggests the formal diversity of God's word" (*Hebrews*, 37).

2. See Craig R. Koester, *Hebrews: A New Translation with Introduction and Commentary*, Anchor Bible (New York: Doubleday, 2001), 20.

out by looking first at the three uses of the Greek personal pronouns by which God has spoken in the Son and then the five activities that give a sense of the Son's agency.

> **God has spoken in the Son . . .**
>
> **1. whom (*hon*, accusative) God placed or appointed (*ethēken*) heir (*klēronomon*) of all things,**
>
> **2. through whom (*di' ou*, genitive of means or agency) God also made (*epoiēsen*) the worlds;**
>
> **3. who (*hos*, nominative). . . .**

The grammar here matters. Jesus is first the object of God's action. God sets, places, or appoints him as "heir" of all things. Here Jesus does not act. God acts upon him. Second, Jesus is the means by which God acts. They work together. Through him God "made" the worlds. Note the confusing intertwining of the relationship between God, the Son, and creation in these first two modes of God's speech. In the first one the Son is silent, but is rewarded as the one who receives all things. In the second the Son speaks with God to make all things. This raises the question, if God through the Son made all the worlds, what then does it mean that the Son also inherits all things? Is the Son not already entitled to them if he is the agent by which they came to be? And notice that it is not "the world," as if all that matters is the earth and its inhabitants. God through the Son creates in the plural, as God did in Genesis 1 when God made the heavens and the earth. How does the Son both accomplish an act that makes him heir and be the one through whom all things are made? An answer to that question will take us into the heart of Hebrews' argument, for here we have an "economy" in which Jesus becomes just like us (2:17) and makes something as a human agent, which as we shall see is purification and perfection that makes him eternal high priest. But he is also the "exact imprint" (1:3) of God and therefore makes something as God. Jesus' singular agency is both human and divine. This brings us back to the third use of the relative pronoun for Jesus in the prologue, the nominative form *hos* (who). Here Jesus is the subject who acts in five specific ways, which are both human and divine.

Having used three different cases of relative pronouns to expand on how God has definitively spoken in the Son, the author now uses three participial phrases to set forth the Son's agency: being, bearing, making. The third participial phrase is followed by two actions, one done by Jesus: "he sat down at the right hand of the Majesty on high," which is a theme Hebrews comes back to again and again in diverse forms. And in the other the subject who does the acting is not explicitly stated: "the name he has inherited." Who gave him which name? The word *onoma* (name) concludes the single sentence that constitutes the first four verses of chapter 1. The three participles and two actions that explain Jesus' agency can be set forth like this:

God has spoken in the Son . . .

3.1 who being (*hos ōn*) the reflection of God's glory and the exact imprint of God's very being (*hypostaseōs*),

3.2 who sustains (*pherōn*) all things by his powerful word,

3.3.1 who having made (*poiēsamenos*) purification for sins,

3.3.2 sat down at the right hand of the Majesty on high,

3.3.3 having become as much superior to the angels as more excellent than them he inherited the name (or "as the name he has inherited is more excellent than theirs").

We find first an ontological claim stating who Jesus is (3.1), which is followed by two claims about his mission (3.2 and 3.3.1). Having stated the work Jesus accomplished in 3.3.1, Hebrews then sets forth Christ's entrance into God's holy presence (3.3.2), followed by his final accomplishment (3.3.3): he inherits the name.

Note the symmetry between the participial phrases in 3.1–3.3.1 and the use of the pronouns in 1–3. That Jesus bears or sustains all things by his words (3.2) further expands the claim that he is the means by which God makes all things (2). That he sits at the right hand of God (the session) and is given the name (3.3.2 and 3.3.3) illumines the accusative use where God placed or appointed him heir of all things (1). The form used to present Jesus' person and work in these first four verses says as much as the content. The form and content together convey the significance of who Jesus is and what he has done.

Who is Jesus in these verses? He is both *apaugasma tēs doxēs* (radiance [NIV] or reflection of glory) and the *charactēr tēs hypostaseōs autou* (exact imprint of his very being or nature). The former expression became a statement identifying Jesus' sameness with God. The latter identified his distinct person. What has Jesus done? He creates, sustains, purifies, and receives authority. Hebrews raises the central issue of the Christian economy in these first four verses: Who is Jesus and what has he done? It has been raised with a specific order. If we are to understand what he has done, we must first see who he is. These four verses played a central role in Christian tradition to answer who he is so that we can understand what he has done. A theological interpretation of them requires attention both to the specific argument in these verses and to their reception in the tradition.

Who Is Jesus? The Doctrine of the Incarnation

What does it mean for Jesus to be the *charactēr* of God's *hypostasis* (Heb. 1:3)? The first Greek word is used only here in the New Testament, and means a reproduction or exact representation. *Hypostasis* eventually became a technical term in Christian theology, which signifies the "person" in the Trinity, but it does not yet have that technical sense. Obviously, the author of Hebrews could not have drawn upon the meaning of *hypostasis* as it would be used in the christological and Trinitarian controversies of the fourth and fifth centuries. Here it most likely means "substantial nature." The term is used two other times in Hebrews. In 3:14 it expresses the "first substance" of what we are to "hold firm to the end," and in 12:1 it means the "confidence," "assurance," or "possession" associated with faith. But the three uses share a common meaning. *Hypostasis* is the "essence" or "fundamental reality" of something.[3] Such a meaning does not stand in any contradiction to how the term will be used in the fourth and fifth centuries, although its meaning will undergo revision for it to express well the central mystery of the Christian faith.

Christian tradition interprets Hebrews' exordium as providing biblical support for the orthodox teaching that the Son is of the same essence as the Father and Spirit, but distinct from them in Person. Although they were basically synonyms in the fourth century, the

3. Attridge, *Hebrews*, 44.

term *ousia* came to express the sameness, and *hypostasis,* the distinction. *Ousia* as essence or nature expresses the fundamental reality of the oneness of the Trinity. *Hypostasis* expresses the distinct acting person. This will cause confusion because once these synonyms take on a new meaning, the result will be that a person acts but not a nature. One of the ongoing controversies is what then is a nature. When the Son became flesh, he maintained both natures as a single acting historical subject who is Jesus of Nazareth. The church fathers gathered in council in the fourth and fifth centuries interpreted Hebrews' exordium as supporting this distinction. This gives rise to two questions. First, were the Fathers correct in finding in Hebrews an orthodox Christology that could be used to settle disputes with heretics who denied this? Second, are their decisions now part of the "confession" that we should "hold fast," part of our attentive listening to Hebrews? First we will examine what that confession is and the role Hebrews played in it, especially in the Nicene Creed and the Chalcedonian Definition. Then we will take a look at some diverse reasons contemporary theologians have for no longer holding fast to such a confession.

The Anglican theologian A. N. Williams would support Hebrews' theological beginning point: "it is not in the first instance what Christ does that saves us, but who he is." History is replete with victims, willing and unwilling, who were sacrifices for others, many in much more horrific fashion than Jesus. What makes his sacrifice redemptive is not that it is sacrifice, but who offers it. This is why there are no heresies about Christ's work but many about his person, four of which are particularly important.[4] Williams finds an "order" to these four heresies and their correction. First comes the condemnation of Arianism and Apollinarianism, then Nestorianism and Eutychianism. The first condemnations establish Christ's two natures. He is fully divine and fully human. Arianism denied the divine nature, Apollinarianism the human nature. First the church established that the Word who was not yet flesh, the eternal Son, was coeternal with the Father. This is a statement about the immanent Trinity, who God

4. "Nestorianism," in *Heresies and How to Avoid Them: Why It Matters What Christians Believe,* ed. Ben Quash and Michael Ward (Peabody, MA: Hendrickson, 2008), 38.

is in God's self. Then it established that this same Word, without any diminution or change, became incarnate and was fully human. The church fathers, often drawing upon Hebrews 1:1–4, affirmed that Jesus is both fully human and divine, the same as the Eternal Word by which God creates and sustains. The Son reflects exactly who the Father is, but he does this by repeating differently the Father's shared essence. He does this both in the immanent Trinity (God as God is in God's self) and the economic Trinity (God as God is for us). In the immanent Trinity he reflects sameness with God's *ousia* and distinction from the Father and Spirit by his *hypostasis*. In the economic Trinity he reflects the same agency as God purifying and restoring creation, but in his temporality.[5] This became the most common and traditional interpretation of the exordium, much as did John 1:1, where "the Word was with God" (1:1a) signifies the difference between God and the Word, and "the Word was God" (1:1b) represents the identity. For Hebrews, the "radiance of God's glory" (NIV) expresses the coeternity whereas the "exact imprint" (*charactēr*) of his substance (*hypostasis*) reflects the distinct agency of his person.

The distinction here is undoubtedly a dogmatic interpretation of Hebrews 1. It is how we read Hebrews in light of ecumenical conciliar decisions. Both Harold Attridge and John Webster rightly find in it a rereading of Hebrews that does not fit the author's intention, although we should be mindful that such a recontextualization is what the author does in the catena of OT Scriptures that follow the exordium. Attridge finds it anachronistic to read "later dogmatic Christology" where *apaugasma* (radiance) equals the shared divine nature and *charactēr* (exact imprint) Christ's distinct person.[6] Likewise Webster denies that "exact imprint" relates to "differentiation": "The dogmatics is beyond reproach but the exegesis surely flawed. The metaphor of imprinting does not take us in a different direction from that of effulgence, but reinforces it by speaking of the Son as the exact representation of the divine essence."[7] If we asked the

5. Greer, *Captain of Our Salvation*, 44–46. See Origen, *De. Princ.* 1.2.7, 8.
6. Attridge, *Hebrews*, 44.
7. John Webster, "One Who Is Son: Theological Reflections on the Exordium to the Epistle to the Hebrews," in *The Epistle to the Hebrews and Christian Theology*, ed. Richard Bauckham et al. (Grand Rapids: Eerdmans, 2009), 87.

author of Hebrews at the time of his writing if Attridge and Webster were correct, surely he would answer yes. "Exact imprint" reinforces "radiance" (or reflection or effulgence). But we should not forget that it does so in the dogmatic tradition as well. "Person" does not differentiate from "essence," but from the other persons. Each *hypostasis* or person is the essence of God. The differentiation is never at the expense of the essence. The Father is the essence, as are the Son and the Spirit. Likewise, the Father, Son, and Spirit are the essence. Yet there is only one essence, not three (or four).

That *charactēr tēs hypostaseōs* duplicates *apaugasma* (radiance) restates rather than critiques the exegesis at Nicaea and its defenders. Theodore, among others, interprets Hebrews 1:3 this way. "The brightness of his glory" indicates the sameness between God and Word, but he interprets "the very stamp of his nature" as identifying the "distinction between the two *hypostaseis*."[8] Note that it indicates not a distinction between God's essence and the person, but among the persons. Such an interpretation becomes commonplace among the orthodox, found equally among the Antiochenes and Alexandrians.[9] This is one reason the language "light from light" was used, finding its way into the creed, language reminiscent of Hebrews 1:3 and Wisdom 7:25–26. The question this exegesis addressed is, why the duplication? Why not just say the Son is the radiance of God, rather than restating it by saying he is the radiance and the exact imprint? The duplication suggests the Son shares the essence of God, but does so in a unique way. He is the "repetition" of God through a distinct agency. To express this requires language that expresses both sameness of essence (radiance) and distinction of person (exact imprint), without the latter opposing the former.

That Hebrews was an important source for Nicaea came as something of a surprise to the Arians, who insisted that the Son was "made" and not "eternally begotten." Hebrews also explicitly refers to Jesus as "made." Theodoret claims Arians refused to recognize Hebrews in their canon because of Hebrews 1:3.[10] Nonetheless Hebrews 1:1–4

Nicean Creed

8. Greer, *Captain of Our Salvation*, 244.

9. Ibid., 244: "The interpretation of Hebrews 1.3 which became fixed during the Arian controversy is one agreed upon by Antioch and Alexandria alike."

10. Erik M. Heen and Philip D. W. Krey, eds., *Hebrews*, Ancient Christian Commentary on Scripture 10 (Downers Grove, IL: InterVarsity Press, 2005), xxv.

and other passages in the sermon could support Arian interpretation. Verse 4 states Jesus "became" greater than the angels. How can he "become" and be coeternal with God? Hebrews 3:2 states he was "made."[11] That Hebrews could provide proof texts for either position suggests that something more than mere proof-texting took place in these debates, for they were resolved in the fourth and fifth centuries, and it should not be forgotten that they were resolved without violence. The resolution was not a bald power move.

What resolved these disputes? It was the inherent logic in Christian worship and practice. Christians worshiped Jesus as God without confusing humanity and divinity. The first commandment forbade that, and the orthodox, unlike many of the early heretics, affirmed that the God of the Old Testament was identical to the triune God. The first commandment was still in effect. Creatures were not to be worshiped, but Jesus could be. This basic practice guided the need to speak about this mystery and hold fast the central Christian practice of gathering in order to worship Jesus, something Hebrews affirms. This can especially be seen in the next logical development in the fifth century's Chalcedonian Definition. After establishing that the Son is fully divine and fully human against Arianism and Apollinarianism, by condemning Nestorianism and Eutychianism the church in council in 451 then affirmed that those natures are neither divided nor mixed. The church came to recognize that Nestorianism divided the natures too thoroughly and Eutychianism collapsed them into one.

These conciliar judgments were not abstract metaphysical speculations. What was at stake was how to read the biblical stories such that Jesus represents only one acting subject so that the Christian practice of reconciliation in all its dimensions would be affirmed. If divinity and humanity are unified as the biblical narrative of Jesus' agency expresses, then the uncreated Creator and creation are not two entities set over and against each other in strife. Instead creation has a place in the life of the Uncreated such that we can even say that in giving birth to Jesus, according to his human nature, Mary gives birth to God. No greater intimacy between God and creatures could be proclaimed than this. It was taught at Chalcedon.

11. See Koester, *Hebrews*, 24.

Chalcedonian Definition

The Chalcedonian Definition states Jesus was "born of the Virgin Mary, the Mother of God, according to the Manhood; one and the same Christ, Son, Lord, only begotten, to be acknowledged in two natures, without confusion, without change, without division, without separation; the distinction of natures being by no means taken away by the union, but rather the property of each nature being preserved, and concurring in one Person and one Subsistence, not parted or divided into two persons, but one and the same Son, and only begotten, God the Word, the Lord Jesus Christ."

http://christologia.org/creeds.html

The Fathers who developed this language clearly thought they faithfully interpreted Hebrews, and at the same time taught us how to read Scripture well so that we might be attentive hearers who communicate again what God has spoken. They never taught that the creed and definition should replace Scripture. The later statements should not supplant but guide our hearing of Scripture so we could recognize who was speaking in it. For instance, Cyril's theology emphasized "a single subject referent in all the incarnate acts."[12] He drew upon Hebrews 1:2 to express the unity of Christ's person: "The Son spoke to us in his own voice through his own body. For the flesh belonged to the only begotten and not to anyone else."[13] God no longer speaks by using instruments like prophets and ancestors. God, who is not body, speaks "through his own body."

Speaking is a temporal, human activity. It requires organs located in time and space. God has none of these; God is eternal. Nonetheless neither the divine nor human nature acts when Jesus acts but the single subject, the Word made flesh. His actions represent the rest or peace that characterizes God's intended relation with God's creation. God and creatures remain distinct, but act in the most natural, intimate unity.[14] God intends their glorification (as we shall see in 2:5–18). In his second letter to Nestorius, Cyril wrote, "We do

12. John Anthony McGuckin, *Saint Cyril of Alexandria and the Christological Controversy: Its History, Theology, and Texts* (Crestwood, NY: St. Vladimir's Seminary Press, 2004), 195–96.
13. Cited in Heen and Krey, eds., *Hebrews*, 8.
14. By emphasizing this, Cyril stands in the tradition of Irenaeus and Athanasius.

not divide out the sayings of our Saviour in the Gospels as if to two hypostases or prosopa [persons]."[15] For this reason, Cyril taught, and the church adopted and preserved, an insistence on Christ's unity, what is called the "hypostatic union." This is not only an ontological statement about who Christ is; it is also a statement about biblical interpretation and worship.

Hebrews attributes a singular agency to Jesus; he does not act as two different agents. Cyril attends to such biblical confession and restates it well: "To the same one we attribute both the divine and human characteristics, and we also say that to the same one belongs the birth and the suffering on the cross since he appropriated everything that belonged to his own flesh, while ever remaining impassible in the nature of the Godhead."[16] The one person, Jesus, acts singularly without confusing the distinction between the divine and human natures. That he so acts is the source of our perfection. He must be a high priest who is the same "yesterday, today, and forever." This is unlike any merely human priesthood with its inevitable change. But Jesus the person acts in both natures simultaneously without confusion, and that is the heart of the Christian mystery. Of course, that a person acts in a nature is no mystery; it is common sense. When we see any person acting, we do not normally say something silly such as: "Look, there is human nature acting." That would be an odd way to speak. We say, "Look, there is Bill or Sally acting," recognizing that they can only act in their human nature because we know how to distinguish it from the nature of an iguana, horse, tulip, or chair. If we were incapable of distinguishing these natures, we would be unable to make sense of any action, let alone human action. Nonetheless, what seems like common sense has become controversial in modern theology. Why this controversy has arisen is puzzling, but many modern theologians deny the metaphysics of natures, and with that denial the language forged at Nicaea and Chalcedon as well. It should no longer be included in the "confession" that Hebrews exhorts us to "hold fast."

15. McGuckin, *Saint Cyril*, 271; see also 287 in Cyril's "Explanation of the Twelve Chapters."
16. St. Cyril of Alexandria, *On the Unity of Christ*, trans. John McGuckin (Crestwood, NY: St. Vladimir's Seminary Press, 2000), 133.

FURTHER REFLECTIONS
Holding Fast, Revising, or Rejecting Conciliar Confessions

Chalcedon and Nicaea did not resolve everything. Would any of the church fathers or mothers have been so presumptuous as to say, "There, the mystery is now solved. We have 'mastered' divinity"? These councils were not filled with logic-chopping, analytic philosophers attempting to set forth purely rational explanations. They recognized they were listening to and articulating a mystery, which while not completely ineffable would and must remain mysterious. If this mystery were completely ineffable nothing and everything could be said about it, for whatever was said would be meaningless. But if it said everything, it would not need to be repeated.

Can we be attentive hearers of Hebrews' exordium and revise or reject the ecumenical consensus forged in the fourth and fifth centuries often in its name? Some modern theologians find that consensus problematic for laudable reasons, considering it a species of imperial authoritarianism or wedded to an ancient metaphysics no longer intelligible. This critique comes from diverse sources. Some representative examples are the Anabaptist J. Denny Weaver, the Catholic feminist Rosemary Radford Ruether, and the Reformed Bruce McCormack. Although they might all claim we should "hold fast the confession," the metaphysical language used at Nicaea and Chalcedon is not for them central to that confession.

Denny Weaver does not reject that Jesus is fully God and fully human, but he thinks the language used by the Fathers was driven by an inappropriate accommodation to the Roman Empire. He asks, "What is there about these formulas of Nicaea and Chalcedon that express the character of the reign of God, in particular its nonviolent character?" It is an important question. Nicaea and Chalcedon should help us interpret God's gracious economy, not supplant it with something else. God's reign has this nonviolent character, and Hebrews gives evidence of it.[17] When Weaver answers his question with "virtually nothing," however, he fails to see the nonviolent

17. Denny Weaver, *The Nonviolent Atonement* (Grand Rapids: Eerdmans, 2001), 61–66.

reconciliation between humanity and divinity present at Chalcedon.[18] He finds nothing more than "abstract categories" at work in these ecumenical councils, and therefore calls for revision.[19] This significantly misses the essential teaching of these Fathers, and the beauty of what they saw in Hebrews. Jesus' agency in that book is singular even while he acts completely human (2:17–18) and divine (1:3). He is the condition for the possibility of recognizing peace between God and creation as well as among creatures. If God and humanity can become one in the Person of Jesus, and work in perfect harmony, then all those metaphysical views that see an inevitable violence as definitive for the relation between God and creatures misperceive that relation. Athanasius recognized this and stated it explicitly in his treatise *On the Incarnation*. He asked what was the proof of Christ's divinity. He found it in the new life it produced. This is the best answer to Weaver's important question.

While they were yet idolaters, the Greeks and Barbarians were always at war with each other, and were even cruel to their own kith and kin. . . . Indeed, the whole course of their life was carried on with the weapons, and the sword with them replaced the staff and was the mainstay of all aid. . . . But, strange to relate, since they came over to the school of Christ, as men moved with real compunction they have laid aside their murderous cruelty and are war-minded no more. On the contrary, all is peace among them and nothing remains save desire for friendship.

—Athanasius

On the Incarnation (1944; repr. Crestwood, NY: St. Vladimir's Seminary Press, 1996), 90.

The Catholic feminist Ruether finds the traditional doctrine of the incarnation deeply problematic. It represents "the imperial Christ of Nicene theology," which "was constructed by the fusion of two basic symbols from the twin heritages of Christian theology: Hebrew messianism and Greek philosophy."[20] Neither helps us hear God's communication well, so they should be rejected in favor of an iconoclastic interpretation of Jesus. The first source, Hebrew

18. Ibid., 93.
19. Ibid., 94.
20. Rosemary Radford Ruether, *To Change the World: Christology and Cultural Criticism* (1981; repr. New York: Crossroad, 1990), 48.

messianism, "represents the dream of revenge of the oppressed nation which will, through God's help, turn the tables on the great imperial nations, and itself become the new imperial ruling power." Like Nietzsche, she finds Hebrews' apocalypticism to be a form of resentment that seeks the very imperial power it attempts to displace. For Nietzsche the desire in Judaism and Christianity for a "different city" than the one currently in power arises from resentment: "These weak people—some day or other they too intend to be the strong . . . their kingdom too shall come."[21] Christians claim virtue in weakness, but it masquerades as a form of power that leads to resentment. They not only masquerade their desire for power behind a putative weakness, but they also have an inordinate desire for power that seeks it beyond this life throughout eternity: "one needs eternal life, so as to be eternally indemnified in the 'kingdom of God.'" For Nietzsche Christian apocalyptic hides this impotence behind a lust for power that goes far beyond that which the Romans themselves desired.

Ruether's second source is "Greek philosophy," which "added the concept of the divine Logos or Nous of God which discloses the mind of God and manifests, in noetic form, the plan of nature. This Nous of God is not only *demiourgos*, or agent of God in creation, but also the means through which the universe is governed. This concept is set in the context of a hierarchical 'chain of Being.' Just as the Nous of God governs nature, so the Greeks must govern barbarians, masters govern slaves, and men govern women."[22] Like Weaver, the culprit distorting Christianity is Greek metaphysics, and like him she accepts Adolf von Harnack's "hellenization thesis," which interprets the ecumenical consensus of the fourth and fifth centuries as ruled by that metaphysics. Unlike Weaver, she does not want the creed revised but its vision rejected for a completely different Christology. "In this vision, patriarchy, hierarchy, slavery and Graeco-Roman imperialism have all been taken over and baptized by the Christian church. . . . Imperial Christology wins in the fourth

21. Friedrich Nietzsche, *On the Genealogy of Morals*, trans. Walter Kaufmann (New York: Vintage Books, 1989), 48–53.

22. Ruether, *To Change the World*, 48. Curiously Ruether seems to describe Gnosticism here much more so than orthodox Christianity.

century as a sacralized vision of patriarchal, hierarchical and Euro-centred imperial control." How we can have a "Euro-centred imperial control" before there was a "Europe" is perplexing, but Ruether's critique of Nicaea makes Weaver's position seem mild.[23] Nicaea perpetuates most of the evil in Western history. Her counterproposal is to do away with this Christology and replace it with "the prophetic iconoclastic Christ." This is the Christ who always calls into question all unjust structures pointing toward a new future that never quite arrives. This would seem to be another version of modern apocalyptic. It is an apocalyptic that announces a new future order, but at the same time insists that it can never arrive. Its sole purpose is to call into question any actually existing order: "The meaning of Christ is located in a new future order still to come that transcends the power structures of historical societies, including those erected in the Christian era in 'Christ's name.'"[24] Because the fall of Christianity was so thorough in the fourth century, and has remained so until the present, we cannot hear from the past. We can only be attentive hearers to a future that has not arrived.

For different reasons, the Reformed theologian Bruce McCormack also finds revisions to Nicaea and Chalcedon necessary. Although he is more favorable to their intent than the above theologians, he also finds the same culprit distorting Christianity—Greek metaphysics. For McCormack, the Fathers' formulations suffered because they adopted a "substantialist metaphysics" to express the great mysteries of faith. They assumed "substances" that endured over time and were the basis for accidents that would then be attributed to them. According to McCormack the Fathers thought of the triune persons as "members of a class" and God's essence as a substance that was wrongly considered to be impassible.[25] Because they already assumed they knew the "substance" of God, Jesus' own historical

23. Ibid., 48–49. Can we intelligently speak of "Europe" until at least Charlemagne in the eighth century?
24. Ruether, *To Change the World*, 55.
25. Bruce L. McCormack, "'With Loud Cries and Tears': The Humanity of the Son in the Epistle to the Hebrews," in *Epistle to the Hebrews and Christian Theology*, ed. Bauckham et al., 47. This is an odd critique given that the Fathers uniformly rejected claiming God could be placed in a genus.

actualization of that substance was not adequately accounted for in their doctrine of God. The sixteenth-century Reformation and Barth's radical revisions in the twentieth century provide a necessary corrective.

McCormack draws on Hebrews for a revision of Chalcedon. He interprets Hebrews 1, especially 1:2, in terms of election. It is about "the language of election (as a pre-temporal event) and creation (as the event in which time as we know it was created). The time before time is not time as we know it; it is the 'time' which founds time—which is a way of saying that 'eternity' is not to be equated with timelessness. It is also not to be equated with a metaphysical realm."[26] In other words, the election of Jesus founds time. Hebrews then is not about metaphysics because there is no space or time before this election. For McCormack there is no *logos asarkos*, that is, an unfleshed Logos who is the Eternal Word prior to the incarnation. The incarnation as a pretemporal election that is not timelessness constitutes who God is in God's triunity. For this reason he denies any distinction between the immanent and economic Trinity. That means the history of Jesus now constitutes God's being. Karl Barth's theology alone recognized the significance of this shift, and with Barth, according to McCormack, we must now think Christology "*under the conditions of modernity.*"[27] He does so by replacing Chalcedon's metaphysics of "substance" with a dynamic, historicized actualism. McCormack reads Hebrews 5:5–10 in terms of this modern, revisionary, and revolutionary Barthian theology, reading the exordium in light of Hebrews 5.

Crucial to McCormack's reinterpretation of traditional Christology is Hebrews 5:7, "Jesus offered up prayers and supplications, with loud cries and tears." He notes that the "performative agent" here is "clearly the man Jesus." But we do not yet know the "ontological subject," which we were already told in the exordium was the eternal Son. Here is where he offers an interesting revision of Chalcedon. We do not know the ontological subject before, or apart from, the

26. Ibid., 58.

27. Ibid., 48. Could Barth have ever made such a claim? Christology is to be conditioned by modern knowledge? How do we square this with Barth's central thesis that "Revelation is the condition that conditions all things without itself being conditioned"?

performative subject. McCormack traces the "complex" and "composite" subject in Hebrews, coming to one of the troubling passages that the Arians affirmed against the orthodox, "Although he was a Son, he learned obedience through what he suffered" (5:8). He notes the oddness of this claim: "It is the fact that he is the eternal Son that makes the learning of obedience to be surprising." A more traditional interpretation of Hebrews would assume we do know something about human and divine natures. The former suffer and die; the latter does not. So the single subject Jesus suffers and dies manifesting his human nature, but because he does so as at the same time he is divine, that suffering and dying human nature is taken into a divine nature that cannot suffer and die. It is redeemed, deified. McCormack rejects this because he rejects any metaphysics of "nature." He finds Cyril's Christology, with its doctrine of deification, "instrumentalizing" Jesus' humanity. It does not play an adequate role in salvation. He worries it might allow for the natures to be independent actors. This is an important concern, and it was exactly what worried Cyril about Nestorius, who could not imagine a nature without hypostasis, an acting subject.[28] Cyril opposed Nestorius's language of a "prosopoic union" because he thought it made the humanity a mere "mask" and did not unite the humanity with divinity.[29] McCormack shares a similar concern, but now directed against Cyril. For this reason, he claims we must "explore the ontological implications of" Hebrews 5 and offers a radical revision of the tradition.

> What is ruled out, it seems to me, is any "instrumentalizing" of the humanity of Jesus. The subject who here suffers humanly is the *God*-human in his *divine*-human unity. If we did not say this, we would have to confine the suffering to the human "nature" alone, thereby treating the human nature as an independent subject. But no, the "subject" is the eternal Son who is seen to have suffered humanly. Such a conception makes best sense against the background of the thought of

28. For McCormack, the Reformed tradition offers a corrective with its "healthy tilt toward Nestorianism" ("With Loud Cries and Tears," 39).
29. Cyril, *On the Unity,* 83, 128.

> a "communication" of that which is done by and to Jesus to the eternal Son—so that the unity of this "composite Person" is maintained.[30]

This is an intriguing interpretation of Hebrews, which seeks to maintain Jesus' unity that Cyril rightly saw as necessary to read Hebrews well. Nonetheless, it should cause us to pause and take note of the radical revision of the Christian tradition intended here and ask if it speaks the Word definitely spoken differently, or revises things so thoroughly that it borders on speaking a different word. The laudable effort to avoid attributing a twofold agency to Jesus in Hebrews, coupled with the loss of any account of "natures," means that the temporal, human, suffering Jesus communicates something to the eternal Son. What is the communication from Jesus to the eternal Son? It is suffering, and by implication—death. For if it is truly human suffering that is communicated to the eternal Son, then it must also communicate death. Any other interpretation of divine passibility simply refuses this logical conclusion.

Is the logical implication of this move a "Christian" form of atheism? "God is dead, and we have killed him." This is an interpretation some theologians and philosophers offer on Hebrews 5. This expression originally comes from Luther, but then gets mediated through Hegel, and is finally taken up by Nietzsche. It could be a proper Christian declaration, if we maintain as Chalcedon did that the divine and human natures are not to be confused. Having rejected metaphysics, McCormack cannot affirm this. God suffers.

If God suffers, then Christianity promulgates the death of God. No other conclusion satisfies. This revised Christianity does away with all transcendence, leaving us with a purely immanent materialism that can be mapped on a grid. It reduces God to a historical force. As we will see below, more than a few theologians and philosophers see this as the logical consequence of Christianity, and something to be affirmed. We will take this up in the commentary on Hebrews 5. Clearly this is not McCormack's position. His revision is intended to be both "orthodox" and "modern," but if the human

30. McCormack, "With Loud Cries and Tears," 66.

Jesus really constitutes the Trinity and communicates suffering to God, how can we avoid assuming he also communicates death? What possibly prevents this implication?

When we now hear the admonition, "hold fast the confession," should we include the confession as it developed at Nicaea and Chalcedon, or must we reject or revise that confession, listening to Hebrews under the condition of modernity? Although they greatly differ in how this is to occur, Ruether, Weaver, and McCormack agree that it should. Unlike them, A. N. Williams finds in Christian orthodoxy an intriguing way of life because it is both dangerous and beautiful at the same time. Rather than revising our metaphysics and dogma because of modern historical shifts, she suggests that the metaphysics and dogma of orthodoxy invite us to revise how we think about the world for "the immensity of [orthodoxy's] declarations and implications" call us "radically to revise the way we think about the world and act in it as the consequence of our belief."[31] Its "immensity" can be found in calling Mary *theotokos*, the "God-bearer." Its implications are in what it means that God, without ceasing to be God, can become that which is not God, humanity, and act as a single subject made known in both natures without collapsing the distinction between them. Once we know that this is who Jesus is, then what he has done takes on all the more significance. The difference here represents one of the greatest controversies before the church today. Should we revise our metaphysics and dogma in order to fit historical shifts and new contexts, or should we interpret those shifts and contexts within the framework of that metaphysics and dogma? Perhaps Hebrews can help us, once again, resolve our controversy.

What Has Jesus Done? He Creates, Sustains, Purifies, and Receives Authority

The exordium points in two important directions as to what Jesus accomplished, which are then fleshed out in the sermon. First, he "made purification for sins" and then he "sat down at the right hand

31. "Nestorianism," 36.

of God." The Word God speaks in Jesus has a sense of agency that could be confusing. He is God, comes from God, accomplishes something as human, and returns to God. What he accomplishes is this act of purification, including his sacrifice, that then results in his enthronement at God's right hand. This requires a distinction between God's immanent and economic reality. God in God's self is eternally the reflection and return of God's essence. That identical essence takes on flesh in the Son, effecting God's economic reality. The subject remains identical as the Word, who is the eternal, consubstantial Word spoken by the Father, but who has now assumed flesh. This requires that we acknowledge that the "flesh" the Word becomes does not have its own *hypostasis* or acting subject. The Word did not enter into an already acting human subject. The Word became flesh. This acknowledgment is called the doctrine of the *anhypostaton*. It means that the flesh the Word assumed was a nature; it is human, but it has no hypostasis of its own. Its hypostasis is in the eternal, consubstantial Word, which is called the doctrine of the *enhypostaton*.[32] This preserves God's definitive speaking. What Jesus accomplishes, the Word accomplishes.

What Jesus accomplishes is purification. The theme of making purification runs throughout Hebrews. Christ is both priest and victim, whose sacrifice makes perfect. Hebrews relates purification and perfection. Indeed, they are the same act. Purification is a cleansing, a removal of something that does not belong. Christ's obedience is his purification; he is without sin. Perfection is a fulfilling, a completion of something that should be. Hebrews sees Christ as effecting both simultaneously. This crucial theme noted here in the exordium also concludes this first section of Hebrews when in 2:5–18 we are told that Christ perfects through his obedience in becoming like us in all things, sin excepted. He shares all that humanity is, including death, taking to himself and removing as the Eternal Word the thing that cannot and does not belong—the power and fear of

32. Lest this sound like Apollinariansm where the divine Logos replaces the human, we should mind well the counsel of the Orthodox theologian Sergius Bulgakov, who explains "in-hypostatization" not as an "abstract, formal-logical definition without any attention to its ontological meaning." Bulgakov's rich interpretation of "in-hypostatization" can be found in *The Lamb of God*, trans. Boris Jakim (Grand Rapids: Eerdmans, 2008), 182–90.

death (2:14–15). But he does this because he is the fullness of what a priest should be—"merciful and faithful." His sacrifice only works because it comes from this fullness. It is from this fullness that he can cleanse. The cleansing then is not a diminishment, but a completion or perfection. All of these themes will need further discussion. Hebrews' bloody, sacrificial language has become offensive to many. Theologians also challenge the claim that Christ is without sin. We will explore these controversial themes more fully below, but what matters for now is to recognize Hebrews' argument. Christ cleanses and completes by making himself priest and victim. He presents not his death to God, but the blood of his sacrifice, which is his life.[33] It is eternal. For this reason, he "sat down at the right hand of the Majesty on high."

That he "sat down at the right hand of the Majesty on high" is not Hebrews' invention. It is found in a number of OT passages, especially Psalm 110:1 and 4, which are favorite texts of Hebrews.[34] He returns to this theme as the culmination of the catena: "Sit at my right hand until I make your enemies a footstool for your feet" (Heb. 1:13). This theme of subjection gets expanded in 2:5–9, and it forms the heart of the sermon in chapter 7, which directly quotes Psalm 110:4. It is cited three times in Hebrews; and while Psalm 110:1 is used in the Gospels, Acts, and Hebrews, only Hebrews quotes verse 4.[35] Interestingly, none of the places where the psalm is used quote verses 2–3. Psalm 110:1–4 is an enthronement psalm that proclaims:

> (1) The LORD says to my Lord,
> "Sit at my right hand
> until I make your enemies your footstool."
> (2) The LORD sends out from Zion
> your mighty scepter.
> Rule in the midst of your foes.

33. I am indebted to David M. Moffitt for this important distinction.

34. Psalm 110:1 is found in Heb. 1:3, 13; 8:1; 10:12–13; and 12:2. Psalm 110:4 is found or alluded to in Heb. 5:6, 10; 6:20; 7:3, 8, 11, 15–17, 21, 24–25, and 28. See David M. Hay, *Glory at the Right Hand*, Society of Biblical Literature Monograph Series 18 (Nashville: Abingdon Press, 1973), 165–66.

35. Hay, *Glory at the Right Hand*, 37, 47.

(3) Your people will offer themselves willingly
on the day you lead your forces on the holy mountains.
From the womb of the morning,
like dew, your youth will come to you.
(4) The LORD has sworn and will not change his mind,
"You are a priest forever
according to the order of Melchizedek."

Too much should not be made from an argument based on silence, but the use of this psalm in Hebrews gives us some insight. Verses 2–3 fall away; they are never quoted. Verses 1 and 4 provide the framework for Hebrews' Christology. Sometimes doctrine arises as much from what we must forget as what we affirm. We rightly forget interpretations once accepted but that are recognized over time as conflicting with the full biblical witness. The former must decrease while the latter increases. Jesus does not lead "forces" in the same way the psalmist intended. This verse does not fit, nor does it appear in all the New Testament usages of Psalm 110.

Like the Synoptic Gospel writers, Hebrews refers the second use of "Lord" in Psalm 110:1 to Jesus. He first does this in the exordium, where he has already made strong claims that the Word spoken in Jesus is of the same essence as God. "The Lord says to my Lord" has become an intra-Trinitarian conversation. That Word proclaimed invites us to listen in to that eternal speech.

Hebrews returns to this important psalm and its new interpretation. In 1:13 the author employs a well-known ancient rhetorical strategy by contrasting what God says to Jesus in Psalm 110 to what God said to any angel. Then in Hebrews 8:1 he brings together both Psalm 110:1 and 4 to claim that Jesus sits at the right hand of God because he is the true high priest. His priesthood gives him this authority. It is a priesthood of his risen, glorified humanity, which is the basis for the confession they must hold fast.[36] This is more fully elaborated at Hebrews 10:12–13, which states that Christ continues

36. See David M. Moffitt, "'If Another Priest Arises': Jesus' Resurrection and the High Priestly Christology of Hebrews," in *A Cloud of Witnesses: The Theology of Hebrews in Its Ancient Contexts*, ed. Richard Bauckham, Daniel Driver, Trevor Hart, and Nathan MacDonald (New York: T & T Clark, 2008), 68–79.

to wait at the right hand until his enemies are made his footstool. They are not yet that, but Hebrews thinks they will be, which could be a form of resentment, as Ruether suggests; but how Christ conquers avoids such a reproach. Indeed, as we shall see, Hebrews explicitly counsels against resentment even toward one's enemies. In 12:2, using Psalm 110 again, the author tells his listeners to look to Jesus, who sits at the right hand for one reason: "who for the sake of the joy that was set before him endured the cross, disregarding its shame, and has taken his seat at the right hand of the throne of God." This crucial use of Psalm 110 in Hebrews (and we have not even begun to discuss how central Ps. 110:4 is to Hebrews' discussion of Melchizedek in chaps. 5–7) illumines how Christ has conquered his enemies. This is an unmistakable theme in Hebrews. Christ is victorious. But Christ has not conquered as the one who "led forces on the holy mountains." That theme from Psalm 110:3 disappears. He has conquered as "priest."

Rather than Plato's well-known "philosopher-king," who knows both the good and how to exercise military power (more on this below), for Hebrews the "priest-king" builds the truly just city. He does so "after the order of Melchizedek," who is first a "king of righteousness" and then a "king of peace," who knows how to grant rest (7:1–3). Jesus creates, sustains, purifies, and receives authority in order to be the priest-king of God's righteous and peaceful city, a city where those who are attentive to Hebrews' words are already "his house" (3:6). The Word God definitively spoke who reflects God's own being, creating, and sustaining the world—that same Word became in all things like us to create and sustain yet again, this time fashioning a city or household reflecting God's own architectural designs. Hebrews sets forth a profound political theology.

Because the Word made flesh purifies and perfects, completing the true city God initiated at creation, he bears a great "name." Before moving on to the catena, some reflection on how the first four verses end is in order. This section ends, much like Paul's famous hymn in Philippians, with a statement about the "name." Paul writes, "Therefore God also highly exalted him and gave him the name that is above every name, so that at the name of Jesus every knee should bend, in heaven and on earth and under the earth" (Phil. 2:9–10). Hebrews concludes the exordium with a similar theological pronouncement: "having become as much superior to angels as the name he has inherited is more excellent than theirs" (Heb. 1:4). Most English translations do not bring out the form of the Greek text, which as we have already seen is important to its content. The single sentence of the exordium culminates in its concluding word: "name."

The Greek word order is better set forth as, "having become as much superior to the angels as more excellent than them, he inherited the name." Like Paul in Philippians 2, we are not told what the "name" is. The name "Jesus" is certainly not somehow a more excellent name. It was quite common. No one would have bowed before it or viewed it as some kind of inheritance that would make one worthy of sitting at God's right hand. Nor for that matter would the mere term "son"; even the phrase "son of God" would not have that kind of significance. Richard Bauckham states, "The potent imagery of sitting on the cosmic throne has only one attested significance: it indicates his participation in the unique sovereignty of God over the world."[37] If that is the case, along with the fact that Hebrews has already called Jesus "reflection of God's glory" and "exact imprint of God's very being," I think it makes most sense to read "name" here like any good first-century Jew, or even someone who knew Judaism well, would have done. It is "the name" that should not be specified, the name given to Moses on Mount Sinai that made Israel elect from all other nations, the name of God, YHWH. It is also interesting to note that the first participle used to explain Jesus' action as Son (3.1 above), where he is then called "reflection of God's glory" and "exact imprint of God's very being," is *ōn,* the present active nominative participle of the verb "to be." This is the same as the LXX interpretation of God's name in Exodus 3:14: *egō eimi ho ōn* (I am the one who is, or, I am being). Could the use of *ōn* by Hebrews have a double meaning, both the participle stating who Jesus is and an allusion to the divine name? It would depend on how the words were read, what was emphasized, what knowing glances were offered. Such a brilliant use of language is not beyond the author's rich prose. However

37. Bauckham, "The Divinity of Jesus Christ in the Epistle to the Hebrews," in *Epistle to the Hebrews and Christian Theology,* ed. Bauckham et al., 33.

interesting such a suggestion is, it reads too much into the use of the participle. It is also unnecessary, for the author claims Jesus is the Eternal Word without such an interesting use of a participle.

No scholars I know of, ancient or modern, make any explicit connection between *ōn* here and the divine name. Gregory of Nyssa, however, did come close. He explains that the use of the present participle of "to be," *ōn*, here can only be interpreted as saying that the Son exists forever: "The evidence of the 'is' [rather than 'becomes'] explains that the Son exists forever and ever and eternal and above anything that would indicate time."[38] Only God could bear this sense of "is." Richard Bauckham interprets 1:3 similarly: "Though most of the commentators do not think so, this can only refer to the divine name, as must 'the name which is above every name'" (Phil. 2:9).[39] This does not exclude the fact that it is *Jesus*, the human agent, who now bears this name. His name has become "more excellent" because it is also identified with *the* name.

1:5–14

The Catena

Discussing the first four verses (the first sentence) of Hebrews at length was necessary. They contain in seed most of what will then be developed. But that Hebrews continues after the first verse could cause surprise. If God has definitively spoken in the Son, why keep speaking? Why not stop there? One key answer is found in Hebrews' use of the word "today." The Word God definitively speaks, which is eternal, can never be exhausted in our temporal articulations. We are always given "today" to speak this identical Word differently and to hear it afresh. This "today" stretched into the past as Hebrews now shows how the diverse manners of God's previous communication were anticipations of God's definitive Word. The Word God speaks in the Son knows no temporal limitations. It was the same in the

38. Greer, *Captain of Our Salvation*, 101.

39. Richard Bauckham, *God Crucified: Monotheism and Christology in the New Testament* (Grand Rapids: Eerdmans, 1998), 34. Bauckham has a fuller discussion of this in "Divinity of Jesus Christ," 15–36.

past as it is today and as it will be in the future. The catena of seven OT quotes in 1:5–14 makes this plain. Each of these texts employs a common rhetorical strategy showing Christ's excellence by contrasting him with something in itself excellent, but not so in comparison to him. The first three are answers to the rhetorical question, To which of the angels did God say?

1:5a *"You are my Son; today I have begotten you" (Ps. 2:7)*

The first two divine utterances to, and about, Jesus let us know that the name "Son" now participates in the more excellent name Jesus bears. That these passages are from the Old Testament and were already known as applying to David show us that it is not the mere name "Son" that bears this excellence. David would not have been worshiped, as is claimed for the Son in Hebrews 1:6. "Son" has now come to mean something more than it did in the Davidic covenant, even though that covenant is necessary to understand what it means for Jesus to be "Son."

The use of Psalm 2 could pose a dilemma for an orthodox Christology. Bart Ehrman suggests it is the original reading of Luke 3:22 found in some of the most ancient manuscripts. So rather than what we find in most present translations, "You are my Son, the Beloved; with you I am well pleased," Luke 3:22 may have been identical to Hebrews 1:5a, "You are my Son; today I have begotten you." It was most likely changed, Ehrman suggests, by an orthodox scribe who made certain the text did not give any credence to an adoptionistic Christology in which Jesus becomes the Son at his baptism rather than his birth. The original was supposedly "doctrinally suspect."[40]

Whether or not that is the case with Luke 3:22, the biblical authors and church fathers seldom shied away from using Psalm 2:7 as a standard OT text for Christology. Hebrews' eschatological use of "today" prompted the church fathers to read it other than adoptionistically. They did not seem to think they needed to alter the text for it to suit their Christology. The "today" in Hebrews is already a clear

40. Bart Ehrman, *The Orthodox Corruption of Scripture* (Oxford: Oxford University Press, 1993), 63.

confession of God's eternal rest, the opening to transcendence in the immanent that makes it possible to still enter that "rest" because it does not disappear with the flux of time. It is the dual nature of the "today" that makes it so theologically rich. It is both God's eternal rest and its temporal presence.

Athanasius interpreted the "today" as a reference to the eternal generation of the Son, whereas Gregory of Nyssa interpreted it as a reference to incarnation. Like Gregory, Theodore of Mopsuestia read it in relation to the mission of the Son in the incarnation.[41] At a much later date Thomas Aquinas finds both the eternal generation and the historical mission in the passage. He claims that "today" is an "adverb of the present time," while "I have begotten" is a verb implying completion and perfection. Therefore when God says, "today I have begotten you," he does so that we might "know that this generation is always and is perfect and so permanence is signified in *Today* and perfection in *I have begotten*." Here "today" refers to the eternal generation of the Son, but it could also signify "temporal generation," referring to the incarnation. The same passage can be read in two ways, one referring to the eternal generation of the Son, the other to the Son's temporal incarnate mission. Aquinas read 1:5 with this twofold significance by noting the two different locations for Jesus in the first two chapters. Those two locations will help us understand Hebrews' use of "today." In 1:4, and throughout the catena, the triumphant Jesus takes his place above the angels. But this would seem to contradict 2:9, where he is made lower than the angels "for a little while." Can he be both higher and lower? Aquinas resolved this by understanding Christ's humanity in two ways. Hebrews 2:9 is understood in terms of the "infirmity of the flesh." Because of his suffering, Jesus is made lower than the angels, whereas 1:4 and the catena refer to the "plenitude of grace" present in Christ's flesh, which makes him triumph over death. The "today" of the Son includes both his eternal generation that makes this plenitude possible and his economic mission that takes place in a temporal sequence.

41. Greer, *Captain of Our Salvation*, 118.

1:5b *"I will be his Father, and he will be my Son"* *(2 Sam. 7:14)*

For Hebrews, Jesus inherits the promise given to David in 2 Samuel 7. He is the "Son" who is the fulfillment of God's promise to David. Second Samuel 7 plays a crucial role in Hebrews. It begins with the intriguing statement, "Now when the king was settled in his house, and the LORD had given him rest from all his enemies" (2 Sam. 7:1). Although this passage is never cited in Hebrews, the sermon could easily be interpreted as a commentary on it. Jesus is presented in Hebrews 3:5, 6 as a king who constructs a house even greater than Moses did. This house provides "rest" for God's people, which brings not only settledness but also disruption. It calls its listeners to look for a different city than the one they currently inhabit.

In the Davidic covenant David attempts to make God as "settled" as he has become. He tells the prophet Nathan that he now lives in a house while God remains in a "tent," that movable dwelling whereby God wandered with Israel, the tabernacle. Nathan, without consulting God in prayer, tells David to do what he has in mind, which is to build God a house. But the "word of the LORD" comes to the prophet that night and reverses expectations. Here we find an example of God speaking to an ancestor through the prophet. God asks, "Are you the one to build me a house to live in?" The question is double-edged.

The word of the LORD came to Nathan: Go and tell my servant David: Thus says the LORD: Are you the one to build me a house to live in? I have not lived in a house since the day I brought up the people of Israel from Egypt to this day, but I have been moving about in a tent and a tabernacle. Wherever I have moved about among all the people of Israel, did I ever speak a word with any of the tribal leaders of Israel, . . . saying, "Why have you not built me a house of cedar?"

—2 Samuel 7:4–7

On the one hand, God's question reveals David's foolishness. God never asked to live in a settled dwelling.

In one sense, then, David's question gets it all wrong: God does not seek the security of a "house." But in another sense it is the right question, even the most important one. God's question—"Are you the one to build me a house to live in?"—gets turned back on David. God says, "Moreover the LORD declares to you that the LORD will make you a house," and that house will give "you rest from all your enemies" (2 Sam. 7:11). Of course, one manifestation of God's promise to David will be the temple, a house for God built not by David but by his son Solomon. Patterned after the tabernacle and preserving the ark of the covenant where God's glory dwells (Exod. 40:34), it is one answer to the question God puts to David—"Would you build my house?"

The temple is a word from God about God's presence and glory. But for Hebrews and NT authors, it was not the definitive Word. That would be Jesus' own body, which is the temple or tabernacle where the glory of God also came to dwell. This is a common theme throughout Scripture as the story of transfiguration in Luke and Matthew proclaims (Luke 9:28–36; Matt. 17:1–8). Likewise the prologue of John affirms this when it tells us Jesus "lived [*eskēnōsen*] among us," revealing the "glory" of God. The verb *eskēnōsen* draws on the language for the tabernacle, *skēnē,* which is also a favorite of Hebrews. Hebrews' argument makes sense only when read in the canonical context of the Davidic covenant, for it also gives an answer to the question God put to David. The author of Hebrews offers the answer directly to his readers, telling them, "we are his house if we hold firm the confidence and the pride that belong to hope" (3:6b). When he tells us this, he refers back to this second OT passage in the catena, reminding us, "Christ . . . was faithful over God's house as a son" (3:6a).

1:6 *"Let all God's angels worship him" (Deut 32:43)*

This third citation from the Old Testament draws on listeners' recognition of the Jewish tradition that angels or intermediary beings were not to be worshiped. It is the case that angels worshiped glorified humans in Jewish apocalyptic.[42] Jesus enters into heaven analogous to such glorified humans, but this should not cause us to think that Hebrews confuses the worship of God and creatures. For Hebrews, Jesus as human is also God. The rhetorical strategy

42. See *Life of Adam and Eve,* and *1 Enoch.*

of comparing Jesus to the angels primarily works because Hebrews' audience knew not to worship angels. The exclusive worship given to God, even by "gods" in Deuteronomy 32, is now exclusively associated with Jesus. How can Jesus, a creature who could be pointed to and identified, be an object of worship? How is this not a scandal?

Orthodox Jews still recognize that it is. My wife worked at a hospital with numerous Orthodox Jews, with whom she became friends. At one point, one of those friends became sufficiently assured of their friendship that she raised a question that troubled her: "Here is what I don't understand about you Christians. Why are you not idolaters?" My wife was at first taken aback by the question, so she asked her what she meant. Her friend's response suggested that Christianity violated the first two commandments. We had other gods besides God, which we turned into an image in Jesus. It is an understandable question and concern. The doctrines of the Trinity and incarnation are the only possible defense.

The average first-century religious Roman or Greek would most likely not have raised the question, any more than a religious pluralist might feel compelled to raise it today. If "divinity" is a genus that contains numerous individual representations, then exclusive worship of one God as opposed to others constitutes no problem. Indeed, it would seem to be a recipe for toleration. We all have our particular representation of some larger genus called "God," but no one's particular representation should be assumed to exhaust the category of that larger genus. If first-century Jews had become slack in their devotion to God as some interpreters from the history of religions school suggest, then this would not have constituted a problem for such syncretistic Jews. It could only constitute a problem if Hebrews' audience still adhered to that exclusive worship. Surely that assumption is the most reasonable way to make sense of the comparison used here in the catena. If the listeners could have said, "Sure we will worship him, and we will worship the angels, and the divine spark inside each of us," then the sermon would have failed. Only because the intended audience knows this is impermissible does it work.

The next Scripture citation reminds the readers what the angels are.

1:7 *"You make the winds your messengers, fire and flame your ministers" (Ps. 104:4)*

They are ministering spirits. This is their mission. Then follows three citations contrasting the angels' mission with that of the Son. They repeat almost identically who the Son is and what he does in the exordium. The final one (1:13) concludes by an allusion to Psalm 110, which we already found alluded to in 1:3. They also lead us into Hebrews' complicated understanding of creation, especially anthropology, and its function in redemption.

1:8–9 *"Your throne, O God, is forever and ever, and the righteous scepter is the scepter of your kingdom. You have loved righteousness and hated wickedness; therefore God, your God, has anointed you with the oil of gladness beyond your companions" (Ps. 45:6–7)*

We already know from the exordium that Jesus occupies the eternal "throne." Here we find another important element. It is not only who Christ is that entitles him to occupy that throne, it is also what he has done. He perfects righteousness, his own and others, and he does so as human.

1:10–12 *"In the beginning, Lord, you founded the earth, and the heavens are the work of your hands; they will perish, but you remain; they will all wear out like clothing; like a cloak you will roll them up, and like clothing they will be changed. But you are the same, and your years will never end" (Ps. 102:25–27)*

The use of Psalm 102 returns to a theme in the exordium—creation, which will be more fully discussed by the use of Psalm 8 in Hebrews 2:6b–8. Hebrews gives us not only a Christology, but also a profound doctrine of creation. Does it assume that creation will be destroyed? If so, then this lends support to Ruether's critique of Jewish apocalyptic. It creates a cosmic dualism where creation is so utterly devoid of goodness that it must be destroyed and thoroughly replaced. Hebrews can certainly be read this way. Kenneth Schenck states, "The earthly realm in Hebrews is transitory and will eventually be 'removed.'"[43] Besides 1:11, 12:27 suggests this. In the latter God shakes creation so that only what can withstand God's voice remains. The "created things" are then *metathesin,* which the NRSV (and most English translations) render as "removed," although it also means "transformed."

Christopher Hitchens finds this kind of thinking one reason Christianity is poisonous: "With a necessary part of its collective mind, religion looks forward to the destruction of the world."[44] Perhaps, but the idea that God intends to destroy creation stands in tension both with 1:11–12 and the claims Hebrews makes for Jesus throughout the sermon, especially in 2:17. After all, he becomes like us "in every respect." If creation is destined for destruction, then why would Hebrews insist on Jesus' creatureliness? He does not shed it when he "sits at the right hand." Is it adequate to read Hebrews' understanding the purpose of creation as "destruction" and on its way to perish, or is it better to read it as destined for "change," to take on the "perfection" and "completion" for which it was intended? This is an important question. The answer to it will affect how we read *metathesin* in 12:27. The answer, I will suggest, is to be found in Hebrews' Christology and its inevitable relation to anthropology. The answer can be found in the glorification of humanity God intends.

1:13 *"Sit at my right hand until I make your enemies a footstool for your feet" (Ps. 110:1)*

The catena concludes with a second use of Psalm 110 forming an inclusion with what was already stated in 1:3. But now it raises the question, What does it mean for Jesus to be at God's right hand? After all, neither the enemies of Jesus nor those of Hebrews' audience are his footstool. Chapter 2 will provide some answers to these questions.

The statements about Christ's person and mission in the exordium

43. Kenneth L. Schenck, *Cosmology and Eschatology in Hebrews: The Settings of the Sacrifice,* SNTSMS 143 (Cambridge: Cambridge University Press, 2007), 73.
44. Christopher Hitchens, *God Is Not Great: How Religion Poisons Everything* (New York: Twelve, 2007), 59.

and catena mutually reinforce each other. That Jesus is Son receives its significance from his session at the right hand and the name he bears. He is to be worshiped. Moreover, the first reference to "God" in verse 6 and to "Lord" in verse 10 make best sense if we understood the Word as their antecedent. The first describes Christ's work that culminates in his session on the throne. The second relates back to 1:2, where we were already told the Word was the Eternal One through whom all things were made. The claim for immutability will also be directly attributed to Jesus in the close of the letter (13:8).

2:1–4

Exhorting the Hearers

"Therefore" or "on this account" begins chapter 2. Hebrews employs this term, or something like it, throughout the sermon to exhort and encourage the listeners to embody what God spoke and the author repeated. Teachings about Jesus entail particular activities. Here we see the close link between doctrine and ethics. The act of listening already done in chapter 1 was itself a central ethical act. The words or doctrines heard are not intended to be answers to abstract, speculative puzzles. They are a way of life. To hear them is to be changed; not to hear is to "drift away." For this reason, the first admonition found in 2:1–4 is "Be attentive!" How interesting it is that we are told this *after* we already heard the central christological affirmations read. Normally we do the reverse: if we are to read something significant to others we announce it to our listeners *before* we begin. Everyone who teaches has done this. We say things such as: "Pay attention to what I am about to say, for this is really important." But Hebrews reverses expectations. We are first told what is most important and then encouraged to "pay greater attention." This attention engages not only our auditory sense, but also the visual. If we are attentive to what we heard, we will see something we could not otherwise see—we see Jesus, the "pioneer" or "anchor" of our salvation (2:10).

To have been addressed by God's communication is already to have received gifts of the Spirit's dispensation (2:4). The first admonition questions if we can still hear, if we are attentive. Because this is who Christ is and what he has done it is imperative for us "to be more greatly attentive [*prosechō*] to what we have heard," which prevents us from "drifting away." Hebrews may be playing on a nautical theme, for in 2:10 it tells us that Christ is the "captain [*archēgos*] of their salvation" (KJV), although that term has a variety of meanings and can also mean "pioneer" (NRSV) or "leader." In Numbers 13:2 and 14:4 the term is used to describe the "leaders" (NIV) selected to "spy out the land of Canaan" or to "captain" the people back to Egypt. Such allusions are most likely present here.[45] Whether he is our "captain" or "pioneer" who guides us, the result is the same. Attention to him, keeping our eyes fixed on Jesus, will prevent us from drifting away. He is the "anchor of our soul" (6:19). He leads us forward, not backward. The admonition is straightforward. First the author reminds them of who Christ is, and then he tells them to attend to what they have heard.

Next he states they did not hear directly from Christ, but from those who did directly hear from him (Heb. 2:3). We are not told if this is chronological or spatial. That is, we are not told if they heard it from those who directly heard it from Christ and are still living, or from those who directly heard it and have died. The first assumes spatial distance that divides them from the original witnesses, the second chronological. Most commentators assume the latter and use this to date Hebrews. What is written here does not give us enough information to decide for the spatial or chronological distance. It does nonetheless suggest distance. This distance, however, has been overcome by God's own direct actions to them. God himself "added his testimony" or "bore witness" to what they heard through "signs and wonders" (v. 4). We have circled back around to one of the important themes in the hymn. God has spoken; we have heard it. We heard it in Christ by hearing directly from those who first heard it from him, and repeated it to us. God himself testified to it. So be attentive because that same word is being spoken yet again. Two options exist. Attend to it and move forward, or seek out a different "captain" and return to Egypt.

45. I am indebted to David Moffitt for this reference.

FURTHER REFLECTIONS

Attentiveness

Attentiveness is a central but demanding ethical practice. My friend Dan Bell regularly reminds me of a bumper sticker he once saw, "If you are not outraged, you are not paying attention." This could be a slogan written for Hebrews. Inattentiveness keeps us from seeing Jesus. Of course, we have good reasons for our inattentiveness. Sometimes it helps us cope. Attentiveness is exhausting. Anyone who has sat through dull sermons or lectures knows this, as do those of us who have given them. The mind wanders nearly uncontrollably. Attention to suffering and oppression is all the more exhausting, if not repellent. Are there Christians who, having meditated on the cross, did not have the irreligious thought cross their minds, "Who asked you to suffer on my behalf?" It could be so manipulative, like that *Far Side* cartoon where a large nun with a weapon-sized ruler stands over a diminutive schoolboy who repeatedly writes on a chalkboard, "I am personally responsible for the sufferings and agonies of Christ." Why should we be attentive to this? Is it not only exhausting but also morbid?

I went to see Mel Gibson's *Passion of the Christ* with a Sunday school class and must admit I was horrified. The brutality of Christ's torturers was vividly and endlessly portrayed on the screen while viewers/voyeurs ate popcorn and drank slushies. The crucifixion had become entertainment, reduced to a "spectacle," a practice the Romans perfected but with which the early Christians refused cooperation. Attentiveness is not voyeuristic; it is not spectacle. The author of Hebrews reminds his readers they were once made such a spectacle: "But recall those earlier days when, after you had been enlightened, you endured a hard struggle with sufferings, sometimes being publicly exposed [*theatrizomenoi*] to abuse and persecution and sometimes being partners with those so treated" (10:32–33). They did not gaze at spectacles, at the "theater" of human suffering. They either received it, or were called to be partners with those so exposed. Gazing at suffering like voyeurs does not make us attentive; it has the opposite effect. But it is hard for us to escape. As I write this, television news programs run reel after reel of the devastating earthquake in Haiti. Dead bodies are scooped up by front-end loaders, placed in sanitation trucks, and carted off to mass graves. Then we break for commercial where happy, beautiful people sell me something to whiten my teeth. How is it possible to be attentive? By the time you read this, we will have moved on from one catastrophic image to the next. The very media we use to see the suffering around us seems to have more of a narcotizing effect. Attentiveness requires us to be something more than spectators.

Hebrews says, "be attentive." "Don't lose your focus." But the attention has a specific object. We are not to be attentive to suffering in general. We are to be attentive to Jesus, to his triumphant suffering that "tasted death" for everyone. We are not to attend to a cultivated despair in the face of suffering, or to capitulate to the tragic; we are to attend to the one who is "now crowned with glory and honor because of the suffering of death" (2:9). This means that some of our attention will require ordinary, everyday activities, as is the case with Hebrews' anticlimactic concluding admonitions.

I once taught a class on violence, forgiveness, and reconciliation that culminated by taking primarily Catholic students to work and live in Protestant households in Northern Ireland. This took place before the Easter Accords that brought some peace to "the troubles." We would attend various ministries that brought Catholics and Protestants together during the fighting. One was a day care center set up at the intersection between Protestant and Catholic neighborhoods notorious for providing men for the various paramilitary organizations on both sides of the conflict. Protestant and Catholic women came together and created a day care center so babies could be cared for. While some of their husbands plotted violence against each other, the women found it necessary to come outside their respective camps and work together even when they did not trust each other. When we asked why, they did not offer theological or philosophical pronouncements. One woman simply said, "Look, even in the midst of fighting, diapers need to be changed." Attentiveness to God's Word does not always entail the extraordinary gesture; most often it is found in the ordinary. Be faithful to your spouse. Welcome the stranger who comes into your neighborhood. Find ways to do good to those near you. Learn to use your resources properly. These are not admonitions to people who expect a cataclysmic end to descend on them at any moment. They are for a people who know they are in it for the long haul. Nonetheless, endurance can be confidently expected because "we do see Jesus." While admonishing and encouraging, Hebrews never ventures far from its christological meditation.

2:5–18

The Glory of Creatures

The attention we give to God's Word has an end. God seeks to glorify creatures. Irenaeus once wrote, "The glory of God is man fully alive."[46] Although Irenaeus did not appear to include Hebrews in his list of Scriptures, his quote fits perfectly what comes next in our text. For like his quote, it has a twofold meaning. It could mean that the incarnate Son is the glory of God. It could also mean that our purpose is, like his, to reflect this glory. Hebrews' use of Psalm 8 plays on both senses. Attention to the Word of God reveals his glory and ours.

Hebrews builds to this conclusion by first setting forth how God bears witness to God's Word. This occurs in two ways: first by "signs and wonders," and second by "gifts of the Holy Spirit." Thomas Aquinas found theological significance in the use of both expressions. Rather than seeing "wonders" as a rhetorical repetition of "signs," he sees two ways God testifies about Jesus. A "sign" differs from a "wonder" or "miracle." Signs are ordinary, natural realities that indicate something extraordinary. A wonder, however, is "what is against nature, as birth from a virgin, or the raising of the dead." God acts both congruent with and against nature in order to make Jesus the sign. This leads Aquinas into an interesting christological reading of Hebrews' use of Psalm 8. God's primary "sign and wonder" is Jesus, who as a sign is both congruent with nature and yet exceeds it. But as a wonder he is miraculously both born from the virgin and raised from the dead.[47]

46. This can be found in *Against Heresies* 4.20.7. See also Eric Osborne, *Irenaeus of Lyons* (Cambridge: Cambridge University Press, 2001), 251.
47. Aquinas, *Hebrews*, 51.

Moderns might not find Aquinas's parsing of these terms compelling, but he draws our attention to the central role of Psalm 8 in Hebrews. Its importance cannot be overstated. Kenneth Schenck finds in it the "ultimate goal of the plot" for Hebrews' narrative, which is "glory for humanity."[48] Psalm 8 offers us Hebrews' soteriology and anthropology. Whereas Aquinas interpreted Psalm 8 christologically, however, Schenck primarily interprets it anthropologically. Although *humanity* is made lower than the angels, God "crowned them with glory and honor, subjecting all things under their feet." God's intention is to share God's glory with humanity. For Schenck, then, the referent of the question "What is man [*anthrōpos*]?" (NIV, KJV) is "humanity." For Aquinas, the referent of that question is Jesus. Yet the differences between Schenck and Aquinas should not be sharply drawn. Schenck admits, "It would easily fit the train of thought to say that because of Christ, humanity also fulfills the psalm."[49] In other words, Schenck reads it primarily but not exclusively about God's intention for humanity. Aquinas reads it primarily but not exclusively about Christ. Christ is the pattern for the answer to this question, "What is humanity?" Christology illumines anthropology. Both Christ and humanity are the answer to the question posed by Psalm 8.

For Aquinas, the use of this psalm testifies to three great christological mysteries: incarnation, passion, and exaltation.[50] The first is found in Hebrews 2:6: "What are human beings that you are mindful of them, or mortals, that you care for them?" The answer to that question is found in the incarnation. Aquinas answers, "humanity was assumed by the Word into the unity of the *supposit*."[51] By *supposit* he means the hypostatic union, that mysterious intimate union between Christ and humanity whereby Jesus is the one subject acting in both natures. No greater glory for humanity is found than in the fact that God assumes it in the hypostasis of the second person. Christ's passion and crucifixion are found in Hebrews 2:7a, which quotes Psalm 8 about the "little while" humanity is made "lower"

48. Schenck, *Cosmology and Eschatology in Hebrews*, 58.
49. Ibid., 57.
50. Aquinas, *Hebrews*, 54.
51. Ibid., 55.

than the angels. This is the lowliness Christ takes on in the incarnation and crucifixion. This is the "making" Jesus does, and it is a human making. This is why Arians misread this passage. They were unable to distinguish between the immanent and economic Trinity. God does not "make" the second person of the Trinity. But Jesus in his humanity "makes" or performs an action in the economy that accomplishes purification and perfection. In other words, his exaltation only makes sense because Jesus, the Eternal Word, accomplished his act of obedience as human. Nonetheless, divinity is not somehow an honor given to Christ. His honor comes by what he does as human. Aquinas states, "But Christ insofar as He is God is not set over all things, but born so; but He is set over insofar as He is man."[52] The ascension and exaltation are accomplished by Jesus' humanity. This is a profound interpretation of Hebrews.

Christ's exaltation is found in Hebrews 2:7b–8, which draws on Psalm 8: God crowns humanity "with glory and honor, subjecting all things under their feet." Christ's exaltation is due to his human obedience. Aquinas even states that the Eternal takes on "passibility" by taking on Christ's humanity, although he does not take on the "vice" often associated with it.[53] This taking on and redeeming of human passibility is genuine, but not debilitating. Jesus "tastes" death as a human creature, but through the hypostatic union he also does so as God. Therefore unlike all other human creatures, he does not remain in death. He exceeds it. As Aquinas poignantly puts it, "The wayfarer hastens."[54] His end is not death. If God suffers as humans suffer, then God too is dead and the result would be atheism. This is unavoidable if we lose divine impassibility. Jesus' very real human suffering and death are not final; they are a stop on the way through which he must pass to accomplish his mission. His passion merits impassibility, which makes possible our salvation.[55] Here is where Christology and anthropology meet. If his end were only death, atheism would make best sense of his mission, but humanity would have no share in his impassible victory. If he does not truly

52. Ibid., 58.
53. Ibid., 68.
54. Ibid., 62.
55. Ibid., 61.

die, then he does nothing to glorify us in our situation. But if death is a "way" over which he hastens and overcomes, then it no longer has the security and certainty we have come to expect. Only because he triumphed over death can he offer us a different security than that death offers. Death is not our glory; eternal life through Christ's humanity is.

The use of Psalm 8 is both christological and anthropological, as is clearly seen in Hebrews 2:8b–10, which suggested that "they," human creatures, would share in Christ's glory. Not everything is now subject "to them." We do not yet see it. The violent continue to bear it away. Evil still triumphs over good. Nonetheless, Hebrews encourages its readers that we do see the triumph in part. "But we do see Jesus" (2:9). What do we see? We see his exaltation from the dead that makes possible such exaltation for all. (This could not occur without the resurrection of his flesh.)[56] Because he "tastes death" for all, consumes it without being consumed by it, a way is made for creatures into the holy of holies: God's glorious presence.

What is so intriguing and difficult in interpreting Hebrews is tracking with the author's understanding of agency. Hebrews 2:10 raises a question of agency similar to verse 6. The NRSV translates, "It was fitting that God, for whom and through whom all things exist, in bringing many children to glory, should make the pioneer of their salvation perfect through sufferings." "God" does not appear in the Greek. The subject of the action is "the one for whom and through whom all things exist." The addition of "God" makes good sense in that the subject here both "leads" (*agagonta*) many children and "perfects" their "leader" or "pioneer" (*archēgos*) through suffering. The latter is clearly a reference to Jesus. Thus it makes good sense to read the "for whom and through whom all things exist" as referring to God, except for the one caveat that Hebrews has already used a similar term to refer to Christ.

In 1:2 the author designated Jesus as the one "through whom [*di' ou*] he also created the worlds." Here in 2:10 he uses the same expression. Could the author so easily have forgotten he used this

56. See David Moffitt's convincing defense of Hebrews' emphasis on resurrection despite the majority of biblical scholars dismissing or neglecting this central theme: "If Another Priest Arises."

expression twenty-two verses earlier? Would those who heard it not hear the similarity? If so, then the agency involved here is complex and confusing. Can Jesus be the one "for whom and through whom" all things are made, and at the same time be a leader who is perfected by the one "for whom and through whom" all things are made? He would have to be both the subject and object of the sentence. That stretches the language of agency nearly beyond the breaking point. It would then read like this: "It was fitting that Jesus, for whom and through whom all things exist, in bringing many children to glory, should make Jesus, the pioneer of their salvation, perfect through sufferings." This makes little sense, so it is more reasonable to place God as the first actor and understand Jesus as the subject acted upon. But this is still unsatisfying. For now it also seems to make God the one who "brings many children to glory," and we should not forget that the term "glory" has also already been used for Jesus in 1:3: Jesus is "the reflection of God's glory."

The term *doxa* or "glory" is a name for God. God is glory. When Moses finished building God's house, the first tabernacle, God filled it with God's glory. This is found in the concluding verses of Exodus, "Then the cloud covered the tent of meeting, and the glory of the LORD filled the tabernacle. Moses was not able to enter the tent of meeting because the cloud settled upon it, and the glory of the LORD filled the tabernacle" (Exod. 40:34–35). This is a common theme throughout Exodus. When God appears, it is an event—God does not show up without "glory." For this reason, the author of Hebrews can refer to "glory" and his readers understand whom he intends. He did this in 1:2 and now he mentions "glory" again in 2:10 after proclaiming through the use of Psalm 8 that creatures were made to share God's glory. What then can it mean that the *archēgos* leads children to "glory," except that he leads them to God? If we specify "glory" as God, as we must, this makes the agency in this verse all the more confusing. Then it would read like this: "It was fitting that God, for whom and through whom all things exist, in bringing many children to God [glory], should make Jesus, the pioneer of their salvation, perfect through sufferings." Now we have the same difficulty in figuring out the sense of agency when we substituted "Jesus" for the first "God." Who is leading whom where? The best resolution is that God, in whom the Word preexists, becomes flesh and in his humanity leads other creatures to glory. To understand this requires examining the next stage of the argument: Jesus is our faithful and merciful high priest.

FURTHER REFLECTIONS
Source(s) and Canon(s)

The odd sense of agency found in Christ's "leading" resulted in much speculation about the sources that would render this agency intelligible. That Jesus is the "leader" who comes down from heaven and then returns produced numerous speculations by scholars that Hebrews drew and developed its Christology from a gnostic source. Ernst Käsemann, following the history of religions school, claimed Gnosticism and Hebrews share a common myth because they both viewed one of the deities as leading people through the heavens back to God. Käsemann notes that "an indispensable condition" in Gnosticism "for the soul's journey to heaven is the forsaking of the body as a component of the material world." Clearly Hebrews does not teach this, but that fact did not qualify his affirmation of a common myth between Hebrews and Gnosticism.[57] Two champions of the history of religions school, Wilhelm Bousset and Richard Reitzenstein, found a "gnostic redeemer myth" as the source that explained Christian origins.[58] This idea has been challenged since the 1950s, although it continues to live on in those trained in that school in the '50s and '60s.

The crucial question is whether Gnosticism is a distortion of Christianity emerging in the second century and thus could not be a source, or if it is a source for Christianity in the first century. Scholars remain somewhat divided. Among others, Simone Pétrement makes a convincing case that it arises within Christianity. She

57. Ernst Käsemann, *The Wandering People of God*, trans. Roy A. Harrisville and Irving L. Sandberg (Minneapolis: Augsburg, 1984), 87–96.
58. See Wilhelm Bousset, *Kyrios Christos* (Nashville, TN: Abingdon Press, 1970) and Richard Reitzenstein, *Helenist Mystery-Religions: Their Basic Ideas and Significance* (Eugene, OR: Pickwick Publications, 1978).

recognizes the similarities between Gnosticism and Christianity. She notes, "No Gnostic text has been found that we can date with certainty, or even with a degree of probability to a pre-Christian time." Moreover, she asks if the church fathers were thoroughly unreliable witnesses when they claimed it was a Christian heresy.[59] Pétrement convincingly narrates central gnostic texts as versions of Christianity. If she is correct, it may be that Gnosticism was less a source for Scripture than a canon within which some were tempted to read it. We will revisit this below in the commentary on Hebrews 4 and discuss how Gnosticism returns in modernity tempting us to read Scripture through its "canonical" lens.

Few biblical scholars today follow Käsemann or the original history of religions school and find a gnostic redeemer myth as the source for Hebrews. Indeed, James Dunn argues that the search for some kind of "divine man" figure as a source led scholars on a "wild goose chase."[60] This seems to have garnered general agreement. Nonetheless he still finds other sources for Hebrews. He ascribes its "ambivalence" and "awkward tension" between Christ's preexistence and an adoptionistic Christology to "Platonic idealism," coupled with "Philo's teaching on the Logos. . . . What we may have to accept is that the author of Hebrews ultimately has in mind an *ideal* pre-existence, the existence of an idea in the mind of God, his divine intention for the last days."[61] For Dunn, Christ's preexistence in Hebrews is more of an "idea" than a "person."[62] Plato's idealism provides a source making sense of who is leading and to where. But this does not seem fitting to the interesting agency Hebrews develops in chapter 2.

Harold Attridge also finds various religious sources behind Christ as leader, *archēgos*, and God's action of leading, *agagonta*. Christ's "leading," he writes, "fulfills the function of various guides on

59. Simone Pétrement, *A Separate God: The Christian Origins of Gnosticism*, trans. Carol Harrison (San Francisco: HarperSanFrancisco, 1990), 10, 15.
60. Dunn, *Christology in the Making*, 16.
61. Ibid., 52–53. He states this despite rightly cautioning against "offering hasty hypotheses concerning Hellenistic influences of the first (Jewish) Christians" (p. 22). For a convincing argument against the Platonic influence see Schenck, *Cosmology and Eschatology in Hebrews*, 117–22.
62. Dunn, *Christology in the Making*, 61.

the heavenly path found in Greek, Jewish, and Gnostic sources."[63] This suggests a gnostic source, although Attridge questions this elsewhere: "What we find in Hebrews, then, is not a specific gnostic redeemer myth, but its elder cousin, an early form of the common Christian salvation myth, distinct from the sapientially inspired mythical pattern of the exordium based on the common redemption myth of various traditions of the Hellenistic period."[64] Can we establish a "common redemption myth" historically? That is, were there broad transcultural narratives of redemption such that one person from one culture would recognize something identical or similar in that of another and see them as a source? Or does this modern account of what a source should be tempt us to read Hebrews through some other canon than the one Christians canonized?

Here we find a significant difference between some scholars who use the history of religions method to read Scripture and theologians who do not. The difference is based on which canon it is read within. Notice that I am not arguing that the difference is whether we engage in canonical criticism—the difference is *which* canonical criticism we employ. Hebrews is never read in isolation. No one comes upon it without having already read it within the context of some kind of canon. Should we read it in the context of Jewish apocalyptic? Gnosticism? Philo? Plato? The Dead Sea Scrolls? A modern hermeneutics of suspicion? All of these contexts may be illuminating, but much of the discussion of sources seeks a historical causality whereby what is already broadly present in culture(s) provides a causal explanation for the role Christians gave Christ in early Jewish Christian thought. We read those sources asking them to illumine what we then read in Hebrews. Is that a reasonable *historical* approach, or an ahistorical *methodological* commitment, a canon?

Contrast this approach of reading Scripture with how the dogmatic theologian Karl Barth interprets the first two chapters of Hebrews. He was not taken in by the history of religions school's search for a secondary or intermediate divine being, such as the "divine man," even before historians discredited it. Barth recognizes

63. Attridge, *Hebrews*, 88.
64. Ibid., 81.

that the NT writers did not need any kind of intermediary being because they already had "wisdom." Wisdom is not a mediating or secondary being between God and creation because God does not need such in order to create or to relate to creation. Barth writes, "we do not have (1) any metaphysical principle to unite the God-concept with the riddle of the universe. . . . And so the 'wisdom' of the Old Testament is not in any sense (2) an intermediate being—a kind of third existence—between God and the world." Instead, the disciples represented the "shattering message of the kingdom of God" putting to an end all "mediating" principles.[65] God directly relates to creation in his definitive speech in Christ and does so in the most intimate manner possible. Hebrews fits well Barth's interpretation, but has to be forced into Käsemann's.

By reading Hebrews in the context of the Christian canon rather than other canons, Barth discovered an intriguing family resemblance among Hebrews, John, and Colossians:

> Far more important than the question of religious history is the factual question how the writers of the New Testament for their part understood the *di' autou* [through him] or *en autō* [in him]; what they meant by associating with God the Father His Son or Word or Jesus Christ in creation. It is clear from all the passages quoted—we have only to think of the most important, Jn. 1:3f., Heb. 1:2f. and Col. 1:15f.—that we are dealing with a special emphasising and distinction of the person of Jesus Christ. It is not God or the world and their relation which is the problem of these passages but the lordship of Jesus Christ. The starting point is not that deity is so exalted and holy or that the world is so dark; nor is it the affirmation that there is something like a mediation between the two which bears the name of Jesus Christ. What they have in view is the kingdom of God drawn near; the turning point of the times, revealed in the name of Jesus Christ, as the fulfilment of all the promises of the covenant of grace. To give the Bearer of this name the honour due to Him, or rather to bear witness to

65. Karl Barth, *Church Dogmatics*, III/1, *The Doctrine of Creation*, trans. J. W. Edwards et al., ed. Geoffrey W. Bromiley and Thomas F. Torrance (repr. Edinburgh: T & T Clark, 1986), 52–53. I think this passage can help explain Barth's unfortunate opposition to metaphysics. He primarily sees it as having this intermediary role.

> the honour which He has, they venture the tremendous assertion that the world was created through Him and in Him as through God and in God, in God's eternal will and purpose.[66]

This illumines the odd sense of agency found in Hebrews 2:10–18 better than the methodological quest for external sources. Both God and Jesus cause creation. Both lead creation back to God, but Jesus has a distinct role to play in this "leading," a role no one else can play. He does so by being made a creature as we are and perfecting what it means to be creature through suffering. Whether Barth himself used a general account of apocalyptic to understand this inbreaking of the kingdom that did full justice to Christ's humanity remains an open question, which we will revisit when we discuss the place of apocalyptic in Hebrews.

The canonical Christian Scriptures do not share the cosmic dualism found in some gnostic texts that find no direct relation between God's perfect goodness and creation. The latter is evil, and the result of the fall of Sophia or Wisdom. But in Hebrews, as throughout Christian Scripture, God directly creates through God's own Wisdom, which is the "very stamp" of God's nature. The instrumental use of the Word in creation and redemption is not mediating in the sense that God needs something lesser to deal with a corrupt creation. The instrumental use identifies the Word with God such that that kind of mediation is forever rendered unnecessary. To continue to look for mediators as sources misses the point of Hebrews altogether.

Barth's interpretation, much more so than Käsemann's, fits with how Christ is *archēgos*—pioneer, leader, or author—in Hebrews. He perfects by becoming perfectly human, suffering, and then ascending as our high priest. Any mediation in Hebrews comes from the human Jesus to God. He presents his sacrifice to him in the holy of holies. This section ends with this: "Therefore he had to become like his brothers and sisters in every respect, so that he might be a merciful and faithful high priest in the service of God, to make a sacrifice of atonement for the sins of the people" (2:17). Jesus does not perfect by shedding his body. Nowhere in Hebrews is there any

66. Ibid., 53–54.

hint that in his ascension he leaves his body behind. We are told explicitly the opposite. He enters the heavenly "Holy Place . . . with his own blood" (9:12). We are "sanctified through the offering of the *body* of Jesus Christ once for all" (10:10). Moreover, his "flesh" is the "curtain" that gains us access to the holy place (10:19–20). This contrasts markedly with most texts we call "gnostic." For Hebrews the body is not to be despised; it is a source of salvation and sanctification. It is to be perfected.

3:1–6:20

Christ: Faithful and Merciful High Priest

The words that describe Jesus in the concluding section of chapter 2—"merciful and faithful high priest"—are the basis for the next two sections of the sermon, 3:1–4:14 and 4:15–5:10. They are also essential to the confession that Hebrews' audience must hold fast. In the first section we are told what it means for Jesus to be high priest "worthy of faith." This section concludes with a similar use of this expression in 4:14 followed by another admonition to us: "Since, then, we have a great high priest who has passed through the heavens, Jesus, the Son of God, let us hold fast to our confession." After this conclusion we are told what it means for Jesus to be the "merciful" high priest, which idea is developed in 4:15–5:10. Beginning with 4:15 the author circles back to the claim in 2:17 that he was like us "in every respect." This is the foundation for Jesus' role as merciful high priest. "For we do not have a high priest who is unable to sympathize with our weaknesses, but we have one who in every respect has been tested as we are, yet without sin" (4:15). This culminates in a profound account of how Christ's mercy was "learned" through "what he suffered." He exercises his office as a human, but does so directly in God's presence. As is Hebrews' custom, these profound christological pronouncements are followed by exhortation in 5:11–6:20. Now we examine each of these sections in turn: 3:1–4:14; 4:15–5:10; 5:11–6:20.

3:1–4:14

High Priest: Worthy of Faith

Chapter 3 begins, like chapter 2 (and chap. 4), with a "therefore." Although different Greek words are used in 2:1 and 3:1, they share a similar function. They connect what is coming next with what came before. The argument in Hebrews is not like that Monty Python skit in which a commentator says, "And now for something completely different." It builds layer upon layer, making a point and then showing its connection to others. Albert Vanhoye demonstrates how this is done with the use of key terms.[1] A key term will be noted in one section, and then elaborated upon in the next. In the section under consideration, the key term is "faithful high priest." The author draws on the earlier statement that Jesus is "high priest" (2:17) and expands it—"High priest of our confession." He will continue to do so until he gets to the heart of the sermon and tells us explicitly his "main point," which is "we have such a high priest" (8:1). We are to hold fast to this confession.

Confession is at the heart of Hebrews' admonition. Hebrews repeatedly tells us to hold it fast. Twice in the passage currently under consideration, the author admonishes his listeners to "hold firm." Although the same verb is used, it has different objects. For what is to be held firm is both the act of confession (3:6) and its substance (3:14). In the first admonition we are to "hold firm the confidence [*parrēsia*]" (3:6). In the second, we are to "hold our first confidence [*hypostaseōs*] firm to the end." The different terms suggest that we are to be bold in the act of confession and grounded in its substance. To be bold without being grounded in the substance of faith would be recklessness. To be grounded without being bold would be cowardice. Both are flaws to be avoided, and at times Hebrews implies that his listeners are failing, or potentially failing, on one of these two counts.

The term *parrēsia* means the boldness that a citizen would use in public speech. It had political connotations, which makes sense in

1. Albert Vanhoye, S.J., *Structure and Message of the Epistle to the Hebrews,* trans. James Swetnam, S.J. (Rome: Editrice Pontificio Istituto Biblico, 1989), 33.

that the author of Hebrews repeatedly claims his listeners are members of a "house" or "city" other than the "city" in which they find themselves situated. *Parrēsia* or "confidence" is not some abstract belief they are to confess privately while every head is bowed and every eye closed; it is a public confession, a boldness of speech that they should be willing to make even if it costs them. Calvin so emphasized this that he rejected "implicit faith," which he found in Roman Catholicism. It suggested that the church is the primary agent of belief, and someone who did not explicitly consent to, or understand, the mysteries of faith could still be baptized and be a member of Christ's body by "implicit faith." Calvin found this to be a denial of the "boldness" of public confession Hebrews demands, rejecting it as a "papal monstrosity" that brought with it a "license to err." Instead, each believer must explicitly make a confession both as act and substance. Calvin states, "What stability of confidence can there be when men do not know what they are to believe?"[2] An explicit confession must be made; otherwise we neglect the "boldness" Hebrews demands.

This rejection of any "implicit faith" found its way into the discussion of "liberty of conscience" in the 1646 Westminster Confession: "God alone is Lord of the conscience, and hath left it free from the doctrines and commandments of men which are in any thing contrary to his Word, or beside it in matters of faith or worship. So that to believe such doctrines or to obey such commands out of conscience, is to betray true liberty of conscience; and the requiring of an implicit faith, and an absolute and blind obedience, is to destroy liberty of conscience and reason also."[3]

Such a passage easily lends itself to a modern interpretation of an autonomous individual free to make judgments solely based on his or her own conscience, but this would be an insufficient and uncharitable interpretation of Reformed Christianity. This affirmation of "conscience" comes in the context of a common confession. A Reformed Christian is not "free" as an individual to decide whether this common confession fits her or his conscience. The difference

2. Calvin, *Hebrews*, 37.

3. Westminster Confession, 20.2, in *Creeds of the Churches: A Reader in Christian Doctrine, from the Bible to the Present*, ed. John H. Leith, 3rd ed. (Atlanta: John Knox Press, 1982), 216.

between Reformed Christianity and Catholicism is not one of individuals versus community, but which community requires the boldness of confession Hebrews demands, the Reformed or Catholic understanding of the church. Calvin and the Reformed tradition's concern is with a "blind" obedience that divides faith from reason and says I believe it because the church demands it of me even though I do not, and cannot, understand it. The Reformed are worried about a Catholic fideism that reduces the act of faith to a bare act of will. Does such an implicit faith and fideism adequately characterize Catholicism?

Implicit faith has a long tradition in Catholicism. Thomas Aquinas discussed it in the context of the question, "whether man is bound to believe anything explicitly."[4] He begins with the objection that this is not expected because such belief is beyond human power, and that it is sufficient to be prepared to believe rather than explicitly to believe, which suffices for obedience. Faith consists in blind obedience. But Aquinas rejects these arguments; they do not constitute what he means by "implicit faith." He replies, "Therefore, as regards the primary points or articles of faith, man is bound to believe them, just as he is bound to have faith; but as to other points of faith, man is not bound to believe them explicitly, but only implicitly, or to be ready to believe them, in so far as he is prepared to believe whatever is contained in the Divine Scriptures. Then alone is he bound to believe such things explicitly, when it is clear to him that they are contained in the doctrine of faith." Implicit faith is an exception to the rule. The articles of faith require explicit faith. Implicit faith is a readiness to believe "whatever is contained in the Divine Scriptures" when they become "clear" to the believer. Far from contradicting Calvin or the Westminster Confession, Aquinas would seem to agree.

The "boldness" Hebrews calls for demands explicit faith. Protestants and Catholics agree on this point despite past polemics. The Catholic Catechism does state, "The desire for God is written in the human heart." Perhaps this has led some Catholic theologians to find this natural desire sufficient as a kind of implicit faith, a form of

4. Thomas Aquinas, *Summa theologica* (repr. New York: Benzinger Brothers, Christian Classics, 1981) 2-2, q.2, a.5.

anonymous Christianity? If so, this contradicts the Roman Catholic Church's official teaching. Faith is not some existential orientation that can be had anonymously without its explicit articulation. The catechism makes this clear when it explains the "obedience of faith": "To obey (from the Latin *ob-audire,* to 'hear or listen to') in faith is to submit freely to the word that has been heard, because its truth is guaranteed by God, who is Truth itself."[5] Faith is "personal adherence to God and assent to his truth."[6] The catechism then draws on the understanding of faith in Aquinas. It is an act of both the intellect and the will. "Believing is an act of the intellect assenting to the divine truth by command of the will moved by God through grace."[7] As an act of the intellect, faith is not "intelligible in the light of our natural reason," but it is congruent with reason.[8] It is also communal: "I cannot believe without being carried by the faith of others, and by my faith I help support others in the faith."[9] Perhaps the Reformed critique lies here? In Catholicism the church is the primary agent of faith. Individual believers must have explicit faith, but they are also borne up through the faith of others.

FURTHER REFLECTIONS

Explicit Faith, Pagano-Papalism, and Infant Baptism

The Reformed insistence on an explicit confession and the Catholic possibility of an implicit faith, baptism of desire, or possibly even anonymous Christianity identifies a subtle difference over their respective interpretations of Hebrews. Reformed Christianity focuses on "confessions" to which believers must rationally and volitionally assent. Catholicism does not deny the free act of the intellect and will in assenting to central dogmas as the norm, but it does allow for exception because the church is the first agent of faith. This allows for a "baptism of desire," which assumes an implicit faith

5. *Catechism of the Catholic Church* (Mahwah, NJ: Paulist Press, 1994), §144.
6. Ibid., §150.
7. Aquinas, *Summa theologica* 2-2, q.2, a9; *Catechism of the Catholic Church,* §155.
8. *Catechism of the Catholic Church,* §156.
9. Ibid., §167.

not yet made explicit. The catechism states, "Every man who is ignorant of the Gospel of Christ and of his Church, but seeks the truth of it, can be saved. It may be supposed that such persons would have *desired baptism explicitly* if they had known its necessity."[10] This can lend itself to an affirmation of "nature as it is" in Catholic theology. We are born with a "fundamental option" for the good, or a supernatural existential ordering us to God. Even if we do not explicitly confess faith, by affirming that fundamental option or supernatural existential ordering we are as much as confessing faith. Some Protestants worry that this tempts Catholic theology to a neo-paganism. That is, rather than grace perfecting nature, grace merely affirms it. It baptizes what is, without the conversion and reordering of our desires and nature Christ demands. Let me give an example.

I was once in Rome, a city I find beautiful and a witness to God's glory. Whenever I have been in Rome, I am always glad the Puritans were not present in early Christianity. They would have torn down the Pantheon rather than seeing its beauty and converting it into architecture that became one of the great churches of that city. I see in that architecture and city a fine example of "grace perfecting nature." Grace takes what is good among the nations and reorders it. Music, art, culture, politics can be found in every nation or peoples and brought before God as a pleasing offering. On this particular occasion in Rome I was to attend a "private audience" with the pope, which was his Wednesday teaching in a hall that seated approximately five thousand people. People were celebrating with song as we waited for the pope to arrive. When he did, the crowd erupted, standing, cheering, waving, and yelling. A friend sitting next to me leaned over and said, "This is what it must have been like for the emperor to return to Rome!" He meant it positively, but it struck me otherwise. It seemed more like succumbing to a Catholic temptation—to affirm "nature" without its conversion to the way of Jesus, to see God's presence in the emperor's return to Rome and forget that true beauty resides in the Savior's entry into Jerusalem on a donkey.

That implicit faith invites a Catholic temptation suggests that, unlike Calvin, I do not find it a "papal monstrosity." It is nonetheless

10. Ibid., §1260.

a temptation that can be found among some contemporary Catholic theologians. Perhaps it is why ecofeminism, especially the neo-pagan version, arose initially among Catholic theologians? Perhaps only a Catholic biblical scholar could affirm a religious studies approach that critiques the early church's opposition to a "pagan other" and instead argues that Catholicism, unlike Protestantism, can make common cause with pagan religion calling on Christianity to find "light among the Gentiles," rather than being a "light to the Gentiles."[11] Celsus seems to have been right all along! If Origen had a doctrine of "implicit faith," he could have affirmed Celsus's critique of Christianity's opposition to antiquity's national religions and told him that they just do not understand what they truly desire.

But if a "pagano-papalism" has been a temptation for Catholics, to make confession *only* an explicit act of will has been a temptation for Protestants. It produces an anxiety and hermeneutics of suspicion that a true explicit confession has not been made, whether this be the act of affirming some doctrinal confession or a politically correct "progressivist" one. A suspicion lingers that the confession was not sufficiently explicit, not measuring up to Hebrews' demand for boldness. Rather than producing charity, this suspicion invites dissension and division. Protestants can learn charity by recalling the words from the Catholic Catechism: "God has bound salvation to the sacrament of Baptism [and I would add the assumed confession that goes with it], but he himself is not bound by his sacraments."[12] Of course this assumes baptism requires intellectual assent and not just an act of will. Both constitute the "obedience of faith."

Perhaps no communion of Christians has opposed "implicit faith" as consistently as the Anabaptists. Surely they would object to Calvin and the magisterial Reformers that they too must have a doctrine of "implicit faith" because they practice infant baptism. The Catholic priest turned radical reformer Menno Simons stated, "where there is no renewing, regenerating faith leading to obedience there is no

11. See Luke Timothy Johnson, *Among the Gentiles: Greco-Roman Religion and Christianity* (New Haven: Yale University Press, 2009).

12. This of course is not only a Catholic teaching; the Anglican John Wesley repeated this common understanding of God's actions in his sermon "The Means of Grace." See *Catechism of the Catholic Church*, §1257.

baptism." Based on this need for an explicit obedience he also found the Communion table too open in Roman Catholicism: "It is true the mouth of the Lord has ordained a breaking of bread or communion in the New Testament, but not in the manner in which you celebrate it. Your Lord's Supper admits all, no matter who or what: the avaricious, the proud, the ostentatious, the drunkards, the hateful, the idolatrous ones, those who frequent houses of ill fame, yes, harlots and scamps. Evidently it is celebrated moreover with offensive pomp and splendor, with hypocrisy and idolatry."[13] Simons's anti-Catholic rhetoric, like Calvin's, no longer serves a useful purpose, but his insistence on the "obedience of faith" now echoes the current Roman Catholic catechism. Of course, the Anabaptists find infant baptism an explicit rejection of such obedience. How can explicit faith be the norm and the church still practice infant baptism?

The Roman Catholic biblical scholar Gerhard Lohfink provides one of the best defenses of infant baptism. He acknowledges that the "experiment" of the imperial church "is truly at an end and can never be resumed, for it left people no chance to make a free decision for faith."[14] If infant baptism means that, it should be rejected. He does not then defend infant baptism as some kind of rite of passage into Western civilization. Instead baptism signifies a "change of rulers."[15] This suggests the norm of adult baptism; do we not need to be adults to pledge allegiance to Christ as our priest-king? Lohfink denies such a consequence. To leave it to children to decide for themselves wrongly assumes "a neutral space" where people somehow decide rulers through a liberty of indifference. "That sounds enlightened, but only superficially. In reality this position ignores the reality of the world and its inhabitants. It is not only false because there are no 'neutral spaces' in our society. It is also a complete mistake with regard to the nature of human existence." Life is a gift; no one decides for it. Indeed, we all need "representatives" who will stand in for us at some point in our life. Baptism functions

13. Menno Simons, "Foundation of Christian Doctrine," in *The Complete Writings of Menno Simons* (Scottdale, PA: Herald Press, 1956), 139, 142.
14. Gerhard Lohfink, *Does God Need the Church? Toward a Theology of the People of God*, trans. Linda M. Maloney (Collegeville, MN: Liturgical Press, 1999), 217.
15. Ibid., 211.

> as one such moment of "representation." Not only children, but also everyone needs the faith of others to sustain us in our exodus from the rulers of this age to the rule of the eternal priest-king. Lohfink concludes, "The baptism of the still *immature* child expresses the truth that the life of faith cannot be created by human effort. Faith cannot be instilled. It can only be received. It is always a gift, a grace. Therefore believing parents may not withhold baptism from their child any more than they may withhold food, clothing, play, playmates, language, or education."[16] This should not be interpreted to deny explicit faith, which must include volitional and intellectual assent. Although we burden our children with the rule of the priest-king through baptism, they must take that rule upon themselves. But his rule also always has a place for those to be baptized who do not have the ability to reason for themselves; their bodies too can be brought and marked with the death and resurrection of Christ. But this is an exception. Explicit faith, both as an intellectual and volitional response, must be the norm, which assumes baptism and confession. Hebrews teaches as much.

Can faith be present without both the formal act of confession and assent to the substance of that confession? Hebrews returns to this theme in 3:14: "For we have become partners of Christ, if only we hold our first confidence [*hypostaseōs*] firm to the end." Whereas the first admonition emphasizes the public act of holding fast the confidence (*parrēsia*), this second one emphasizes its substance (*hypostaseōs,* the second use of this important term). Both work together. The confidence or boldness of speech required of them is not a reckless jeremiad or prophetic posturing that seeks merely to provoke; it is grounded in the substance of that which they have seen and heard. As we will see in 11:1, this "confidence" as *hypostaseōs* is the "assurance [or substance] of things hoped for." It is the heart of faith. Confession requires an act of both the will and the intellect. To will confession without acknowledging the truth of its substance fosters fideism. It can only be an act of power. To acknowledge its truth without the will seeking to embody that truth as its own good

16. Ibid., 270–71.

produces an arid scholastic rationalism. Faith entails an act of the entire person, both will and intellect. This does not mean theologians make the best Christians. For the act of intellect here is not critical scrutiny or accumulation of information, but love of what is true, which brings the will and intellect into an inseparable unity. As Aquinas recognized: the milkmaid who knows Jesus, knows more than Aristotle.[17]

Both Catholic and Reformed theology suggest that explicit faith, as an act of will and intellect, is normative, but they seem to differ over exceptions. Perhaps some adjudication on this difference can be found in the reason why Hebrews admonishes its listeners to "hold firm the confession." Was the audience in danger of forsaking it? If so, was it a hypothetical or actual danger? Every preacher knows that he or she sometimes preaches against a temptation to which the congregation may not yet have succumbed. Such preaching is prophylactic. One reminds the people of God what they should not do if they find themselves in a situation that would tempt them. If this is what Hebrews is doing in this sermon, then the danger is hypothetical. This may be, but the admonitions are so stark at places that the danger seems more than hypothetical. If it is an actual danger, what is it? One of the oldest interpretations is that this congregation is tempted to return to Jewish practice. The temptation is "judaizing." The strong contrast between the temple cult, the law, and the Levitical priesthood on the one hand, and on the other hand Jesus as high priest, could suggest this interpretation. Yet perhaps the author desires to show them the continuity with the Jewish cult? If Hebrews was written after the destruction of the temple in AD 70 it could be an attempt not so much to keep them from judaizing, but to demonstrate that the cult continues even though the temple does not. Jesus as the high priest makes possible the continuation of a Jewish sacrificial practice even though the temple cult has been destroyed.

Another reason they might have been tempted to give up the

17. Aquinas actually stated, "none of the philosophers before the advent of Christ was able, with all of his effort, to know as much about God and the things necessary for eternal life, as a little old lady, after the advent of Christ, knows through faith." In *Collationes de symbolorum apostolorum* in http://www.corpusthomisticum.org/csv.html. I am grateful to Mark Johnson for the reference and translation.

confession was persecution. Several passages suggest that some in their community have been persecuted and many have lost possessions. This interpretation seems persuasive when Hebrews reminds them of how they had been "publicly exposed to abuse and persecution" or were "partners with those so treated" (10:33). They "cheerfully accepted the plundering" of their "possessions" (10:34). After reminding them of this, Hebrews returns to the same admonition we witnessed in 3:6 to maintain and not abandon their "confidence" (*parrēsia*; 10:32–35). This suggests that their temptation might be to lose the boldness of their public witness because of persecution. However, that Hebrews writes of these persecutions in the past tense might also suggest that what they face is not a present persecution, but an altogether different kind of temptation: sloth. Persecution seems to have inspired them more to a profound confession than to forsaking it. Perhaps the persecution has passed and now they face the arduous task of everyday faith where they must learn to maintain their boldness in the midst of the banal? This interpretation also seems to have some merit in Hebrews. One of the things they are accused of is "slothfulness." In the third section under consideration Hebrews contrasts the "full assurance of hope" that they should have until the end (6:11) with a tempting "sluggishness" or sloth (6:12).

What tempts the people to abandon their confidence and confession of faith such that Hebrews repeats again and again that they must hold it fast? Is it a temptation to return to Jewish practice and abandon Christ as their true high priest? Is it cowardice in the face of persecution? Is it sloth in the face of settledness? And are any of these temptations actual, or are they merely hypothetical? We do not know. We will never know, and any attempt to settle on one of these answers rather than another is speculation. This should cause no alarm, for the meaning of the text is not found in the material words penned only by the original author and sent to the original community. If meaning were that tied to a particular historical artifact and its materiality, then Holy Scripture would have its significance either ossified into an antiquarian museum piece or lost altogether. It is *good* that we do not have these concrete material indications that would ossify the meaning, for if we did the Word of God could not be what the author of Hebrews himself understands it to be: "living and active, sharper than any two-edged sword, piercing until it divides soul from spirit, joints from marrow; it is able to judge the thoughts and intentions of the heart" (4:12). Anyone who would confine its meaning to the original material conditions of its production (the author, the original autograph, the concrete people who first heard and received it), would neglect the *ongoing* material conditions that make Scripture to be Scripture: those who preserve it, continue to receive it as holy, and seek to hear it, repeating its words in nonidentical situations. This is what matters most.

Our lack of knowledge as to why the author admonished his listeners helps us recognize when exceptions to explicit confession, in act and substance, may and may not be warranted. Neither persecution nor sloth makes for a legitimate reason to neglect confession. True faith must be bold both when it is under attack and when it is not. I saw the former while attending a church service in China. Because being a Christian brings with it accusations of anti-Chinese activity, Christians can suffer loss of goods, reputation, or profession. For this reason, the sacraments take on a political reality they seldom explicitly have where Christianity is more settled and the temptation is sloth. I was present for a service of Holy Communion one Sunday morning in a Chinese church. After the pastor said the words of institution, and before people communed, he asked all of those who were baptized to stand in order to receive the elements. Because worship services occur under the threat of surveillance, to stand in that place is to make a bold confession. It is *parrēsia*. All those unwilling to stand are not permitted to receive because they have refused that witness. Contrast this with the lack of boldness present in more settled Western churches where sloth toward confession has taken over. Rather than asking for any explicit confession, they invite everyone to Communion whether they are willing to take the intellectual and volitional risk of faith or not. The new practice of "open communion" that divides baptism and confession from Holy Communion is clearly a sign of sloth that demonstrates how the "implicit faith" against which Calvin railed has now overtaken much of Protestantism. Open communion refuses to connect discipleship with confession. The same boldness present in Chinese Christianity where persecution could break out should be required in the more settled Christianity of the "West." Hebrews speaks to both those who are in an actual situation of persecution and those who have become lazy because of settledness.

FURTHER REFLECTIONS
"Judaizing"

The threat of "judaizing" represents a more difficult issue for Christians today. We receive Hebrews' word in a time when the threat of judaizing takes on a profound difference from what it could have meant in earlier generations. Both the Spanish Inquisition and the history of pogroms and holocausts against the Jews requires us to be more circumspect so that we do not read into Hebrews' admonition either an anti-Judaism or an anti-Semitism that would reproduce that history and neglect the central positive teaching of Hebrews: those who attend well to its message must be filled with faith, hope, and charity (10:22–24). We should always read Hebrews with this admonition in mind: "let us consider how to provoke one another to love and good deeds" (10:24).

During the time of that state project known as the Spanish Inquisition, which sometimes had the church's blessings and sometimes its opprobrium, this lesson was forgotten. In an effort to solidify national unity, the Spanish crown required Jews either to convert to Christianity or to leave Spain. Although some left, many "converted." But forced explicit confessions are meaningless. Many continued to practice Judaism. The very people who required forced conversions then began to question their authenticity, accusing others of judaizing. Techniques of torture were used, including water boarding, to determine the authenticity of their confession. Although those who were tortured and killed were minuscule in comparison to those tortured and killed in the name of democracy or communism from the nineteenth century on, this does not excuse the practice, and we should no longer speak of "judaizing" without remembering what it meant for those placed on the rack, or suspended until their arms were pulled out of their sockets. That this happened in Spain is all the more sad because Spain was one of the countries that had earlier refused to make Jewish inhabitants wear the yellow star as other European countries demanded. We know how that history ended.

Of course, whatever judaizing the original readers of Hebrews might have faced, it was not identical with the anti-Judaism and anti-Semitism that occurred in European politics at a much later date. That Hebrews could have been misused to support those later practices does not mean it is somehow less than Holy Scripture. To quote an old adage: "the abuse of a thing does not take away from its use." But we must be attentive to how Hebrews is used. The boldness it demands of us looks very different when Christians are in power and use it against the powerless rather than when they were out of power and suffered for it.

The first question the author puts to the community is if they will hold fast to the form of confession, to the boldness required. A second question that emerges from this section is the content of the confession. The author expects them to hold to it, but does not tell us exactly what it is. Is it a set baptismal confession, perhaps something like the exordium? Is it the public profession of who Jesus is? Is it something they would have known but the author does not explicitly mention? Or is it the argument in the letter as a whole? Or is it the "main point" that Jesus is our high priest who intercedes on our behalf? Although all of these possibilities have merit, the last suggestion is the most promising. That Jesus is "faithful high priest" is that to which they should cling. But as faithful and high priest Jesus also accomplishes something—he builds a house.

The substance of the confession has to do with the "house" Jesus our priest builds. The explication of this confession begins with the claim that God "appointed" Jesus as high priest (3:2). But the expression used is troubling. The NRSV translates the passage: "Jesus was faithful to the one who *appointed* him." That is a good theological judgment about the verse, which uses a term that literally means "made." To translate it as "made" could suggest Arianism. Aquinas recognized this and nonetheless translated it "made." But he qualified what was "made": "Who made Him the Apostle and High Priest according to his human nature and not according to His divine nature, because as divine He is neither made nor created, but begotten."[18] God made Christ's human nature and not without assistance from other human agents—especially Mary. This is important and should not be neglected. It fits well Hebrews' teaching. Jesus performs what he does as a human in the way other humans act. He "builds" or "makes" a house analogous to Moses, except Moses did it as servant and Jesus does it as Son.

Central to the confession Hebrews sets forth is the claim in 3:6, "we are his house if we hold firm the confidence and the pride that belong to hope." Here the conditional admonition to "hold firm the confidence" is given its purpose—so that we might be made God's house. This draws upon two OT passages, both of which are alluded to in the first three chapters. Hebrews 3:5 refers to Numbers 12:5–7, where God's glory appears at the "entrance of the tent," and God says: "When there are prophets among you, I the LORD make myself known to them in visions; I speak to them in dreams. Not so with my servant Moses; he is entrusted with all my house." This house was the inheritance promised to Abraham and Sarah. It comes through Moses and Miriam to David, who was alluded to in Hebrews 1:5. The important passage from 2 Samuel 7 is alluded to in Hebrews 3:6 when we are told that, even more so than Moses, Jesus is "faithful over God's house as a son." The allusion to 2 Samuel 7 is important, for the words found in Hebrews 1:5 and now elaborated in 3:6 were first spoken to David when God promised to build David a "house." If we hold fast the substance of the confession, the result is that we are made God's house.

God says to David, "And I will appoint a place for my people Israel and will plant them, so that they may live in their own place, and be disturbed no more; and evildoers shall afflict them no more, as formerly, from the time that I appointed judges over my people Israel; and I will give you rest from all your enemies. Moreover the LORD declares to you that the LORD will make you a house."

—2 Samuel 7:10–11

What does it mean to be the house of God? This is the most important question God poses in Holy Scripture, which we already

18. Aquinas, *Hebrews*, 78.

posed in the commentary on 1:5b. Scripture itself can never be read well without keeping this question in mind. From the creation story in Genesis 1 to the image of the new Jerusalem that concludes Revelation, the biblical stories are an answer to God's question posed to David, "Would you build me a house to live in?" Hebrews sees Jesus as "the Son" who fulfills the promise to David and gives God's house "rest."

This rest can be missed as it was "on the day of testing" in the wilderness (Heb. 3:8). But Hebrews sets forth a different time, a time other than "that day" such that it does not need to define our lives. Instead we have "Today."

"Today" is the day the Spirit speaks (3:7). It is the time of Christ, which is a time unlike any other time. It is not transitory or perishable, it is the "same yesterday and today and forever" (13:8). It is the day we "hear his voice" (3:15). But it is not yet ultimate. Like Israel standing before the promised land, Hebrews' audience stands before God's eternal rest. But unlike them, their leader, Jesus, is already in that rest. The ultimate merges with the penultimate, making "Today" the day to hear his voice. Hebrews returns again to the theme of hearing the Word and attending to it. To hear it well is to enter into his rest. This produces an interesting tension in Hebrews. On the one hand we are called to be unsettled, to look for a different city. On the other, we are promised rest. These two dispositions fit together because of our location, on the verge of God's eternal rest, but connected to Jesus, who already inherited it.

The goal of being God's house, people, city, or temple is to enter into God's own rest—a clear reference to the act of creation and what God does on the seventh day, on the *Today* still available to us. Related to this rest is "inheritance." The Son's work has inherited the rest—he sits at the right hand of God. So one of the reasons he is worthy is because he can share that rest with the people. This "rest" reflects God's own activity. It is what God did on the seventh day when God finished his work (Gen. 2:2).

Hebrews 4:1–14 develops this theme of rest. It is first and foremost God's (4:4). God gives it to God's people. For the ancient rabbis, the rest on the seventh day was also an act of creation. Abraham Heschel explains this, quoting a midrash by Rashi on Genesis

2:2: "After the six days of creation—what did the universe still lack? *Menuha*. Came the Sabbath, came *menuha* [rest] and the universe was complete." Hebrew *menuha*, which we usually render as "rest," means here much more than withdrawal from labor and exertion, more than freedom from toil, strain, or activity of any kind. *Menuha* is not a negative concept but real and intrinsically positive. This must have been the view of the ancient rabbis if they believed that it took a special act of creation to bring it into being, that the universe would be incomplete without it. "'What was created on the seventh day? *Tranquility, serenity, peace* and *repose*.' . . . In later times, *menuha* became a synonym for the life in the world to come, for eternal life."[19] Of course, Rashi lived one thousand years after the author of Hebrews. Rabbinic Judaism was not yet beginning to form when the book of Hebrews was written, but the striking similarity to this hoped-for rest and that of Hebrews shows how thoroughly it draws on central Jewish concepts. They both draw on the same Scriptures to explain a common hope.

This common scriptural background also helps us make sense of the term *hypodeigma* in 4:11. This term, found three times in Hebrews (also 8:5; 9:23), is often translated as "copy" (NRSV prefers "sketch") and supposedly demonstrates the Platonic and Philonic influence on the author. As L. D. Hurst has shown, however, Philo uses this term only four times throughout his many works, and Plato normally uses *mimēma* or *eikōn* for the "copy" of an original ideal. *Hypodeigma* is more often used as "example" than "copy."[20] We have an instance of that in 4:11: "Let us therefore make every effort to enter that rest, so that no one may fall through the example (*hypodeigmati*) of their disobedience" (my trans.). After having established that his listeners are "the house" Christ builds, Hebrews then goes on to contrast the "example" (*hypodeigma*) of Israel's disobedience with the "example" they are called to follow. This not only helps us make sense of the exhortations that then follow in 5:11–6:20, but it also gives us insight into how to interpret

19. Abraham Heschel, "A Palace in Time," in *The Ten Commandments: The Reciprocity of Faithfulness*, ed. William P. Brown (Louisville: Westminster John Knox Press, 2004), 221.
20. L. D. Hurst, *The Epistle to the Hebrews: Its Background of Thought*, SNTSMS 65 (Cambridge: Cambridge University Press, 1990), 13–14.

the two tents or tabernacles at the heart of the sermon in chapters 8–9. They are not a caricatured Platonism that juxtaposes a static ideal and a material, temporal copy that must be abandoned. They are "examples" of two kinds of houses. That the house of Moses is good has already been established. The house Jesus builds, however, is perfect. Moses' house is an "example" of what Christ's house is, because it is his body. Because his body now bears God's own essence, participation in that body will bring the rest that characterizes God.

4:15–5:10

A Merciful High Priest

Whereas the previous section (3:1–4:14) developed the theme from 2:17 that Christ is a high priest who is "*worthy of faith*," this section picks up on the second theme in 2:17, that Christ is a "*merciful*" high priest. This too is central to the confession—not only that he is priest but what kind of priest he is. Where the first section ended with the reminder that not all called to the rest received it, this section gives hope that a better way has been opened up by Christ because he can "sympathize with our weaknesses," for he was as we are in all respects but "without sin" (4:15). That expression finds its way into the Chalcedonian Definition in 451, which has sustained the church's faith in Christ throughout the ages. Jesus' sinlessness is crucial for Hebrews' argument because it sets the stage for Christ to make a single sacrificial offering, unlike the Levitical priests, who had to offer a sacrifice for themselves as well as the people year after year because of their sinfulness (5:1 and 9:7).

One can read 4:14 as either concluding the previous section or opening the next or perhaps as fulfilling both roles. Notice that it picks up again on this theme of Jesus as high priest. Now it adds that he has "passed through the heavens." What could it mean to say Jesus passed through the *heavens*? How many are there? Where are they found, and why did he have to "pass through" them rather than "into" them? If heaven is the dwelling place of God, why did Jesus overshoot it, as it were, passing beyond it? Answers to these questions are important in contemporary Christian theology because of the gnostic sources/canons within which some read Hebrews, to which we alluded earlier and must now return.

Ernst Käsemann wrote, "Both the drafting of the entire theme and the Christology of the letter in particular were possible only on soil made ready by Gnosticism."[21] Gnosticism is a loosely associated group of teachings traceable to documents that originate primarily from the second and third centuries AD. The early church fathers, especially Irenaeus, Hippolytus, and Tertullian, classified these teachings as heresies. These teachings share some common themes, but not all of these themes are present in every text we would call gnostic. First, they often make a sharp distinction between the God of the Old Testament and the God of the New. The OT God is depicted as arrogant and wicked and denies knowledge of the true God to creatures. Second, creation is a mistake. Creation is fall. Creation is often attributed in gnostic teaching to Sophia, whose presumption causes her to seek to be like the true God. Third, creation itself is evil or at least deficient. Redemption occurs by overcoming creation's deficiency. For this reason gnostic teachings often have a strong soul-matter distinction. Redemption requires shedding the body and being, or becoming, "pneumatic." This is a higher form of being than the "psychics," who can still become pneumatic, usually through rigorous ascetic practices. They are higher than the "material kind" who, according to the *Tripartite Tractate*, are "alien in every respect" and only subject to "perish."[22] The Christology in Gnosticism is often, but not always, docetic. Jesus only feigns to be human. He does not really suffer or die. Fourth, gnostic teachings are often theodicies. It is the god(s) who need to be justified, especially those liable for the mess that creation is. Creation is evil because of what the gods or aeons did. They are the ones in need of redemption, and they are the ones whose ways must be justified.

These themes can be found in what are known as "gnostic sources," especially as they denigrate the Jewish story of Yahweh's creation.[23]

21. Käsemann, *Wandering People of God*, 174.

22. *The Nag Hammadi Scriptures*, ed. Marvin W. Meyer (New York: HarperOne, 2007), 93.

23. See also in ibid.: *On the Origin of the World*, 205–6; *Holy Book of the Great Invisible Spirit*, 263; and *Second Revelation of James*, 338.

***Secret Book of John*: "When he saw creation surrounding him and the throng of angels around him that had come forth from him, Yaldabaoth said to them, 'I am a jealous god and there is no other god beside me.' But by announcing this, he suggested to the angels with him that there is another god. For if there were no other god, of whom would he be jealous?" —*Nag Hammadi Scriptures*, 117**	***The Second Great Discourse of Seth*: "Then the voice of the world ruler announced to the angels, 'I am God, and there is no other beside me.' I laughed heartily when I reflected upon how conceited he was. . . . The whole host of his angels, who had seen Adam and his dwelling place, laughed at its insignificance." —*Nag Hammadi Scriptures*, 479**

The gnostic distortion within Christianity often read it against Judaism. The first commandment is viewed as misguided, the work of a lesser, jealous, and arrogant deity. Creation, like its creator, is riddled with deficiencies. Yahweh seeks to keep from people the true path to God, which comes about by the soul's ascent through and above the aeons by the secret knowledge often given by Jesus after his resurrection to a privileged elite. Sometimes it is the gods or aeons who make this ascent and are in need of redemption. In one of the most famous of all gnostic teachings, the *Tripartite Tractate,* "the Savior himself was in need of redemption after having descended into the world of matter."[24] The materiality of creation shatters the "All," or "Fullness" (*plērōma*), that constitutes an original harmony. Redemption requires shedding that materiality so that the original harmony can be restored. In gnostic teaching Jesus often demonstrates the way through the aeons back to that harmony. Is this what is taking place in Hebrews 4:14? Some church fathers have perhaps pointed in this direction.

Origen interpreted 4:14 in terms of Greek "spheres." He stated that most departed saints "remain on earth" in "paradise," where they receive "instruction." Those who are "pure in heart," however, and are "well-trained" pass through "the region of the air until they reach the kingdom of the heavens, passing through the series of those

24. Einar Thomassen, introduction to *Tripartite Tractate,* in *Nag Hammadi Scriptures,* 58.

'rooms' . . . which the Greeks have termed spheres, that is, globes, but which the divine Scripture calls heavens. In each of these they will first observe all that happens there and then learn the reason why it happens: and thus they will proceed in order through each stage, following him who has 'passed through the heavens, Jesus the Son of God,' and who has said, 'I desire that they also may be with me where I am.' Further he alludes to this diversity of places when he says, 'In my Father's house are many rooms.'"[25] But it would be wrong to see Origen as a gnostic. He explicitly rejected their teachings.[26]

Origen reads the "rooms" of the Gospel of John through a Greek cosmology that sees levels of reality through which Jesus passes. Other interpreters, as diverse as Aquinas and James Moffatt, read Jesus' "passing through the heavens" in terms of the temple. For Aquinas, Christ passed into the "holy of holies," so 4:14 should be read in light of Leviticus 16:2 and Hebrews 9:7, where the high priest enters once a year into the holy of holies. Thus Aquinas writes, "This however especially befits Christ. For the other enters with blood in a holy prefigurement; but Christ through His own blood entered into the holies, that is into the sacred heavens."[27] James Moffatt likewise states, "The greatness of Jesus as *archiereus* consists in his access to God not through any material veil, but through the upper heavens; he has penetrated to the very throne of God."[28] Like Aquinas, he interprets this "passing" not by placing it in the context of a gnostic canon, but in the internal logic of Hebrews.

The temple imagery gets lost once the gnostic canon returns in modernity. Käsemann connects 4:14 to the word that is "difficult to understand" in 5:11 and the claim that Hebrews' listeners are "partakers of the Holy Spirit" in 6:4. By these connections he finds in

25. Cited in Heen and Krey, eds., *Hebrews*, 66.

26. See *Contra Celsum* 5.61, trans. Henry Chadwick (Cambridge: Cambridge University Press, 1980), 311; here Origen distances his account of salvation from the Valentinians with their distinction between people who are "natural" and those who are "spiritual": "What has this to do with us who belong to the Church, who find fault with those who maintain that natures are saved or lost in consequence of the way they are made?"

27. Aquinas, *Hebrews*, 107.

28. James Moffatt, *A Critical and Exegetical Commentary on the Epistle to the Hebrews*, International Critical Commentary (1924; repr. Edinburgh: T & T Clark, 1979), 58.

Hebrews an appeal to a gnostic secret knowledge. "According to no doubt current Gnostic usage, they are no longer psychical . . . but pneumatic."[29] He interprets this gnostic influence over against Judaism. "We must note first that with its penetration of the Hellenistic world it left the influence of Palestinian soil and inner-Jewish history. It was thus compelled to think through and form its content in a new way, so as to make the gospel accessible to new hearers originating in other contexts."[30] Therefore he argues that it is "clearer than ever" that a central influence on Hebrews and early Christian Christology was the gnostic redeemer myth. Hebrews did not reject that myth. By incorporating it into its Christology, "in the history of the church a synthesis of gospel and mysticism has continually resulted" that led "*the gospel, disengaging itself from Palestinian soil,*" to achieve universality. But, Käsemann argues, Hebrews does not allow the myth to absorb the gospel.[31] Hebrews contains no speculation about preexistent souls or dualism of spirit and matter. What allows Hebrews and early Christianity to absorb rather than be absorbed by the myth is its antimetaphysical character: "*the Christian message refuses to become a metaphysic, . . . it rejects the pseudo-theology that bases the reception of revelation and the possibility of redemption on an innate capacity, on the universal and innate nobility of an immortal, divine soul.*"[32]

This is an odd use of the term "metaphysics." For Käsemann it refers to gnostic myths. Yet for Plato, Aristotle, Augustine, and Plotinus "metaphysics" is a rational undertaking that is an alternative to myth, not its exemplification. For this reason Augustine claimed that Christianity is more like natural theology (or metaphysics) taught in the academy than the mythic (fabulous) or civil religion found in the Roman populace. Fabulous theology is presented in the forum by poets and actors where myth predominates. Natural theology is theology for the academy; it is kept out of the hands of the populace,

29. Käsemann, *Wandering People of God*, 187.
30. Ibid., 175.
31. Ibid., 176.
32. Ibid., 177–78.

for it begins with criticism of the mythical theology. It is more akin to metaphysics.[33] For Käsemann, Christianity seems to have no option but to be fabulous. It refuses metaphysics, but it adopts Hellenistic myth in its soteriology, especially in the doctrine of the incarnation: "Early Christianity of the Hellenistic world simply could not convey the significance of Jesus if it ignored the store of ideas about the one sent from heaven, the Son of God and the *Anthropos*, already in existence in that world and universally known."[34] Christ's universality requires Christians to use the Hellenistic myth. He is the telos of all longings, and as such he "gives to all the answer to their questions." To the Jew, he is the answer to their law by displacing it. To the Greeks, he is the answer to the longing present in their myth by revealing that it cannot be accomplished through some innate divinity in creatures. But it was precisely this mythical world that the third-century church father Irenaeus rejects and sees as the source of Gnosticism's errors.

> **In reality they [the gnostics] transfer to their own system what is said in theaters everywhere by actors and splendid voices, or rather they use the same plots and simply change the names.**
>
> **—Irenaeus**
>
> *Against Heresies* 2.14.1, in Robert M. Grant, *Irenaeus of Lyons* (London: Routledge, 1997), 110.

With Käsemann we have moved far away from the "temple," or the "house of God," as the interpretive key to understanding Hebrews' message. Instead, the "gnostic redeemer" supposedly illumines its message. But we have moved far away from the canonical context of shared Scriptures with Judaism as well. For Käsemann, Jesus also "shatters the Jewish law by giving himself to all the world, not merely to the chosen people." Jesus does so by destroying any possibility that human nature possesses anything, or any relation, to divine nature. Only once grace completely destroys nature can the myth be of "use to Christian proclamation."[35] Myth always serves a different politics than that found in Holy Scripture.

33. Augustine, *City of God* 6.5, in *Nicene and Post-Nicene Fathers*, first series, vol. 2 (repr. Grand Rapids: Eerdmans, 1979), 112–13.
34. Käsemann, *Wandering People of God*, 178.
35. Ibid., 179.

FURTHER REFLECTIONS
Protestant Gnosticism and Modernity

Why did this gnostic return have such power in modern biblical scholarship? Why does it continue to return in contemporary theology? Given the oddity of its claims, these are important historical questions. We need to contextualize modern scholarship and ask about the conditions for the "gnostic return." Fortunately Cyril O'Regan has already done much of this work. He argues persuasively that Gnosticism represents a peculiarly Protestant temptation.[36] If neo-paganism tempts Catholicism by its affirmation of "nature," then Gnosticism tempts Protestantism by its disavowal of "nature." O'Regan builds on F. C. Bauer's thesis that "ancient Gnosis" returns in modernity, affirming Bauer's "determinate criterion" for indentifying this gnostic return as a "repetition in modern Christian discourses of a narrative focused on the vicissitudes of (divine) reality's fall from perfection, its agonic middle, and its recollection into perfection."[37] Because the Trinity is misunderstood in modern theology as becoming through the cross, it gets interpreted in terms of a gnostic theodicy that seeks to justify God and explain evil.[38]

O'Regan's use of this thesis provides explanatory power for a genealogical understanding of the prevalence of these "gnostic" readings among contemporary Protestantism from process theologians to peculiar readings of Barth. He suggests "six material conditions" must be satisfied before this gnostic return. First, traditional Christian understandings of God and how God relates to creation are understood as "moribund." Second, although they are inadequate, they are not abandoned but revised. Third, they are revised through a "shift" in biblical exegesis from the "literal to the pneumatic and from community to individual contexts of reading." Fourth, these revisions are "global," affecting all Christian teachings, and fundamentally altering "their community and traditionally based meaning." Fifth, the purpose of these revisions is to address the problem

36. Cyril O'Regan, *Gnostic Return in Modernity* (Albany: SUNY Press, 2001), 20.
37. Ibid., 29.
38. Ibid., 33.

of evil. It "absolves the divine from blame by making narrative development self-legitimating." Finally, although such revisions appear to provide equality among human creatures, they actually underwrite "pneumatic privilege and distinction." Those in the know become, in Orwell's phrase, "more equal than others."[39] Gnosticism emerges in modernity among Protestants because Protestantism assumes most everything we have received from tradition is inadequate and cannot answer the unique questions of our existence, especially the question of evil. In order to do so, Christianity must be globally revised by individuals who have a singular revolutionary insight into what needs to be done.[40] If we are to understand why "gnostic" interpretations of Hebrews cannot seem to die despite their thoroughgoing oddness, I think the answer is found in the contexts within which these material conditions flourish. They provide a new canon within which Hebrews operates.

The conditions that make possible a "gnostic swerve" in modern Protestant theology also contribute to a rejection of the central teaching in Hebrews, present in the Chalcedonian Definition, that Christ is without sin. Because for Hebrews and the orthodox Christian tradition sin is the problem of humanity and not God, it is important that Christ did not sin. Most theologians still assume Christ was without sin, and thus he is both priest and sacrifice—unblemished. Some argue otherwise.

The Episcopalian theologian Marilyn McCord Adams is one such theologian. Her work is an effort to address questions of "horrendous evil" through a Chalcedonian Christology. On the one hand, she defends Chalcedon and seeks to "hold firm the confession." On the other, her work revises Christianity in order to address evil. For her, evil is not an accident that emerges from creaturely abuse of the freedom God gives us, resulting in the "fall." Instead, evil is God's responsibility. It is a necessary metaphysical feature of God's desire to create something other than God. "God is responsible for creating human beings in such a framework," where that framework is a "metaphysical misfit" between God's own being and creaturely

39. Ibid., 183–84.

40. "These conditions are specific to related but distinct contexts in the unfolding of Protestant thought" (ibid., 184).

being. God cannot but create with this "metaphysical misfit."[41] She then jettisons traditional doctrines of impassibility and immutability in order to address the question why horrendous evils exist. For the only way God defeats horrendous evils is through "divine participation." The key term here is "divine," for this participation requires more than the traditional doctrine that God participates in the human suffering of the one person Jesus without confusing the divine and human natures. More is required to "defeat" horrendous evils. God must participate in them such that God suffers and changes in divinity.[42] Indeed, she goes as far as to suggest that this takes place "when God participates in the horrors God has perpetrated on us."[43] Note the language is not "permits" but "perpetrates." God is not only responsible for evil, God "perpetrates" it. This entails a global revision of Christianity while trying to affirm essential Christian teaching. "My cosmological hypothesis promises to describe a cosmos held together by Christ and to exhibit the coherence of Christology!"[44] The incarnation holds the cosmos together because it is the reason God is justified in perpetuating evils on us. God can only create and perpetrate the evils of the metaphysical mismatch because God also becomes incarnate and receives the horrendous evils God perpetrates.

For this reason, Adams defends a version of the "logic" of Chalcedon that Jesus is one person truly human and truly divine. But for this same reason she also rejects that statement in Chalcedon from Hebrews 4:15 that says Jesus "is like us in all respects, sin only excepted": "Contrary to patristic/medieval and turn of the twentieth century consensus, Jesus' NT roles as teacher, preacher and healer do not by themselves require sinlessness or moral infallibility."[45] Neither Christ's sinlessness nor his perfection are required for his two natures to come together into a harmony across the "metaphysical size-gap between Divine and human consciousness." Jesus' perfect

41. Marilyn McCord Adams, *Christ and Horrors: The Coherence of Christology* (Cambridge: Cambridge University Press, 2006), 36.
42. It "defeats their *prima facie* life-ruining powers" (ibid., 40).
43. Ibid., 41.
44. Ibid., 44.
45. Ibid., 73.

obedience is unnecessary for salvation. Instead what matters is his "mutual indwelling across the gap." It is a "harmony humanly aimed-at through the filter of limited understanding and affective scope."[46] We do not need Jesus' sinlessness for this.

Adams finds that Hebrews 4:15 has been both misread and overread by the tradition when it advances the claim that Jesus was without sin: "Hebrews 4:15 (tempted as we are yet without sin) is cited as a fully explicit affirmation of Christ's sinlessness. Yet, the focus of the epistle is not sin in general, but apostasy in particular. The whole letter 'cheerleads' its recipients to persevere by holding up the example and the surpassing worth of Christ. Thus the thrust of the passage might be the more limited one: 'Christ was tempted, had to struggle to maintain His loyalty in the face of death, but he didn't betray His calling. You shouldn't either.'"[47] This is a very strained reading of Hebrews. It neglects the central role "perfection" and "purification" play throughout the letter, as well as the importance of Jesus' human obedience. Such a reading is best understood in terms of the neo-gnostic question that animates it: Given that God must perpetrate evil against us in order to create, how might we construe the relation between God and creatures so that we can justify God's evil actions and find a return to a harmonious whole? Once this becomes the basic theological question addressed, then we find a global revisioning of traditional Christian themes that fundamentally alters their meaning even while affirming them. Indeed, evil becomes so decisive that one wonders if it can be defeated. The Eucharist itself is the source not of communion and reconciliation, but of violence and agonism. Adams states that in the Eucharist, "Christ's donation of Himself to be bitten, chomped and chewed exposes Himself to our anger and frustration—anger and frustration so great that we would kill and cannibalize, even destroy God."[48]

Why might it matter that Jesus is without sin? For Hebrews not only who Jesus is matters for salvation, but also what he has done. This

46. Ibid., 73–74.
47. Ibid., 75.
48. Ibid., 310.

was stated in the exordium, "When he had made purification for sins, he sat down at the right hand of the Majesty on high" (1:3b). The purification he makes for sins is both related to, and distinct from, the sacrifices of the Jewish cult. If they are taken out of that context, out of the question posed in the Davidic covenant, Hebrews makes no sense. Hebrews never denies the validity of Jewish priests. They appear very human and limited, but this is no detriment. It allows these priests to "deal gently with the ignorant and wayward" because they recognize their own sin, weaknesses, and limitations (5:2). Because of this they offer sacrifices not only for the sins of others, but also for their own. They are indeed "called by God" (5:4). Christ is like them in this regard. Like them Christ is "merciful," for he too suffered and "learned obedience" (5:8). But as good and significant as these priests are, Christ is more excellent. Unlike them, he is the "source" of salvation (5:9) because his offering of gifts and sacrifices is only done once. Here is the decisive difference from the Levitical priests. Unlike the Levitical priests, he is without sin and therefore does not need to offer continual sacrifices for sins. But like them, his sacrifice works only if he is human. His perfect, creaturely obedience restores God's creation such that he can offer "it," that is, he offers his own performance of this perfection in the holy of holies. This performance takes place "in the days of his flesh" (5:7). This could refer to his entire earthly life, or to the particular moment when he faced death in the Garden of Gethsemane. Either way, Hebrews does not shy away from the fact that what Jesus faced was horrifying and caused him to offer prayers to God "with loud cries and tears" (5:7). Jesus is not Socrates, who faces death as an adventure to be welcomed. He seeks salvation from it. Death is not the answer but the enemy. With death, something has gone wrong. But facing the horror of death does not cause Jesus to recoil in fear, to seek the preservation of life at all costs. He remains "obedient" and actually "learns obedience" in his historical, fleshly life. In so doing, he is "made perfect" and becomes the "source of salvation." He is both priest and victim. Far from being a misread or overread of Hebrews, that Christ is without sin is essential to its message. If that is rejected, so is the entire argument. It leads up to the "main point" in 8:1–2.

5:11–6:20

More Exhortations

The main point, already stated in the exordium, alluded to here, and explicitly spelled out in 8:1–2, is this: "We have such a high priest, one who is seated at the right hand of the throne of the Majesty in the heavens, a minister in the sanctuary and the true tent that the Lord, and not any mortal, has set up." But we are not yet at the point where we can rightly hear this word. First the author prepares the soil in order to plant this word more firmly. This is one of several metaphors used to prepare his hearers for the "main point." The first is the metaphor of instruction as food for athletic training (5:11–14). Related to this is the "tasting" that a profitable cultivation of the soil produces versus that which is worthless (6:1–8). In case the hearers miss the point of the metaphor, Hebrews pauses to explain its meaning, noting what will be the hearers' proper response if they hear rightly—faith, endurance, hope, and patience in order to inherit God's promises (6:9–13). The exhortations conclude with a different metaphor, a nautical one. Jesus' perfect obedience and exaltation is an "anchor of the soul," drawing them forward in hope. He is this anchor because he himself is the "forerunner." He is ahead of them, securely present "behind the curtain." So the race for which they are training is not one they run alone. It is as if they are tied to Christ who is always ahead of them, securely anchoring and drawing them forward (6:14–20). The purpose of these metaphors and admonitions is to call us to go on toward perfection. Each of these metaphors and admonitions needs fuller elaboration.

5:11–14 *Solid Food for Discerning Good from Evil*

Having just been told that Christ was made perfect (*teleiōtheis,* 5:9), we are now exhorted in this section and the beginning of the next to "go on toward perfection" (5:14; 6:1). We are to move beyond basic elements to "solid food" that will allow us to discern good from evil. Such discernment presses on toward perfection, which is first and foremost Christ's. Perfection is something that happens to him because of what he does. Three times Hebrews notes the "perfecting of Christ": 2:10; 5:9; and 7:28. In each of these cases Christ is made perfect by his suffering and obedience. But Hebrews also presents Christ three times as the source of perfection: 10:14; 11:40; 12:23. Between the claim that Christ was made perfect and that he is the source of perfection, Hebrews contrasts Christ's ability to perfect with the inability of the old covenant to do so four times (7:11, 19; 9:9; 10:1).[49] The placement of these passages demonstrates the unfolding of a central argument. First the author establishes that Christ has been made perfect. This theme was alluded to in the exordium (1:3b–4) and then expanded in the first part of the sermon. Once Christ's perfection has been established, then Hebrews contrasts it with the inability of the old covenant to cause it. This shows that Hebrews is less concerned to demonstrate that the old covenant was wrong than that it was incomplete. It was a "shadow of the good things to come" (10:1), but it was not those things themselves. This can only be seen because the "good thing" has come and we see it in Christ. His perfection is the excellence that allows us to see the former things as good but partial. Hebrews contrasts the good with the perfect. Far from supersessionism, Hebrews affirms those former things for what they could accomplish.[50]

The author then uses OT passages to demonstrate that his argument is neither novel nor unique; it stands within the Old Testament itself. If the first covenant made perfect, we would not need another house beyond that of Moses and David (chap. 3). If the first covenant made perfect, Joshua's rest would have been sufficient (chap. 4). If the first covenant made perfect, the Levitical priests would not have to repeat their sacrifice (chaps. 5, 7, 9, 10). If the first covenant made perfect, we would not need the other priesthood of Melchizedek (chaps. 5, 7). If the first covenant made perfect, God would not have promised another one in Jeremiah (chap. 8). If the first covenant made perfect, the prophets would not have prophesied, "Sacrifices and offerings you have not desired, but a body you

49. David Peterson, *Hebrews and Perfection: An Examination of the Concept of Perfection in the 'Epistle to the Hebrews,'* SNTSMS 47 (Cambridge: Cambridge University Press, 1982), 1.
50. For an excellent discussion on whether Hebrews teaches supersessionism see Richard B. Hays, "'Here We Have No Lasting City': New Covenantalism in Hebrews," in *Epistle to the Hebrews and Christian Theology*, ed. Bauckham et al., 151–73.

have prepared for me" (chap. 10). If the first covenant made perfect, then Abel, Noah, Abraham, Sarah, Isaac, Jacob, and Moses would have already received the rest, but they still wait. For what are they waiting? That they might be "made perfect" with us (11:39–40). If the first covenant made perfect, Mount Sinai would have sufficed and we would not hope for Mount Zion (chap. 12). The incompleteness in the first covenant is found in the hope that Christ's perfection secures the inheritance, the "rest."

All of the above conditional sentences could have also been written, "If the first covenant had not pointed in the direction of this perfection, then Christ could not make perfect." The comparison here does not denigrate Israel. Indeed, even though it claims that covenant is "passing away," it is only passing away because of the "greater thing" that has come which is perfect. Only as it is measured against the perfect is it found inadequate. But if Hebrews did not recognize the legitimacy of the law, our author would not concern himself with making an argument as to why Jesus can be high priest even though he is from the wrong tribe.[51]

The difference between the old covenant and Christ's sacrifice in Hebrews cannot be explained in terms of ritual versus moral, external versus internal, or law versus grace. None of those oppositions illumines Hebrews. The difference between them is Christ's own perfection and his subsequent ability to perfect. It is only Christ's perfection that renders the former words and covenant partial. For this reason, getting some sense of what this "perfection" is matters greatly.

Perfection is what happens to Christ and what he makes possible, but scholars are divided in explaining more fully the content of that perfection, often making differentiations and arguing for one rather than another by fragmenting life into distinct components. Answers include: Perfection is ritualistic and cultic. It is moral. It is "formal," bringing to wholeness or maturity what was not yet attained. It is knowledge, whether in the form of mysteries or an avowed confession. It is metaphysical in the sense of a stable, transcendent realm that secures the unstable temporal one, if not dissolving it

51. David Moffitt pointed this out to me.

altogether. It is eschatological, coming to us from the future in a new age. It is Adamic, bringing to completion what was lost in Adam.[52] Which answer a scholar prefers will often be determined by which "canon" she or he employs to read Hebrews. If read in the context of the gnostics, perfection entails knowledge; if Jewish apocalyptic, then it is eschatological; if Platonism or Philo, then it will be moral, formal, and/or metaphysical; if the Old Testament, then it is ritualistic and cultic. The canon within which we read Hebrews makes a significant difference. But even these divisions are too neat and tidy. Each of these "canons" cannot be defined solely by one answer. Take for instance George Nickelsburg's claim about the relation between space and time found in the Jewish apocalyptic work *1 Enoch*, "A spatial dualism between this world and heaven and a temporal dualism between this age and the age to come are important components of the worldview of 1 Enoch."[53] If that is true of *1 Enoch*, then we have a first-century apocalyptic work that does not fit the false dichotomy of a spatialized Greek metaphysics or temporalized Jewish eschatology. The same must be said of Hebrews, which makes any sharp distinction among metaphysics and eschatology or Plato, Philo, and Judaism difficult to sustain. This helps us interpret "perfection." We should refuse to offer a single answer, but recognize the fullness of the term itself.

For Hebrews, perfection is first and foremost Jesus. It is who he is, what he does, and what happens to him. For this reason we do not need to choose between a focus on the "incarnation" or "atonement" as the locus for Christ's perfection.[54] Christ is perfect because he is "the reflection of God's glory and the exact imprint of God's very being" (1:3). For this reason he is the permanent and indestructible source of salvation that will be the "same yesterday and today and forever" (13:8). As the fullness of God's being, Christ appears in

52. Peterson, *Hebrews and Perfection*, 2–20.

53. George Nickelsburg, *1 Enoch 1: A Commentary on the Book of 1 Enoch, Chapters 1–36; 81–108*, Hermeneia (Minneapolis: Fortress Press, 2001), 5.

54. Peterson posits this either-or, finding a focus on the incarnation in Catholic thinkers like Vanhoye. Peterson prefers an understanding that focuses primarily on atonement. So he writes, "Man is perfected in relation to God *when the promises of the New Covenant are realised in individual experience*" (*Hebrews and Perfection*, 155). But where does Hebrews ever mention "individual experience"?

time and becomes like us in all things "except sin." He was tempted toward our "weakness," but did not succumb to it (4:15). Unlike priests who share our weakness and must offer a sacrifice for their sins and ours, Christ is a high priest who shared all that we are, can "sympathize" with our weakness, and nonetheless it does not characterize his identity (4:15; 5:2–3). His obedience, learned through his suffering, makes him perfect. In other words, he brings his perfection as the "exact imprint" of God into creation, into its space and time, and achieves it there. He becomes what he is. Because he achieves perfection, he then becomes the source for our own perfection, leading creation into it (5:9).

Hebrews acknowledges this is a difficult teaching: "About this we have much to say that is hard to explain . . ." (5:11). This expression makes best sense when the antecedent for "this" refers back to Christ as the source of perfection (5:9), and to Christ as "high priest according to the order of Melchizedek" (5:10). Because Hebrews equates Christ's priesthood and his causal power as perfecting, what follows is unsurprising. First we get a discussion of what it means for Christ to be the source of our perfection (chap. 6), and then we get a discussion on Melchizedek (chap. 7). Hebrews then turns to the "main point" in 8:1–3 reminding us yet again that we have a high priest who is the source of perfection. The heart of the sermon emphasizes perfection.

In explaining what perfection should be for us, Hebrews begins by drawing on our bodily development as human creatures. The author contrasts *nēpios,* "immature" or "infant," with *teleiōn,* "mature" or "perfect." The importance of this terminology can easily be lost in English translations, most of which render the clause "solid food belongs for the mature" rather than for the "perfect." This rendering could prevent seeing the continuity between 5:14 and the admonition in 6:1 to "go on toward perfection," which could also be translated "go on to maturity" (so NIV). The contrast between infancy and maturity or perfection is key. We are called to go on to perfection, which, like the full development of our humanity itself, takes on maturity and leaves immaturity behind. This requires growth in both knowledge and practice, or intellect and will. These two come together in the important admonition that the purpose of this maturation is to "distinguish good from evil" (5:14). Clearly, then, knowledge and ethics constitute perfection. It is theoretical and practical at the same time. Chapter 6 establishes this. But perfection is also cultic and ritual, as the end of chapter 6 and the discussion of Melchizedek in chapter 7 demonstrate. Doctrine, ethics, and ritual are woven tightly together such that one can only differentiate them by forcing apart what Hebrews keeps together. Their interwoven character is a participation in the "Holy Spirit," the "goodness of the word of God," and the "powers of the age to come" all at the same time (6:5–6). It is metaphysical and eschatological.

6:1–12 *"Going on to perfection"*

Starting from the "foundations" of the "basic teaching of Christ," our perfection develops like a fruitful crop (6:7) toward the "better things . . . that belong to salvation" (6:9). It is characterized by a "full" hope, faith, and patience that imitate the saints (6:11–12). The author sets forth concrete examples of these three theological virtues in chapter 11. They demonstrate perfection, which is the fulfillment of the promise made to Abraham, a promise that is perfection itself because it comes from an unchangeable God. It is "sure and steadfast" because it is like an anchor securing us within the holy of holies (6:19), the place of God's own dwelling, where Jesus exercises his priesthood through his "indestructible life" (7:16). The perfection of his own body through his obedience, now identified with the perfection he always had as the exact imprint of God, is a sure and certain cause of perfection. It ensures that we too can become what we were intended to be. As previously noted, Irenaeus saw this well: "For the glory of God is a living man, while the life of man is the vision of God."[55] Or as the Orthodox Father Dumitru Staniloae states, "The glory to which man is called is that he should grow more godlike by growing ever more human."[56] In the Orthodox tradition

55. *Against Heresies* 4.20.7, cited in Norman Russell, *Fellow Workers with God: Orthodox Thinking on Theosis* (Crestwood, NY: St. Vladimir's Seminary Press, 2009), 40.
56. Kallistos Ware, *The Orthodox Way*, rev. ed. (Crestwood, NY: St. Vladimir's Seminary Press, 1995), 66.

this is known as "deification," which is very similar to the perfection for which Hebrews calls.

The central biblical text for deification in Orthodoxy does not come from Hebrews, but from 2 Peter, which was most likely written after Hebrews. It offers a teaching of redemption in line with that of Hebrews. The crucial passage is 2 Peter 1:3–8. Reading Hebrews in light of it helps us understand "perfection" in Holy Scripture.

Two central themes, even using the same words, demonstrate a strong similarity between Hebrews and 2 Peter's teaching: calling and promise. Hebrews' entire sermon addresses those who are "partners/participants/partakers [*metochoi*] in a heavenly calling" (3:1), "partners [*metochoi*] of Christ" (3:14). In 6:4 his hearers are told not to turn away from being "partners" [*metochous*] in the Holy Spirit. Here Hebrews uses *metochos,* one of the two important terms the Orthodox draw upon to explain "participation in Christ." Second Peter 1:4 sounds a very similar theme when it tells us that our calling is to be "participants of the divine nature," but it uses the term *koinōnoi* rather than *metochoi*. Both terms are important for the doctrine of deification. They share a family resemblance in meaning. Our calling is to be "partakers" or "participants" in a heavenly calling. The calling, for both Hebrews and 2 Peter, is grounded in God's promise (*epangelia*). This promise requires that we "make every effort," which translates the phrase *spoudēn pasan pareisenegkantes* (2 Pet. 1:5). The term *spoudēn* is the same term Hebrews uses

His divine power has given us everything needed for life and godliness, through the knowledge of him who called us by his own glory and goodness. Thus he has given us, through these things, his precious and very great promises, so that through them you may escape from the corruption that is in the world because of lust, and may become participants of the divine nature. For this very reason, you must make every effort to support your faith with goodness, and goodness with knowledge, and knowledge with self-control, and self-control with endurance, and endurance with godliness, and godliness with mutual affection, and mutual affection with love. For if these things are yours and are increasing among you, they keep you from being ineffective and unfruitful in the knowledge of our Lord Jesus Christ.

—2 Peter 1:3–8

in 6:11, which admonishes its hearers to "show the same diligence" in accomplishing the end for which they hope. Both 2 Peter and Hebrews call for "effort" or "diligence" in striving for faith and hope.

They also do so with a remarkably consistent list of "excellences" or virtues, although the well-known Greek moral philosophical term for this, *aretē,* is found only in 2 Peter (and Philemon). Interestingly *hexis,* the well-known Greek moral philosophical term for the exercise of virtue that produces character, is only found at Hebrews 5:14. Both are drawing upon a commonplace Greek moral vocabulary, but relating it to faith in Christ, in order to explain the pursuit of goodness. For 2 Peter, faith is "supported" by moral excellence or "goodness" (*aretē*), and then "knowledge," "self-control" (*enkrateia*), "endurance" (*hypomonē*), "godliness" (*eusebia*), "mutual affection" (*philadelphia*), and "love" (*agapē*). Hebrews employs all these terms except *aretē* and *enkrateia* for a similar purpose. For instance, in the concluding admonition in chapter 13 we are told, "Let mutual love [*philadelphia*] continue." The term *hypomonē* is Hebrews' central admonition in 12:1. Chapter 6 shows us what this endurance or perseverance entails. Indeed, it warns that those who fail in it cannot be restored "again to repentance." We will return to this controversial passage once we establish more fully what this call to perfection entails.

FURTHER REFLECTIONS
Perfection and Deification

Along with 2 Peter, the long tradition of "perfection" or "deification" in the Orthodox tradition assists in understanding perfection. Of course, this is a teaching that also resonates in Western Christianity. Norman Russell explains this ancient Orthodox account of redemption: "Theosis is our restoration as persons to integrity and wholeness by participation in Christ through the Holy Spirit, in a process which is initiated in this world through our life of ecclesial communion and moral striving and finds ultimate fulfillment in our union with the Father—all within the broad context of the divine economy."[57] Although he does not present this as a definition of "perfection" in Hebrews, he could have.

Hebrews' teaching on perfection lends strong support to the Eastern doctrine of *theosis*. Russell also defines it concretely. It is "to live as a faithful member of the Church, attending the Liturgy, receiving the sacraments and keeping the commandments."[58] But for many Orthodox theologians deification presumes theological doctrines the West rejects or at least neglects. In particular, deification requires the distinction of God's essence and energies. God's essence is always unknowable. God's energies, which are God's activity in the world, produce a union between divinity and humanity that is both the source of union with God and, at the same time, the only source for the knowledge of God. This is a personal union and knowledge that many in the Eastern tradition find violated especially by the role reason plays in Western scholastic theology. Aristotle Papanikolaou explains this, interpreting the thought of Vladimir Lossky: "Union with God is not knowledge of God as an object but an experience of God, a mystical experience that surpasses all understanding and description."[59] For Lossky, this union can only occur because of the essence and energies distinction. He claims it provides a "dogmatic basis for *union with God*."[60] Coupled with this teaching is another the majority of Eastern theologians find lacking in the West, the *monarchia* of the Father. It demands that the Father alone processes the Holy Spirit. Unlike the West, where Christians confess that the "Spirit proceeds from the Father and the Son [*Filioque* in Latin, which translates 'and the Son']," the East confesses that the Spirit proceeds from the Father alone. This makes the Father the "monarch" who in his person generates the Son and processes the Spirit. Eastern theologians often claim that for Western theologians the divine essence generates the persons of the Trinity, and that makes their origin impersonal, losing the

57. Russell, *Fellow Workers with God*, 21.
58. Ibid., 170.
59. Aristotle Papanikolaou, *Being with God: Trinity, Apophaticism, and Divine-Human Communion* (Notre Dame, IN: University of Notre Dame Press, 2006), 21.
60. Vladimir Lossky, *The Mystical Theology of the Eastern Church* (Crestwood, NY: St. Vladimir's Seminary Press, 1976), 71. Papanikolaou italicized "union with God" in his quotation, *Being with God*, 25.

necessary distinction between the unknowable essence and the divine persons. The result, as Lossky put it, is that "by the dogma of the *Filioque*, the God of the philosophers and savants is introduced into the heart of the Living God."[61] Papanikolaou bluntly states the significance of this for Orthodox theologians: "And the fatal existential consequence of this introduction is that it precludes full personal communion with the divine."[62] Or as he puts it elsewhere, drawing upon both Lossky and John Zizioulas, "To err in relation to a doctrine of God would result in misconceiving the nature of salvation, which itself would create obstacles to that saving union/communion with God."[63] We would lose deification.

It is difficult to fathom that three words, "and the Son," could create such an existential crisis that it prevents Western Christians from achieving the perfection God intends for God's creatures. It also seems ironic that the Eastern tradition regularly critiques the Western for its "rationalism," but then argues that its misconstrual of the doctrine of God produces an "obstacle" to union or communion with God. Is it possible that because we confess the Spirit processes from the Father and the Son that we cannot achieve deification? Does anyone truly believe that removing those three words from the creed would open the floodgates to God's activities and allow God's holiness to pour into the Western churches in a way it is not now present? Would that it were so. But Lossky's point is less that the mere doctrine of the *Filioque* produces this crisis, and more that it keeps Western Christians from the ascetical practices, including the intellectual practice of ridding oneself of a rational conceptuality for knowledge of God, that would allow in practice the experiential union present in the divine energies that alone makes knowledge of God and deification possible. This difference is no small matter in the life of the church. It has split the church between the East and the West since the eleventh century. Differing interpretations of Hebrews did not contribute to this split, but the different theological frameworks surrounding deification produce yet another

61. Cited in Papanikolaou, *Being with God*, 69.
62. Ibid.
63. Ibid., 91.

controversy in reading and hearing Hebrews' call to "go on to perfection."

For the Orthodox the call to perfection occurs through a participation in the divine energies, which are a mode of God's existence in the world.[64] For Hebrews the only cause and source for this perfection is Christ, who receives it through what he suffered and offers it to others through his eternal high priesthood (5:8–10). A common critique the Western tradition brings against the East is that they replaced the action of the second person of the Trinity with the "divine energies." Some Orthodox theologians refuse any sharp distinction between God's energies and the Son. The Orthodox theologian John Zizioulas, however, "breaks with his peers by discussing salvation not in terms of participation in the divine energies, but in terms of the divine 'hypostasis' of the Son."[65] The energies are not distinct from the work of the persons of the Son and the Spirit. If they were, they would constitute a fourth person in the Trinity, which Orthodox theologians consistently reject. Yet if this is the case, then are the Western and Eastern theologians that far apart?

Some theologians within Western Christianity also seek to lay claim to the tradition of deification. A. N. Williams finds this theme central in the work of Thomas Aquinas.[66] Recent work on Luther has argued, not without controversy, that the best way to understand his account of salvation is through the doctrine of theosis. Perfection characterizes the distinct charism the Wesleyans bring to the church catholic through the teaching of the Anglican theologian John Wesley, and many of its most able theologians find it similar to the Eastern tradition of theosis.

Drawing on 2 Peter 1:4, Aquinas relates God's gracious action to our deification. "Now the gift of grace surpasses every capability of created nature, since it is nothing short of a partaking of the Divine Nature, which exceeds every other nature. . . . For it is as necessary that God alone should deify, bestowing a partaking of the Divine Nature by a participated likeness."[67] "Partaking of the Divine

64. Ibid., 26–27.
65. Ibid., 106.
66. A. N. Williams, *The Ground of Union* (Oxford: Oxford University Press, 1999).
67. Aquinas, *Summa theologica* 1-2, q.112, a.1.

Nature" occurs through grace that helps us attain perfection. God alone contains the perfection of all things, giving to God a *scientia* (knowledge) of things outside God. For Aquinas, "all that makes for perfection in any creature is to be found first in God, and is contained in him in an eminent degree."[68] But God does not grow in knowledge by learning these things as we do. For God is the cause of all things and knows them intimately by knowing God's own self. God knows all things in the fullness in which they were intended to be, for God caused them. Our perfection consists in becoming by God's grace what God intends us to be. For Aquinas this requires that grace also be a "principle" that is created so that we participate in our perfection by our creaturely reality. This is an issue that still divides Catholics and Orthodox. For the latter, grace remains uncreated because the energies are God's own mode of existence and not a created reality.

Lutherans are internally divided on the question of deification. Some deny Luther taught this, finding it repugnant to his doctrine of justification by faith alone. A clear statement of this can be found in the "radical Lutheran" school of Gerhard Forde, with his insistence on an "eschatological" interpretation of Christ's work. For him, eschatology "is more the story not so much of how we shall fare in the future cataclysmic end, but how the future will come to us in Jesus, how the end and the new beginning breaks in upon us in Jesus' life and deeds among us, especially his death and resurrection."[69] Eschatology provides the true form for faith because it is the "new" that breaks with the old. To deny this is to "ontologize" Jesus. Ontology is the study of being or what something is, its nature. For Forde, if we do not emphasize the new that comes with Christian faith, then we reject the "eschatological" for the "ontological": "The question about grace—whether it is a quality in the soul or the sheer divine promise *is* a question of ontology versus eschatology. Is 'grace' a new eschatological reality that comes *extra nos* and breaks in upon us bringing new being to faith, the death of the old and

68. Ibid., 1-1, q.14, a.6.

69. Gerhard O. Forde, "The Apocalyptic No and the Eschatological Yes: Reflections, Suspicions, Fears, and Hopes," in *A More Radical Gospel: Essays on Eschatology, Authority, Atonement, and Ecumenism*, ed. Mark C. Mattes and Steven D. Paulson (Grand Rapids: Eerdmans, 2004), 21.

the life of the new, or is it rather to be understood in ontological terms as an infused power that transforms old being?"[70] For Forde it is clearly the former, but this is confusing since he still speaks of the "new being" that this eschatological reality brings, which seems to imply the ontology he rejects. But a new school of Lutheran interpretation finds more continuity between Luther and the Christian tradition of deification.

The "new school" of Lutheran interpretation began with the work of Tuomo Mannerma. It claims that the kind of interpretation of Luther one finds among the "radical Lutherans" has more to do with Melanchthon's reaction to Catholic teaching than to Luther's own understanding.[71] Veli-Matti Kärkkäinen is a theologian who draws on this interpretation of Luther.[72] Rather than a "forensic" doctrine of justification, Kärkkäinen finds Luther setting forth a doctrine of theosis. In Christ, God exists in the believer in a "real-ontic" manner.[73] Luther preached, "For it is true that a man helped by grace is more than a man; indeed, the grace of God gives him the form of God and deifies him, so that even the Scriptures call him 'God' and God's son."[74] Like all doctrines of deification, Luther did not teach a violation of the Creator/creation distinction. Deification is a "community of being" brought on by grace; it is not that God's essence becomes the human essence or vice versa. It is the union of the divine and human natures in Christ that makes this possible, a union that neither "confuses" nor "changes" one nature into the other.

The Wesleyan tradition affirms the possibility of perfection in this lifetime more so than most Christian traditions. Methodists still require ordinands to answer positively the question, "Do you expect to be made perfect in love in this life?" The ordination service itself asks God for this to be fulfilled, "May God, who has given you the will to do these things, give you grace to perform them that the

70. Ibid., 32.

71. See Veli-Matti Kärkkäinen, *One with God* (Collegeville, MN: Liturgical Press, 2004), 37.

72. Veli-Matti Kärkäinen, *One with God: Salvation as Deification and* Justification (Collegeville, MN: Liturgical Press, 2004), 37–67. A Lutheran theologian who develops theology along these lines is Olli-Pekka Vainio.

73. Kärkkäinen, *One with God*, 37.

74. Luther, *Sermons*, 1, ed. and trans. John W. Doberstein, LW 51 (Philadelphia: Muhlenberg, 1959), 58 (cited by Kärkkäinen, *One with God*, 47).

work begun in you may be brought to perfection."[75] The doctrine is found in Charles Wesley's great hymn "Love Divine, All Loves Excelling," which states well the Methodist teaching in this verse: "Finish then thy new creation; pure and spotless let us be. Let us see thy great salvation perfectly restored in thee."

Like the Orthodox, the Wesleyan teaching makes following commandments central. The Wesleyan quest for perfection began by following three "General Rules," which once defined the movement: first, "by doing no harm"; second, "by doing good"; third, "by attending upon all the ordinances of God." The first two rules were Wesley's reinterpretation of the commandments. Under each of them were placed specific obligations. Sometimes they were directly from the Ten Commandments, such as avoiding "taking the name of God in vain" or "profaning the day of the Lord" (second and third commandments). Others demonstrated the implications of the commands, such as avoiding slaveholding in order neither to kill nor steal (fifth and seventh commandments). Also like the Orthodox, following the commandments included and was made possible by the "Liturgy." This was required by the third general rule, which mandated attendance at public worship, preaching, and the Eucharist along with fasting, prayer, and Scripture reading. One pursued these means in order to be made holy, even though holiness was never an achievement, but always a gift.

Wesley was not that concerned with the language used to explain "perfection." He warned Methodists to be "cautious" in making reference to it. "Avoid all magnificent, pompous words; indeed, you need give it no general name; neither perfection, sanctification, the second blessing, nor the having attained." Instead, he suggested speaking "of the particulars" of it, which is "a fullness of love to God and to all mankind."[76] However, when he explained what it is, Wesley related Christian perfection to the "rest" promised in Hebrews. "He createth them anew in Christ Jesus; he cometh into them with his Son and blessed Spirit, and, fixing his abode in their souls, bringeth

75. *The United Methodist Book of Worship* (Nashville: United Methodist Publishing House, 1992), 666, 676.
76. John Wesley, *A Plain Account of Christian Perfection* (repr. Peabody, MA: Hendrickson, 2007), vii.

them into the 'rest which remaineth' for the people of God."[77] Following Hebrews, he emphasized that this perfection is only possible because of Christ's "intercession" as "high priest," an intercession that never comes to an end. Those to whom perfection comes will always stand in need of a "mediator."[78] Christ's high priestly intercessions are what cultivate perfection.

The instantaneous character of perfection might suggest perfection is only a mystical event that comes all of a sudden, but Wesley explains it as analogous to dying and death. Someone may be dying for a very long time, but his or her "death" will be instantaneous. Likewise, the death to sin that perfection brings might require a very long process of dying. For this reason most persons receive it only right before they actually die.

Wesley offered a fourfold definition of perfection:

1. **That Christian perfection is that love of God and our neighbor, which implies deliverance from *all* sin.**
2. **That this is received merely by *faith*.**
3. **That it is given *instantaneously*, in one moment.**
4. **That we are to expect it, not at death, but every *moment*; that *now* is the accepted time, *now* is the day of this salvation.**

—*Plain Account of Christian Perfection*, 51

Hebrews supports the Wesleyan teaching on perfection and the Orthodox claim that deification gives shape to the Christian doctrine of salvation. Some contemporary theologians affirm this understanding of salvation at the expense of the Western teaching on the atonement. They argue the West should abandon any sense of Christ as a sacrifice who vicariously substitutes for us. Two responses should be made to this. First, it would be inaccurate to find a sacrificial and substitutionary teaching on the atonement only in the West. Second, that teaching has as much support from Hebrews as does deification. Hebrews does not ask us to choose between them. I will take up the second response in commenting on chapter 9, which will entail further reflections on the contemporary

77. Ibid., 30. See also the hymn and theme of rest on 31–32.
78. Ibid., 55–56.

> theological critique of sacrificial language and substitutionary atonement. I have already attempted to respond to the first through demonstrating how deification and perfection are also present in Western Christianity. One commitment that keeps the East and West together, despite different emphases, is their common love of Scripture. Because "deification" is so clearly present in Scripture, no decent theologian in either tradition should neglect it.

Does this teaching on perfection entail a rigorism that invites deceit because it cannot possibly be lived? This is also a possibility when striving for perfection. But perfection in light of Hebrews 6:4 could easily exacerbate this possibility. It has caused consternation and controversy; for it states that those who were once "enlightened" and became "sharers [*metochous*] of the Holy Spirit," who then "fell away," cannot be "restored again to repentance." Harold Attridge notes that this passage "has occasioned considerable discomfort in the history of interpretation." He also reminds us that its aim is not "addressing systematically the problem of penitential discipline," which is certainly true in its original setting. When Hebrews was written the church had not yet passed through the Decian persecution or the Novatian schism. The Donatists were not yet present. However, once Hebrews became canonical it did become part of the theological wisdom that should guide the church in addressing the problem of sin after baptism. Attridge rightly recognizes that Hebrews offers a rigorous either-or, either "continued zeal" or "apostasy." This relates to the contrast between "fertile" and "barren" land (6:7, 8). If apostasy is chosen, Hebrews' hearers have no hope: "There is no indication that apostates have any hope of redemption. The stance is a rigorous one, but its presuppositions are not unique in the early church." Attridge also reminds us that the purpose of this stern warning is rhetorical.[79] It lets Hebrews' readers know the stakes so that they will take the path of continued zeal, which is the outcome the author assumes for them. Of course, this does not mean Hebrews is merely using hyperbole, exaggerating the threat in order to admonish listeners. Hebrews will later give the example

79. Attridge, *Hebrews*, 166–67.

of Esau in a passage that Kenneth Schenck calls "one of the most startling verses in the New Testament."[80] Esau, having sold his birthright, could not find repentance, "even though he sought it with tears" (12:17). Esau sought forgiveness, but none was offered. For Hebrews, this is a real possibility.

Given the rigor of Hebrews, we should be grateful that it has been read in the canonical context of the New Testament and especially the Pauline Epistles. Few ancient or contemporary theologians interpret 6:4 as suggesting sins for which no repentance is possible. Some did. Novatian, presbyter and rival bishop of Rome in the mid-third century, is usually associated with this rigorist position. Although the early church formally excommunicated people for the sins of idolatry, homicide, fornication, and apostasy with little hope of restoration, by the third century the "power of the keys" was thought sufficient to restore them if they were penitent. The Novatian schism assumed a more rigorous position, viewing the church more as a holy community of saints rather than a hospital where the bishops had the power to dispense forgiveness for the lapsed.

In his commentary Thomas Aquinas raises the question whether 6:4 teaches as Novatian claimed. Is there a sin for which repentance could not be done? He rejects this position: "But this position is false, as Athanasius says in the *Epistle to Serapion,* since Paul himself received back the incestuous Corinthian as is clear from II Cor. 2:5ff. as well as Gal. 4:19, where he says, *My little children, of whom I labour again,* etc. It must therefore, be understood, as Augustine says, that he does not say that it is impossible to repent, but that it is impossible *to be renewed again,* that is, baptized."[81] That Aquinas calls upon Athanasius for support here is somewhat odd. His letter to Serapion relates the death of Arius as told to Athanasius by Macarius. Arius was to be received back into communion with the church by the emperor's command, but before this could happen, he died. Athanasius does not want to rejoice in his death, but he thinks it does reveal God's judgment against Arius's heresy. Nowhere in this letter does

80. Kenneth Schenck, *Understanding the Book of Hebrews* (Louisville: Westminster John Knox Press, 2003), 63.

81. Aquinas, *Hebrews,* 127.

Athanasius appeal to Paul or the restoration of the incestuous. But Aquinas must see something similar to such an appeal in a statement by Athanasius concerning those taken in by the Arian heresy: "let no one join himself to the heresy, but let even those who have been deceived repent."[82] Athanasius does not argue Arians should be comforted in the church, but they are called to repent, which suggests it is possible. In other words, if incest and Arianism can be restored, what could not be? Perhaps the best way to think about Hebrews 6:4, reading it after the Novatian schism and the Arian heresy, is to read it in a way that became traditional. Repentance is always possible, but no one should be rebaptized. What cannot be "restored" is the benefits of baptism by baptizing again. What can be claimed are the benefits of one's baptism by a true repentance.

That traditional interpretation reads a great deal into 6:4. I think most would agree it is not the original intention of the author. Nonetheless, it is not a simple fabrication. It reads Hebrews within the canon of the Pauline Epistles and the developing Christian tradition. In so doing, Athanasius, Augustine, and Aquinas find it inconceivable that a sin exists for which repentance is impossible if Paul could call for people involved in an incestuous relationship to repent and be restored, and others called for Arians to repent as well. Nonetheless, the seriousness of apostasy in 6:4 calls into question any easy affirmation of the gospel as "accept that you are accepted." The message of Hebrews could never be enlisted to support that any more than Paul's Epistles could. The message is that you are called to go on to perfection through "faith and patience," holding fast the confession until the end. Failure to do so will mean a failure to inherit the promises.

6:13–20 *"Behind the curtain"*

Perhaps the harshness of 6:4 is mitigated by 6:9–12, which restates the need not to be "sluggish" but to "inherit the promises" via "faith and patience" (6:12). The exhortation then takes on a hopeful tone, emphasizing how certain the promises are since Jesus is a priest in the

82. http://www.ccel.org/ccel/schaff/npnf204.xxv.iii.iv.ix.html.

order of Melchizedek. This is a return to the theme that was noted in 5:1, and will then constitute the center of the argument, which takes place in three parts from 7:1 to 10:39. Throughout chapter 6 the problem does not seem to be that they are in danger of persecution but that they are slothful. They have not advanced in the confession, which means they have not yet "trained" the "faculties" to "distinguish good from evil" (5:14). This is the problem Hebrews' listeners face. How might they attain the perfection necessary to have a *hexis*, or trained character, that would allow them to distinguish good from evil? The answer is found in the example of Abraham, the exercise of Jesus' priesthood, and God's immutable promise.

The answer Hebrews gives is that Abraham "patiently endured" (*makrothymēsas,* 6:15). Hebrews does not argue that faith alone ensures the promise. Faith points in the direction of the promise, but to it must be added endurance, hope, and love. Hebrews calls upon its listeners to endure patiently whatever comes in the hope that they will inherit the promise. It finds faith, patient endurance, hope, and love as necessary *human* acts by which creatures can participate in the Holy Spirit's work and thereby receive the promises. The promise is certain; it is unchangeable. It alone secures our ability to endure. Creaturely participation is not certain. It is all too changeable. The sermon makes no sense if humans have little to no power to endure patiently and in the process express and attain faith. Faith emerges in and through patient endurance. This is why the admonition (*paraklēsin*) culminates in the claim, "we who have taken refuge might be strongly encouraged to seize the hope set before us" (6:18). Here we see a, if not the, central term in Hebrews that has a "wide semantic range"—*paraklēsin.*[83] It means both encouragement and admonition. The admonition is at the same time an encouragement. The admonition in 5:11–6:8 turns into the encouragement in 6:9–20.

The encouragement is possible only because God is unchangeable. As Attridge notes, "The widespread [Jewish] tradition about God's immutability underlies Hebrews' affirmations."[84] Any challenge to God's immutability (and therefore impassibility) would

83. Attridge, *Hebrews,* 182.
84. Ibid., 181.

render Hebrews' very Jewish argument untenable. It would read it instead within the context of the modern, gnostic canon. For Hebrews, the God who is not changed or affected by creation will shake it such that only what is unshakable endures. Like a mighty flood that turns everything upside down, God will act. Hebrews' listeners need not fear because they have an "anchor" in Jesus, who has entered "the inner shrine behind the curtain." They can take "refuge" in Christ in the midst of the storm. It is the stability of God's presence there, and Jesus' mediation of that presence, that makes possible their "steadfastness" and "hope."

Hope anchors the believer "behind the curtain" (6:19). This is a reference to the Jewish temple, which alone renders Hebrews' argument intelligible. This claim that Jesus goes behind the curtain where God's glory dwells is key, and it represents one of the central means by which it challenges our flat world. Not all places are equal. Some are more sacred than others because God is present in them in a way God is not present everywhere. God communicated with Adam and Eve in the garden, but they fell and were expelled. In turn, an angel with a fiery sword guarded that sacred place from creaturely usurpation. But God did not abandon God's people. God called Israel and existed with them "behind the curtain." This was God's holy dwelling place over the ark of the covenant, kept first in the tabernacle and then in the temple, and guarded by two cherubim. God commanded the building of the tabernacle as the means by which Israel could keep the Sabbath holy (Exod. 35:2–3). The people brought "the Lord's offering" in order to construct what God commanded. This holy offering contrasted with the decadent offering collected for the construction of the golden calf (32:1–6), which represented the construction of Egyptian religiosity in the midst of Israel. God now demands a different space as God's dwelling place. When the people made all that God commanded, "The LORD spoke to Moses" and told him "to set up the tabernacle of the tent of meeting," to "put in it the ark of the covenant," and then to "screen the ark with the curtain" (40:1–3). God exists behind the curtain in the ark, which the two cherubim surround like the angel who guarded the entrance to God's holy dwelling in the garden. The sons of Aaron were anointed as a "perpetual priesthood throughout all generations to come" (Exod. 40:15). Once everything was in place, "the glory of the LORD filled the tabernacle." A great theophany occurred letting Israel know God was with them. The tabernacle was God's "house."

The tabernacle eventually gave way to the temple, built by David's son Solomon (1 Kings 5). The temple was patterned on the tabernacle, which was patterned on God's instructions to Moses. Solomon built an "inner sanctuary" and placed the ark of the covenant there (1 Kgs. 6:19). Unlike the building of the tabernacle, the people did not come voluntarily and joyfully, bringing more than was necessary; they were conscripted. Two doors were made to divide the inner sanctuary from the rest of the temple. There was no curtain. The inner sanctuary had no windows, and Solomon proclaimed that he built the temple in this way because "the LORD has said that he would dwell in thick darkness" (1 Kgs. 8:12). This temple was later destroyed and rebuilt. According to the Gospel accounts, the Second Temple was constructed with a curtain that was torn in two at Christ's crucifixion (Mark 15:38; Matt. 27:51). This curtain plays an important role in Hebrews' message.

Hebrews refers to the "curtain" that separated the holy from the holy of holies in three places: 6:19; 9:3; 10:20. The author never mentions that the curtain has been torn in two as we find in Mark and Matthew, but consistent with this theme he claims that Christ has passed through the curtain and entered into the holy of holies. He exists "behind the curtain" where God's glory first dwelled in a cloud and fire (Exodus 40) and then in a "thick darkness" (1 Kings 8). In the Synoptic Gospels the curtain is torn. This could be interpreted as God's presence being "emptied" into the world. Some take it so far as an end to transcendence, the death of God, and the beginnings of a thoroughly disenchanted secularism. It could also be interpreted as Jesus' body becoming the temple, the place where God and creatures meet in a new and unique unity. Rather than emptiness, we find fullness, perfection. In Hebrews, God is not emptied out into the world, but remains in part "behind the curtain," a place to which Jesus gives us access through his humanity if we endure, hold fast the confession, and seize the hope.

FURTHER REFLECTIONS
Enchanted Spaces and the Death of God

What should we do with this odd account of a mystical or enchanted space? If the world is flat, it does not make much sense. Every place is equal to every other, and every site is as much a location for the presence or absence of God as any other. Catholics and Orthodox still have this sense of sacred place, rubrics exist by which only the priest enters the holy of holies, and God's presence literally still dwells in the tabernacle, the place where the host resides after the Eucharist. Protestants tend to participate in what Max Weber called the "disenchantment" of the world. It was a correlate of "intellectualization." This does not mean that moderns were more intelligent than those who came before us. Weber rejected such an idea. "The increased intellectualization and rationalization do *not*, therefore, indicate an increased and general knowledge of the conditions under which one lives. It means something else, namely, the knowledge or belief that if one but wish one *could* learn it at any time. Hence, it means that principally there are no mysterious incalculable forces that come into play, but rather that one can, in principle, master all things by calculation. This means that the world is disenchanted."[85] Weber does not argue that we now claim some kind of titanic knowledge. He argues that our approach to things no longer has a sense of mystical space. Everything could potentially be rendered intelligible by the laws of scientific causality that helped produce the tremendous technological gains of the modern era. Does it still have a place for the enchanted space "behind the curtain," or has it been penetrated and emptied of all meaning?

Weber named our reality well. We live in a "disenchanted world." We seldom expect any holy of holies that functions as the meeting place where heaven and earth come together, where God dwells with creatures and creatures with God. It is interesting, however, how this theme reoccurs in Western culture. We see it, for instance, in literature and film. Steven Spielberg's *Raiders of the Lost Ark* holds

85. Max Weber, "Science as a Vocation," in *From Max Weber: Essays in Sociology*, trans. and ed. H. H. Gerth and C. Wright Mills (1946; repr. New York: Oxford University Press, 1958), 139.

forth this possibility of a sacred space as the central motif in Indiana Jones's adventure. Nazis want to harness the power of the ark of the covenant for evil ends. When they discover it, they open it, initially finding only sand. But soon the frightening glory of God does them in. Not knowing Scripture well, they gaze upon it and it kills them, for "no one shall see [God] and live" (Exod. 33:20). Of course, Indiana Jones knows better. He and his friend do not look upon it and are spared. This thoroughly Hollywood film reduces the sacred space to nothing more than a museum piece to be collected. It is entertaining without much theological or political substance, except for the concluding scene. The ark is placed in a box by the United States government and tucked safely away in a warehouse. The sacred space of the tabernacle gives way to the flat space of the warehouse overseen by the nation-state. Does the nation-state have to contain sacred spaces so that their wild insecurity does not destabilize modern life?

In the modern era, sacred spaces are often relegated to children's fantasy. We see this in favorite stories and films like J. K. Rowling's Harry Potter series, C. S. Lewis's Chronicles of Narnia series, and Frank Baum's *Wizard of Oz*. Harry moves from the streets of London into "The Leaky Cauldron." He enters a small room where a wall makes way for him to enter into "Diagon Alley," where the world is no longer straight and narrow but constantly in movement at odd angles. Enchantment arises behind the wall. C. S. Lewis's first book in the Narnia series, *The Lion, the Witch and the Wardrobe,* also had a space, much like the tabernacle, where children passed through the door of the wardrobe into the magical world of Narnia. Frank Baum's children's book, *The Wizard of Oz*, likewise had a passageway into the enchanted land of Oz. However, the wizard who ruled Oz is revealed as nothing more than a circus performer from Omaha, Nebraska (in the book), or Kansas (in the film). His reign is based on trickery and deceit. He hides behind a curtain and makes himself appear as something he is not. Dorothy's little dog Toto recognizes this and exposes the space behind the curtain, where the fearful image of Oz gives way to a nonthreatening jovial Midwesterner. At first he pleads, "Pay no attention to the man behind the curtain." But eventually he concedes who he is. Behind the curtain is nothing but emptiness.

Unlike Spielberg's *Raiders of the Lost Ark*, these children's fantasies do not explicitly draw on the holy of holies behind the curtain. They do, however, betray the lingering influence of sacred space. Perhaps they are reduced to children's fantasy because of our loss of innocence? That is, we long for there to be such spaces but we are convinced they do not exist. We let the children imagine such a space until the time when they too will realize that the most you will find behind the curtain is an avuncular, albeit not so reputable, Kansan. All transcendence has disappeared; our future is found only in a flat immanence.

Christianity itself contributed, in part, to disenchantment. Along with Platonism it destroyed the mythical or "fabulous" theology of the Greeks and Romans. For this reason early Christians were labeled "atheists." Some philosophers, such as Slavoj Žižek, see in Christ's crucifixion and the tearing of the curtain the origin of atheism. Oddly enough, some theologians side with him, especially those influenced by the "death of God" theology. The Methodist theologian Ted Jennings adopts this "death of God" theology, which he explains by telling us why he primarily goes to church only on Good Friday:

> Every year my friend Kunitoshi Sakai and I attend Good Friday services. Those who know us and that we almost never attend church ask about this odd custom. To which Kunitoshi always replies with a mischievous gleam in his eye: we go to make sure that God is still dead.
>
> Since I was a seminary student at Emory in the mid 60s the theology of the death of God has been for me a source of constant provocation, and even consolation....
>
> Some have suggested that the theology of the death of God belongs to another era. I know from my own students that it remains an indispensable challenge to think more seriously, more responsibly, more radically than they had heretofore believed possible....
>
> To ask if the death of God has a future is to ask, more or less, if theology has a future.

> Above all this theme has meant that theology must think the transformations of culture and history together with the gospel, for the gospel of Christian atheism is not a tinkering with church doctrine but a discernment of the relation of the gospel to the history of our culture and the nihilism of our time. . . .
>
> The death of God I have learned is that which realizes itself in history. But this realization or actualization is by no means complete. The stench of the decomposing body of the transcendent or sovereign God wafts through the air of preemptive war and terrorist attack. The name of this lingering transcendent sovereignty, as Altizer has reminded us, following Blake is: Satan. God is not yet dead enough.
>
> If this God does not die fast enough, we will all die in pursuit of our nightmares of sovereignty and transcendence. Thus not only the future of theology and even the gospel but of the planet may be at stake in the question of the future of the death of God.
>
> The good news, if there is any, is that the divine has renounced the dream/nightmare of sovereign transcendence to take on vulnerable flesh in Joyce's vision of Here comes everybody; an everybody of erotic, pleasure sharing flesh—mortal and so pulsing with life and liveliness, varied and chaotic in the promiscuous hospitality of an all in all that is the promise of the fiesta of the excluded. Perhaps, in the more sober hope of Derrida, a democracy to come, or a cosmopolitanism to be realized, or a justice to be done; but above all—a gift to be given away.[86]

This lengthy quote sees in the biblical story of the crucifixion the emptying out of any transcendent and sovereign God into the celebration of a sensuous, erotic, fleshly humanity. God is not found "behind the curtain." The "god" who is to come and bring the transformation of culture and history is found precisely in his demise. A transcendent, sovereign God is dangerous. Such a God is

86. A letter from Ted Jennings intended to be presented at the "Whither the Death of God" seminar, AAR, 2009, posted at http://itself.wordpress.com/2009/12/27/ted-jennings-statement-for-the-aar-death-of-god-panel.

responsible for evil, war, terrorism. The death of this God, not yet sufficiently accomplished according to Jennings, cannot come quick enough. We must hasten his death. We do so through a celebration of an erotic hospitality. The good news for Jennings's apocalyptic a-theology is that God is dead but something—democracy, justice, a new cosmopolitanism, a gift—might arise in God's place (it cannot "break through" because there is no transcendence). This is an apocalyptic vision rooted in the utter apophatic, and therefore a-theistic, theology of postmodernity, which we will discuss below when we take up the theme of apocalyptic in Hebrews, modernity, and postmodernity. It can be useful in deconstructing the idols of modernity that passed as "God," but it bears no relation to the biblical world of Hebrews. In the end it can do nothing but celebrate the flat, nominalistic modern world that blinds us from the odd reality Hebrews calls us to see.

7:1–10:39
Priesthood and Sanctuaries

In Jewish apocalyptic, God's presence, even in the holy of holies, contained an entourage of other created beings, particularly angels. Sometimes even humans would be transported to this holy and frightening place. The ancient Enoch traditions offer such apocalyptic visions. They glimpse behind the curtain and find not absence but an overabundant fullness.

> **1 Enoch 14:18–21**
>
> **And I saw a lofty throne; and its appearance was like ice; and its wheels were like the shining sun; and its "guardians" were cherubim; and from beneath the throne issued streams of flaming fire. And I was unable to see. And the Great Glory sat upon it; his raiment was like the appearance of the sun and whiter than much snow. And no angel could enter into this house and behold his face because of the splendor and glory; and no flesh could behold him.**
>
> Nickelsburg, *1 Enoch*, 257.

What Enoch sees is confusing. He enters in where no flesh can go. He sees into God's house, and sees God, whom no one can behold or into whose presence no one enters. He sees angels there, but no angels can go there. The early Christians, including at least one biblical author, appreciated such apocalyptic visions; Jude 6 quotes *1 Enoch*. That the author of Hebrews would have known these stories seems likely.

We find similarities between Hebrews and the Jewish apocalyptic vision of *1 Enoch*, but we also find significant differences. As George Nickelsburg states, Hebrews "represents the ultimate Christianizing of the [apocalyptic]

Jewish traditions" because it applies to "the exalted Christ functions and characteristics that originally applied to angels."[1] Angels were mediators. They were present in the giving of the law. They spoke God's words on God's behalf, often speaking them to the prophets and fathers who would then speak them to the people. In one sense, Hebrews renders the angels' work unnecessary. "Long ago" God spoke in these "many and various ways," but now God speaks definitively in the Son. He alone now mediates the covenant. We no longer need angels, nor do we need the apocalyptic visions of the Enoch traditions. We do not need a priest who ascends behind the curtain, because Jesus fills that space. Hebrews helps us understand why most of these apocalyptic visions did not make it into the Christian canon. The presence of angels or priests in the "house of God" in the Enochic tradition is confusing; they are not supposed to be there, but they are. But there is no question about the Son's role; he belongs there, sitting at God's right hand. The angels are God's ministers, but only Christ is "high priest forever."

Hebrews 7:1–10:39 develops Christ's priesthood in three parts, which elaborate themes noted in the last section, especially the central role of the priesthood, its sacrifices, and the tabernacle/temple where those sacrifices occurred. In the Scriptures Hebrews alone presents Jesus as the true high priest. As noted above, in the first covenant the sons of Aaron were anointed as a "perpetual priesthood throughout all generations to come" (Exod. 40:15). This creates two problems. First, Jesus is not a "son of Aaron." He is not of the family lineage to be a priest. Second, if they were anointed for this role "perpetually," how can Jesus now usurp it? Interestingly, Hebrews finds the answer in Scripture itself, in the odd story of Melchizedek found in Genesis 14 and drawn upon in Psalm 110. Hebrews' argument develops in three sections:

7:1–28 Priest according to the Order of Melchizedek
8:1–9:28 Perfection, the Better Covenant, and the Heavenly Sanctuary
10:1–39 Christ as the Temple Who Brings Confident Speech,

1. Nickelsburg, *1 Enoch,* 210.

Faith, Hope, and Love. Verses 1–18 presents Christ's sacrifice, followed in verses 19–39 by further exhortations.

These three parts cannot be theologically interpreted without discussing the controversy surrounding Christ as "sacrifice," the figural interpretation of the temple, and the political significance that Hebrews presents Jesus as a priest-king similar to Philo's interpretation of Moses as priest-king.

7:1–28

Priest according to the Order of Melchizedek

Melchizedek is an enigmatic, mysterious character who has prompted much speculation. For most of the Christian tradition the figure of Melchizedek is interpreted typologically. Even when some thought he might be an actual person, or perhaps even Noah's son Shem, they still interpreted his significance as a type of Christ. Christ is the true figure; Melchizedek is a "shadow" of that greater reality. Leo the Great stated this well in the fifth century, "[Christ] himself is the true and eternal bishop whose ministry can neither change nor end. He is the one prefigured by the high priest Melchizedek."[2] Such an understanding continued through the Middle Ages and into the Reformation. Aquinas still referred to him as a "figure" of the "priesthood of Christ."[3] His presence at the beginning of Abraham's journey prefigures Christ. Hebrews' statement that he is "without father" is then a reference to Christ's humanity, which had no father since Mary was a virgin. That he is "without mother" is a reference to his divinity. For although Mary gave birth to God as is proclaimed through the term *theotokos*, she gave birth to God in his "humanity." Divinity has no mother. That he is "without genealogy" is a reference to his eternity.[4] Calvin did not speculate in quite the same terms: "We ought therefore to be content with this moderate knowledge

2. Cited in Heen and Krey, eds., *Hebrews*, 97.
3. Aquinas, *Hebrews*, 144.
4. Ibid., 143.

that in showing us Melchizedek as one who was never born and who never died, Scripture is setting forth as in a picture the truth that for Christ there is neither beginning nor end."[5] Wesley also reads him as "Christ's type."[6]

The Melchizedek character is too fascinating for historians to leave it simply with Calvin's "moderate knowledge." They have repeatedly asked what possible sources informed Hebrews' use of Melchizedek. Was he drawing on Jewish apocalyptic sources that see Melchizedek as a mystical figure such as Metatron, Enoch, the son of man in Daniel 7, or perhaps Michael the archangel referred to in 11QMelchizedek at Qumran? Perhaps Melchizedek is an angelic priest who performed heavenly tasks now taken over by Jesus' humanity, who is set above him? Or is Hebrews' source for Melchizedek Philo's interpretation of him as a personified Logos? Some suggest a historical reference to some king who wanted to function as a priest but did not have the Levitical genealogy. Melchizedek would then authenticate his priesthood. Do we find a hint of this in Ezra 2:61–63 or Nehemiah 7:63–65?[7] The history of religions school found in Melchizedek another example of a hellenized intermediary being. Everywhere they looked in the Bible, and especially in Hebrews, this history of religions school found evidence of the gnostic redeemer myth. It was evidence of Judaism's syncretism with Hellenistic thought, and it is what produced Christ as a divine intermediary.

James Dunn explains this well. "The suggestion that already the writer to the Hebrews thought of Melchizedek as 'a divine being in human form' ('without mother' and 'without father' implying a superhuman origin) expresses the optimism of the earlier History of Religions School that it was possible to trace the origins of the gnostic redeemer myth back to a pre-Christian date." Melchizedek represents a pre-Christian tradition of a divine figure who comes to earth and ministers. But Dunn and most biblical scholars are no longer convinced by this once fashionable interpretation. Nonetheless,

5. Calvin, *Hebrews*, 89–90.

6. John Wesley, *Explanatory Notes upon the New Testament* (repr. London: Epworth Press, 1977), 826.

7. Bruce Demarest, *A History of Interpretation of Hebrews 7,1-10 from the Reformation to the Present*, BGBE 19 (Tübingen: Mohr [Siebeck], 1976), 101.

Dunn does not read Hebrews "without mother, father, and genealogy" in terms of the traditional Christian affirmation of Chalcedon. Instead, he states, "These adjectives are better explained however by reference to the typically rabbinic exegetical principle (what is not in the text, is not), or . . . by recognizing some influence from Philo or Philonic thought on Melchizedek as an embodiment or allegorical expression of the Logos."[8]

So who is Melchizedek? We need to see how he is used in Hebrews' argument to answer better that question. One thing has to be admitted up front: the relation between Jesus and Melchizedek in this passage is confusing. First, Hebrews relates Melchizedek to the Son of God, and not the Son of God to Melchizedek. He "resembles" the Son (7:3). But then Hebrews reverses the terms of the relation stating that Jesus "arises" as a "priest" "resembling" Melchizedek. So which is it? Does Hebrews find Jesus resembling Melchizedek or Melchizedek resembling Jesus? The answer is yes—both, which fits well Hebrews' argument. The first resemblance, Melchizedek to Christ, establishes the authority of Melchizedek. Hebrews draws on the absence of information about Melchizedek's life to assert a theological claim about Melchizedek's *order of priesthood*. It is "forever," which must mean it is eternal. What the Levitical priesthood embodies in time is Melchizedek's eternal, because heavenly, priesthood. In this sense, Melchizedek resembles Jesus in his divinity, the one through whom all things were made. Hebrews finds in the Old Testament not one order of priesthood, but two. There is one done in perpetuity, which is historical and earthly. But there is another, which is eternal. It can only be eternal because Melchizedek is given a share in Christ's priesthood even before it was exercised. But when our author then goes on to compare Melchizedek to the Levitical priesthood he claims Jesus' priesthood resembles Melchizedek. Having already established that Melchizedek exercised in history Christ's eternal priesthood, now Jesus in history participated in the ministry of which Melchizedek was the first priest. This he does through his incarnation, obedience, and sacrificial offering. Once accomplished, like Melchizedek, Jesus' priesthood is eternal, indestructible, and the

8. Dunn, *Christology in the Making*, 20–21.

source for a "better hope." So Jesus authorizes Melchizedek's priesthood, which can only occur if he preexists and is divine. Once he is incarnate, however, Melchizedek authorizes Jesus' temporal priesthood, which is necessary for the human exercise of his office.

The purpose of these comparisons between Jesus and Melchizedek is found in 7:11, which addresses the question why we need a priesthood other than that of the Levites. The Levitical priesthood does not perfect. If it did, it would not need to be repeated again and again. It does not emerge from an "indestructible life" (7:16) where a single sacrifice suffices. It emerges from human finitude and thus must be repeated until such a sacrifice, a priest, and a concomitant change in the law arises as Jeremiah prophesied (Jer. 31:31–34; Heb. 8:8–12). The author of Hebrews sees this fulfilled in Jesus, but he also finds OT precedent for it. He does not invent a priesthood according to Melchizedek; he finds it in the enthronement Psalm 110: "The LORD has sworn and will not change his mind, 'You are a priest forever according to the order of Melchizedek.'" The original setting for the psalm was the kingship of David. Here we see that David is not only "king" but also "priest." Like Melchizedek, and Philo's Moses, he is a "priest-king."

This is important for the political theology not only of Hebrews but also of Holy Scripture in general. Its significance can best be seen by contrasting it to the image of the "philosopher-king" in Plato. If Plato argues political power (the king) must be subordinate to the philosopher (the good), Hebrews reconfigures "power" altogether. Plato addresses the question, How do we curb the power of the king by the good? Hebrews addresses the question, How do we see the true power of the priest who offers a better hope when he does not seem to rule? This priest-king, like Melchizedek, is characterized by "peace" and "righteousness" rather than the dialectical contrast of power and goodness. Power, which is not good, must be exercised. The good, which makes life worth living, must temper power. We will discuss more fully Hebrews' alternative in Jesus as the priest-king once we have established what it means for him to be priest, victim, and temple.

Melchizedek appears early in the biblical narrative, even before God's promised covenant made to Abraham in Genesis 15. In

Genesis 14 Abraham routs King Chedorlaomer and others who conquered the kings of Sodom and Gomorrah, taking away their provisions and Abram's brother Lot. The king of Sodom comes out to meet Abram in "the valley of Shaveh (that is, the King's Valley)" (14:17). King Melchizedek of Salem (Jerusalem?), "the priest of God Most High," comes and blesses him, bringing out bread and wine. He says, "Blessed be Abram by God Most High, maker of heaven and earth; and blessed be God Most High, who has delivered your enemies into your hand" (14:19–20). Abram then gives one-tenth of his bounty to Melchizedek. The importance of all this is not lost on Hebrews. Unlike many of the early church fathers, Hebrews does not mention the "bread and wine." In the early church this becomes associated with the Holy Eucharist. It would be tempting to read Genesis 14 typologically, as Christian tradition often has done, seeing in this offering of bread and wine Christ's body proleptically presented and offered to Abram before he enters into his covenant with God.

For just as he, who was priest of the Gentiles, is not represented as offering outward sacrifices but as blessing Abraham only with wine and bread, so in exactly the same way our Lord and Savior himself first, and then all his priests among all nations, perform the spiritual sacrifice according to the customs of the church and with wine and bread darkly express the mysteries of his body and saving blood.

—Eusebius of Caesarea

Quoted in *Hebrews*, ed. Heen and Krey, 96.

Hebrews, however, makes nothing of this. Instead Melchizedek's name, king of "righteousness" and "peace," his priesthood, the lack of mention of genealogy, and the fact that Abraham gave him a tithe matter most.

Abraham's tithe to Melchizedek, followed by Melchizedek's blessing of Abraham, establishes the possibility of a different kind of priesthood. Because the promise of the priesthood is present in Abraham's body, by blessing him Melchizedek blessed the Levitical priesthood itself. Hebrews does not deny legitimacy to that priesthood; Melchizedek blessed rather than condemned it. But this act of blessing along with Abraham's tithe demonstrates a priesthood above the Levitical. For Hebrews this is clearly the priesthood of

Christ. Here is where Melchizedek resembles Jesus. But Hebrews not only argues that we have such a high priest; it also identifies what he accomplishes. He is a priest who is also "king of righteousness" and "peace." The city over which he reigns is identified as a place of peace (7:2).

Although the author of Hebrews has repeatedly alluded to Christ's high priesthood, only in 7:26–28 does he explicitly state its significance. Three key claims are made: First, Christ is perfect—"holy, blameless, undefiled, separated from sinners." These adjectives describe his role as both priest and victim. They could be used for either. Second, he contrasts with "other high priests" who offer sacrifices for themselves and others continually. Third, Hebrews contrasts the source for these two priesthoods and the sacrifices they offer. The law founds the Levitical priesthood. It is good, but it is a remedy for weakness (7:28). This priesthood and its sacrifices share in the weakness for which they seek to be a remedy. This is why they have to be repeated. Christ's priesthood and sacrifice, however, come from "the word of the oath," an oath found in Psalm 110:4, "You are a priest forever according to the order of Melchizedek," who brings a better covenant. The next section picks up on this theme of a "better covenant" and expands upon it.

8:1–9:28

Perfection, the Better Covenant, and the Heavenly Sanctuary

Now we are at the heart of the letter. We know this because we are directly told it: *Kephalaion de epi tois legomenois,* literally, "The main point now in the things we are saying." F. F. Bruce, a Protestant exegete, interprets *kephalaion* here not as "main point" but as "summary." For him, Jesus as high priest is not the central theme of Hebrews, albeit an important one. Rather than initiating a new cult, Hebrews initiates the theme of "new covenant." As Bruce puts it, "True worship, 'in spirit and in truth,' is thus released from dependence on the externalities of religion."[9] He finds in Hebrews 7, as

9. Bruce, *Hebrews,* 180, 190, 194.

did Calvin, a claim that Christ's "once-for-all oblation sufficed to the end of the world."[10] Such a claim found its way into the Anglican and Methodist Articles of Religion, with a strong anti-Catholic polemic: "The offering of Christ once made is the perfect redemption, propitiation, and satisfaction for all the sins of the whole world, both original and actual; and there is none other satisfaction for sin, but that alone. Wherefore the sacrifice of Masses, in the which it was commonly said that the Priest did offer Christ for the quick and the dead, to have remission of pain or guilt, were blasphemous fables, and dangerous deceits."[11]

The Roman Catholic Church still teaches that "the Eucharistic sacrifice is also offered for *the faithful departed* who 'have died in Christ but are not yet wholly purified,' so that they may be able to enter into the light and peace of Christ."[12] Likewise it unconditionally affirms the Eucharist as a sacrifice. It cites Hebrews 7:25–27 as evidence. "When the Church celebrates the Eucharist, she commemorates Christ's Passover, and it is made present: the sacrifice Christ offered once for all on the cross remains ever present."[13] Catholic theology does not deny that Christ's sacrifice is complete and sufficient; it adds that it is always present and that we can participate in making it so in the Eucharist. This fits well Hebrews' apocalyptic "today."

Bruce is unconvinced of such an interpretation because of 7:27: "In passing we may note that it is not implied that Jesus is continually or repeatedly presenting his offering; this is excluded by 7:27, which contrasts the daily sacrifices of the Aaronic high priests with the offering which the Christian's high priest has already presented once for all."[14] Hebrews teaches that Jesus has no need for daily sacrifices because Jesus, unlike the Aaronic priests, does not sin. His sacrifice is perfect for this reason. Does this exclude this single, sufficient sacrifice from being repeated in time? Perhaps we find the answer in the "main point" elaborated in 8:3, "For every

10. Calvin, *Hebrews*, 103.
11. Anglican Articles of Religion, art. 31; United Methodist Articles of Religion, art. 20.
12. *Catechism of the Catholic Church*, §1371.
13. Ibid., §1364.
14. Bruce, *Hebrews*, 182.

high priest is appointed to offer gifts and sacrifices; hence it is necessary for this priest also to have something to offer." Christ offers himself, but he does so "today," which can be repeated without being other than what it once was because like Melchizedek's priesthood it takes place in the heavenly realm. But it can also be present in history because Christ's humanity makes such an offering possible. Charles Wesley's hymnody expressed this well.

Come, Sinners, to the Gospel Feast

Come and partake the gospel feast, be saved from sin, in Jesus rest; O taste the goodness of our God, and eat his flesh and drink his blood. See him set forth before your eyes; behold the bleeding sacrifice; his offered love make haste to embrace, and freely now be saved by grace.

—Charles Wesley

United Methodist Hymnal (Nashville: United Methodist Publishing House, 1989), #616.

Eight chapters in, Hebrews arrives at the "main point," the *kephalaion*. If we had been listening to the sermon read uninterrupted to this point, we would have been listening for approximately twenty-nine minutes.[15] Now, what comes next resembles a confession or rule of faith. In fact, it repeats the confession found in the exordium, with some important additions. Compare the two verses:

1:3: *ekathisen en dechsia tēs megalōsynēs en hypsēlois*
(he sat down at the right hand of the Majesty on high)

8:1: *ekathisen en dechsia* ***tou thronou*** *tēs megalōsynēs* ***en tois ouranois***
(he sat down at the right hand **of the throne** of the Majesty **in the heavens**)

The two sentences are identical except for the words in bold print. The main point was already established in Hebrews' very first sentence. He is not telling his listeners anything new, except where it

15. This is based on reading aloud the Greek text as one would read it to others. The entire text takes approximately sixty-five minutes to read aloud. Of course, these times would vary based on who was reading (and we do not know if the text was read), or if it was read straight through.

is that Jesus serves as high priest. Christ is enthroned in heaven, in God's dwelling place. His throne is not found in the temporal, transitory spaces that define political rule in the world, which Hebrews' audience finds alien. The true priest-king is enthroned, but he is found in that which is permanent, indestructible, everlasting, unchanging. The attributes that characterized his earthly practice in 7:26: "holy, blameless, undefiled, separated from sinners," now characterize his eternal priesthood in the "main point." Christ serves as the true high priest in the "Holy Place" (*tōn hagiōn*), which is the sanctuary or "holy of holies."[16] This is the "true tabernacle" set up by God, not humans.

The author of Hebrews comes to the main point by bringing together the various threads of his argument. He recapitulates the theme of building and being the house from 3:3–6 with the contrast between Moses and Jesus. The true tent is compared to the "sketch and shadow of the heavenly one" (8:5) that Moses is commanded to build "according to the type God showed him on the mountain." This establishes the fact that the Old Testament itself has two tents or sanctuaries, which also produce two different covenants. Jesus offers a "better covenant" because he offers his in the true sanctuary and not in its earthly representation. Crucial to the biblical warrant for this true tent is Jeremiah 31:31–34 (quoted in Heb. 8:8–13), the lengthiest quotation from the Old Testament in the New. The author of Hebrews does not cite Plato, Philo, Jewish apocalyptic, or some gnostic knowledge as the source for his analogy between the two tabernacles. It comes from Exodus 25:40 (alluded to in Heb. 8:5) and Jeremiah 31, from the Law and the Prophets. The key terms are "covenant" and "house." God promised through the prophet the establishment, renewal, and perfection of what God instituted in Moses, "a new covenant with the *house* of Israel" and with the "*house* of Judah." God proclaims through Jeremiah, "This is the covenant that I will make with the house of Israel . . . I will put my laws in their minds, and write them on their hearts" (Heb. 8:10). God will no

16. Normally Hebrews refers to the sanctuary or holy of holies through the traditional repetition of the term "holy." Here he only makes one reference to it, but most commentators, as does the NRSV, interpret it as the "holy of holies."

longer remember their sins and God will be "merciful." For Hebrews this occurs in Christ. He is this house because he is the faithful and merciful high priest. The author of Hebrews already told us "we are this house." Now he tells us how. In the concluding passages in this section he draws on Psalm 40 and claims that the "body" God prepares is Christ's body. It is what "sanctifies" (Heb. 10:5, 10).

The "main point" that initiated this section and caused us to sit up and take notice now gets fleshed out. It is worth quoting in its entirety because it is both literally and figuratively the center of Hebrews:

> But when Christ came as a high priest of the good things that have come, then through the greater and perfect tent (not made with hands, that is, not of this creation), he entered once for all into the Holy Place, not with the blood of goats and calves, but with his own blood, thus obtaining eternal redemption. For if the blood of goats and bulls, with the sprinkling of the ashes of a heifer, sanctifies those who have been defiled so that their flesh is purified, how much more will the blood of Christ, who through the eternal Spirit offered himself without blemish to God, purify our conscience from dead works to worship the living God! (Heb. 9:11–14)

This central passage is worthy of being read again, pondered, and explored. It brings together Hebrews' central themes: perfection, the true tent or temple, and Christ's enthronement there. It is the heart of the confession they are to hold fast.

The "perfect" tent Christ enters is the heavenly temple (9:11–15), which Hebrews contrasts with the earthly one (9:1–5). Verse 5 closes with a statement that the "cherubim of glory were overshadowing [*kataskiazonta*] the mercy seat [*hilastērion*]" in the earthly temple; it was obviously important. Here we are taken into the most holy of Israel's sacred places, the place of God's own dwelling. Hebrews does not deny that God is present in the Mosaic temple. The word *kataskiazō* is significant. It is similar to the word used in Luke 1:35, *episkiazō*, when Mary is told, "the Most High will overshadow you," and to *skēnoō* in John 1:14, when we are told the *logos* became flesh and "lived" or "tabernacled" among us. The root verb here is related to the tabernacle. The verb speaks of the glory of God filling the tabernacle. We also see this in Exodus 40:34–35 (LXX), where we are told the glory of God filled the tabernacle (*skēnē*) and that Moses could not "enter the tent of meeting because . . . the cloud filled [*episkiazō*] the tabernacle." Likewise the center of Hebrews tells us Christ came as "high priest . . . through the greater and more perfect tent [*dia tēs meizonos kai teleioteras skēnēs*]" (9:11). He is, as the exordium proclaimed, the "glory" of God.

Hebrews does deny that the offerings made in the first tabernacle were useful for the forgiveness of sin. But if they were sufficient, they would not need to be repeated and Jeremiah would not have prophesied about a second covenant. That earthly temple was a figure of the heavenly, God's own dwelling place. Now we see what the "main point" adds to the exordium. *Only* Christ's work allows him, and us, to enter into the true place where God is enthroned, and not just a figure or symbol of it. Not even Moses could enter it when God's glory "overshadowed" it. But Christ enters. His entrance into the "throne" of the temple "in the heavens" is yet another way of stating who he is and what he has done. This is what makes him the "mediator of a new covenant," the one Jeremiah prophesied. Perfection, purification, enthronement, temple, and sacrifice are brought together to explain Jesus as the king-priest.

FURTHER REFLECTIONS

Blood Sacrifices, Innocent Death?

Here in the center of Hebrews' message we come up against yet another significant controversy in the contemporary life of the church, one to which Hebrews contributes and perhaps one it can help us resolve. The language of cross, sacrifice, and blood no longer compels some contemporary Christians as it once did. When I was in seminary preparing for Christian ministry, there was a movement to remove the cross from the center of worship because of the violence associated with it. Ecofeminist theologians would often conduct worship by replacing the cross with a globe. I once worked in a seminary where we did extensive renovations to all our classrooms.

When they were completed a number of us thought nothing distinguished them from the spaces in our secular counterpart in the university. We proposed that we put crosses in each of the rooms so that our teaching and work would take place under the sign of the cross. That proposal was rejected because the cross could be used to perpetrate violence against women and people on the margins of society. What was once true of the Christian "left" or "progressives" now, ironically, the "right" adopts. Megachurches conduct services without the cross because it is an alienating symbol. Instead they use the less abrasive image of a "bridge" or the globe.

Because the cross, and its correlative language of sacrifice, has become controversial within the Christian faith, many have turned from a so-called Western, juridical doctrine of the atonement associated with Hebrews 9 and, as we shall see, with Anselm to an Eastern, participatory doctrine of deification. The latter supposedly emphasizes the incarnation as the site of redemption rather than the cross. But this either-or, either the cross or the incarnation, either atonement or deification, finds no support in Hebrews. Indeed, Hebrews has a broader understanding of incarnation. God's enfleshment in Jesus includes the cross and ascension. Hebrews unites both deification and atonement in its understanding of Christ as priest and victim who heals through his self-offering. It takes seriously both incarnation and crucifixion; one cannot be understood well without the other. Now we must discuss why this has become controversial and seek to find reconciliation in Hebrews.

Hebrews' sacrificial language became problematic when it became associated with a particular interpretation of Anselm, an interpretation that was one of the five fundamentals set forth by the "fundamentalist" movement against the "modernists" in American Protestant Christianity. The five fundamentals are Christ's deity and the virgin birth, a substitutionary theory of the atonement that requires blood sacrifice, bodily resurrection, Christ's second coming, and biblical inerrancy. These were originally set forth as an attempt to bring peace among divided Protestant Christians.[17] Fundamentalists thought Christians could at least agree on these. They did

17. See Brian D. McLaren, *A Generous Orthodoxy* (Grand Rapids: Zondervan, 2004), 197.

not. Nor did they bring peace but rather further division, causing "liberals" and "fundamentalists" to question each other's Christianity. Even confessing the classic creeds of the church such as the Nicene would not assuage some fundamentalists as to the authenticity of one's Christianity. And confessing such creeds is a sure sign of fundamentalism for some "progressives."

When it came to the "fundamental" claim about the substitutionary theory of the atonement and the need for "blood sacrifice" to assuage God's wrath, fundamentalists did and do appeal directly to Hebrews 9 and relate it to Anselm's penal substitutionary theory of the atonement. For many theologians, pastors, and believing Christians these two became linked. It is easy to see why. Hebrews states that Christ's blood, "more so than the blood" of sacrificed animals, will "purify our conscience from dead works to worship the living God" (9:14). It connects this with blood as a purifying agent in the Old Testament. "Indeed, under the law almost everything is purified with blood, and without the shedding of blood there is no forgiveness of sins" (9:22). For some this is proof that Hebrews teaches the penal substitutionary theory of the atonement, and it alone is an adequate account of how Christ saves.

The penal substitutionary theory includes three elements. First, it is "penal" in that it is primarily concerned with punishment. Second, it is "substitutionary" in that Christ is the "substitute" who takes our place and suffers the punishment we deserve. Third, it is God who both wills the sacrifice of the Son and accepts the sacrifice on our behalf. Hebrews would seem to teach the first. Christ's death "redeems . . . from the transgressions under the first covenant" (9:15). However, that a death redeems does not mean that it is the death itself that redeems. As Anselm recognized, Christ's death is the indirect effect of his directly willed obedience. Death itself does not redeem; Christ's obedience does. For Hebrews Jesus assumes the penalty for our transgressions, although it does not explicitly state that the specific punishment Christ endured should have been ours. Nonetheless it clearly implies that such transgressions earn transgressors' judgment, and as we have seen in chapter 6, Hebrews could be stern in its sense of an impending judgment for transgressions. Christ redeems us from the deserved penalty.

The second aspect of the fundamentalist teaching finds less support from Hebrews. It does not explicitly state that Christ's suffering on the cross should have been ours; it does not actually teach that Christ "substitutes" for us in that sense. Christ is a substitute, but for the Levitical priesthood and its sacrificial system. Christ does offer himself as a sacrifice to God on our behalf, but he does so in order to bring an end to sacrifice.

Does it then teach the third element of penal substitution? Is God the primary agent who demands that Christ suffers and dies, and the recipient of the sacrifice? In other words, does God will the death of an innocent person in order to redeem us and then find that death acceptable? This is the most controversial and morally questionable aspect of the fundamentalist teaching. Many see in it a return to paganism in which a vengeful deity must be assuaged by human blood, and in this case innocent human blood. But if we are commanded against willing the death of an innocent, how can God get away with it? Numerous theologians challenge this teaching, feminists, Catholics, Orthodox, Anabaptists, and evangelicals, but for different reasons. Some find the theory of atonement through Christ's sacrifice on the cross so appalling that they dismiss it altogether. Others make a less thorough rejection of Christian teaching and claim atonement theory can and should be revised. Others recognize that the fundamentalists' teaching is a distortion of both Hebrews and Anselm's teaching on atonement. We will examine representative theological rejections, revisions, and defenses of the atonement.

Feminist theologians Joanne Carlson Brown and Rebecca Parker accuse the theory of the atonement of sanctioning suffering and violence. It makes God a tyrant who uses coercion and violence against the innocent to work his will. They find this in Anselm, whom they suggest taught that God "desired the death of the Son." As evidence for this they quote from Anselm's *Cur Deus Homo?*: "The Father desired the death of the Son because he was not willing that the world should be saved in any other way."[18] If God wills the death

18. Joanne Carlson Brown and Rebecca Parker, "For God So Loved the World?" in *Christianity, Patriarchy, and Abuse: A Feminist Critique*, ed. Brown and Carole R. Bohn (New York: Pilgrim Press, 1989), 7.

of the Son, and this is what redeems us, then redemption is immoral. If I singled out one of my children for a horrible, suffering death in order to save the others, you would rightly question what kind of person I am.

These kinds of criticisms do not only come from within Christianity, but also from outside it. A YouTube video entitled "Jesus Loves You" offers a humorous and popular example.[19] The video begins with "some grey bloke" telling us he received an anonymous e-mail saying, "Jesus loves you." The grey bloke then says, "Well I thought, that's nice. But then I read the rest of it which says, 'If you don't worship him, you're going to burn in hell forever.'" He acknowledges this is a "conditional form of love," and that most forms of love are like that, but he expected something more from Jesus since he "should be more noble" than the rest of us. He then asks the anonymous e-mailer, "If Jesus loves me, why does he want to send me to hell?" The reply came back, "He doesn't want to, but unless you accept him, he's just going to have to." Grey bloke then was confused—"doesn't Jesus make the rules? He is God after all." The response was, "Jesus loves you, but his dad thinks you're a shit." That doesn't seem "fair," he adds, but "at least it's clear." But then he was utterly confused by a response, which said, "P.S., Jesus is his own dad."

Christians should neither get defensive nor react negatively to such a witty critique of the mystery of the atonement. Nor should we immediately apologize for it. Christ's sacrifice for us is after all a mystery, and like all mysteries its meaning cannot be elucidated through a few rationalist propositions. Some Christian theologians would side with the "grey bloke" and the feminist critique of the atonement. Some theologians find both Hebrews and Anselm irredeemable. They suggest that deification or theosis should replace Western juridical theories of atonement. Stephen Finlan is one such author. He admonishes Christians to do away with "sacrificial" language altogether because "sacrifice implies pacifying God with payment or gift."[20] Because he approaches theological questions

19. As is often the case, I am indebted to Dan Bell for sharing this humorous critique of Christianity with me. The video can be found at: http://www.youtube.com/watch?v=-2bpc7LSRZc.

20. Stephen Finlan, *Options on Atonement in Christian Thought* (Collegeville, MN: Liturgical Press, 2007), 31.

through a developmental psychology, he finds that "a primitive mentality underlies all sacrificial thinking." It cannot but assume fear and therefore manipulation of the deity.[21] He puts our author on the therapist's couch, cites the work of Donald Capps approvingly, and states, "Because Hebrews speaks of God as chastising, Capps is confident that the author was beaten as a child."[22] In other words, Finlan peers into the psyche of an author whom we do not know and finds his child abuse to be the real cause for the sacrificial language in Hebrews 9. This is because he is dogmatic that modern ethics and psychology represent "advances." These now function as a canon within which we read Hebrews. Finlan places his developmental psychology over Hebrews' message and concludes that the latter is insufficiently biblical.

How can Hebrews, which is a book in the Bible, be insufficiently biblical? Finlan works with two strange and contradictory ideas. The first is that Hebrews is insufficiently supersessionist; it has not yet gone far enough in overcoming the Jewish sacrificial system.[23] If it took more seriously typological fulfillment then it would have rendered sacrifice null and void. But it is also too Greek. It has a "Platonic idealism" that draws upon "Platonizing allegory" rather than "Paul's typology of fulfillment," which is "more biblical" than Hebrews.[24] "Biblical" has become a norm separate from the Bible itself, which Finlan then uses to declare the Bible unbiblical. Odd. Nonetheless he does not reject Hebrews completely. Instead he plays the doctrine of the incarnation present in Hebrews 2–5 against the sacrificial language of atonement in Hebrews 8–10.[25] He is not alone in doing this. Liberal Protestants like Harnack did it first, but he sided with the Western doctrine because it was less "physical" than the Eastern deification. Orthodox theologians like Lossky make a similar rigid distinction between the West and East.[26]

21. Ibid.
22. Ibid., 47.
23. Ibid., 48.
24. Ibid., 52.
25. Ibid., 50.
26. See David Bentley Hart, *The Beauty of the Infinite: The Aesthetics of Christian Truth* (Grand Rapids: Eerdmans, 2003), 360–73, for an excellent discussion of atonement theory.

A more temperate critique of atonement theory and use of Hebrews, which still sides with those who want to do away with blood sacrifice, can be found in the Anabaptist theologian J. Denny Weaver. Key to his argument is what he calls "narrative Christus Victor." It "provides a reading of Jesus' life and work that avoids all the dimensions of violence in traditional atonement imagery."[27] That all violence would be avoided in discussing atonement seems like a tall order to fill. The cross was a violent means of death, and we cannot get around it; at the heart of the Christian mystery is a cross, which our architecture, liturgy, hymnody, and sacred texts obviously manifest. To rid the faith of all these images would take a puritanical cleansing few would countenance today. I take it Weaver does not seek to purify the tradition in that sense. His point is not a denial that Christ died a brutal, violent death; it is that the death itself is not what redeems.

Weaver argues that Hebrews fits his "narrative Christus Victor" well.[28] Hebrews can be separated from Anselm and redeemed. Weaver rightly recognizes that Hebrews' argument actually calls for an end to sacrifice: "The writer of Hebrews places this prophetic critique of sacrifice in the mouth of Christ."[29] Like the prophets, Hebrews argues that God desires not sacrifice but obedience. Mark Baker and Joel Green also bring out this important theme in Hebrews. The "sacrifice of obedience" found in Isaiah 1:10–17, Amos 5:21–25, and Micah 6:6–8 is "explicitly highlighted by the author of Hebrews (Heb. 10:5–10) and is not far from the background of an overall New Testament witness to the faithful obedience of Jesus Christ." As we will see in discussing Hebrews 10, the author explicitly draws on the prophetic tradition to have Christ say, "Sacrifices and offerings you have not desired, but a body you have prepared for me" (10:5).

Yet key to this passage is the plural "sacrifices." I do not find it compelling to then argue Hebrews has no place for sacrifice. Christ's body is our sacrifice. It replaces the repeatable sacrifices of the earthly temple made by human hands; but as I argued above

27. Weaver, *Nonviolent Atonement,* 10.
28. Ibid., 13.
29. Ibid., 61.

in discussing supersessionism in chapter 5, it goes too far to conclude that Hebrews finds no merit in that earlier sacrificial system. Hebrews affirms those former things for what they could accomplish, but what they could accomplish was limited. Hebrews does not deny that God required the sacrifices of the first covenant. Instead Hebrews argues they were shadows of the true covenant that God promised in Jeremiah 31. Jesus brings that covenant to its perfection by his sacrifice, which is both an offering of obedience and an offering of his own blood.

Weaver finds a place for Hebrews, but he rejects Anselm's theory because he thinks it requires God to have "need for a death penalty to balance the sin of humankind as the basis for restoring justice." According to Weaver, "God did not send Jesus to die, but to live, to make visible and present the reign of God. It is obvious that for narrative Christus Victor, the agent of Jesus' death was not God but the powers of evil."[30] Fair enough, but who argues that God is the *direct* agent of Jesus' death other than a few ill-informed fundamentalists? Anselm did not argue this. God only indirectly willed Christ's death. Anselm is explicit about this. Nor has Weaver avoided the question Anselm and others confronted. Why did God deliver the innocent Son into the hands of the "powers of evil"? God surely could have prevented it. Yet it occurred. Thus, like Weaver, Aquinas did not make God the agent of Jesus' death. He explicitly stated there was no force of necessity in God's own being that required Jesus to die. God decreed that Jesus die, but God did not actively kill Jesus. He only removed his protective grace from him so that the evil forces of this world could kill him. Thus both Anselm and Aquinas would agree in part with Weaver that Christ's death "was the result of pursuing another goal."[31] But contrary to Weaver and Finlan, both Anselm and Aquinas would accept that Christ now offers his deed performed, including his sacrificial death, as an offering acceptable to God, and that "in some sense" God willed it. They would affirm with Hebrews: "how much more will the blood of Christ, who through the eternal

30. Ibid., 74.
31. Ibid., 133. Weaver does note in passing on 191 that Anselm argues something like this, but he is so insistent that redemption be nonviolent he cannot find any way to affirm Anselm's theology.

Spirit offered himself without blemish to God, purify our conscience from dead works to worship the living God" (Heb. 9:14).

Joel Green and Mark Baker acknowledge along with the theologians above that the fundamentalist penal substitutionary atonement is a problem. "In fact, for many American Christians, 'penal substitutionary atonement' interprets the significance of Jesus' death fully, completely, without remainder."[32] If they are correct, then surely it is cause for alarm. Deification, theosis, and being brought to perfection are all crucial to interpret the significance of Jesus' death in Hebrews as well as his sacrificial offering for our transgression. But unlike some of the other theologians mentioned, they do not then make the misstep of removing the "scandal of the cross." They draw upon Jesus' own interpretation of his suffering in his resurrection appearance to the two disciples on the road to Emmaus in order to explain why the cross matters (Luke 24). Jesus did not give them a "theory of atonement," but explained how his death was prefigured in the lives of the prophets. "The cross was a scandal that provided an occasion for stumbling for these disciples because they failed to see in what way Jesus fulfilled the prophetic pattern: rejection, suffering, and violent death. Jesus, by correlating the presumed destiny of the prophets with messiahship, contended that the Scriptures portend the figure of an eschatological king who must suffer before entering into his glory."[33] This interpretation fits Hebrews' message well. Christ is the priest-king who restores the household of God through his suffering, which is his entrance into glory. This would seem to be lunacy to most people in the first century, as well as to those of the twenty-first, because the scandal of the cross is a political statement about God's rule, and most rulers do not rule from crosses.[34] However, Baker and Green are as harsh on Anselm's teaching as the theologians already mentioned. His "framework and imagery" are not "taken from the Bible, but from

32. Joel B. Green and Mark D. Baker, *Recovering the Scandal of the Cross: Atonement in New Testament and Contemporary Contexts* (Downers Grove, IL: InterVarsity Press, 2000), 13.

33. Ibid., 14.

34. Ibid.

the feudalistic system of his day."[35] He was too indebted to "feudalism," the "penance system," and "Greek philosophy."[36]

The repetition of concerns about Anselm's theology should cause the reader to ask about their source. Why do so many see the same problem in Anselm? The source behind these critiques is Gustaf Aulén, a Lutheran theologian who wrote a book that has been widely influential, *Christus Victor,* from which Weaver gets his term "narrative Christus victor." In it Aulén found Anselm to be the culmination of the "Latin" theory of the atonement. This provided the basis for the medieval Catholic notion of the Mass as a sacrifice that human creatures offer to God, and therefore produce sufficient merit to have their sins forgiven. As a Lutheran theologian, Aulén found this deeply problematic: "Two points immediately emerge: First, that the whole idea is essentially legalistic; and second, that, in speaking of Christ's work, the emphasis is all laid on that which is done by Christ *as man* in relation to God."[37] This means that, as human, Christ offers an acceptable sacrifice to God, which other humans (earthly priests) can now offer as well. Anselm's theology goes awry because it is legalistic, penitential, grounded in his feudalistic culture, inattentive to the patristic, dramatic, understanding of Christ's work, and focuses on Jesus' action as a human rather than as God. For Aulén, Luther overcomes these limitations and restores the dramatic theory of the atonement of the church fathers, which Aulén called "Christus Victor."

Few theologians defend Anselm's theory today. Following Aulén, Anselm is most often pitted against the "Christus Victor" model of the early church. The Reformed theologian Hans Boersma and the Orthodox David Hart, however, remind us of the historical selectivity in such a reading. Aulén's periodization does not work. Anselm does not abandon crucial patristic themes, nor did the Fathers neglect the significance of the cross and Christ's sacrifice in their soteriology. Boersma cites the second-century *Epistle to Diognetus*

35. Ibid., 131.
36. Ibid., 135.
37. Gustaf Aulén, *Christus Victor: An Historical Study of the Three Main Types of the Idea of Atonement,* trans. A. G. Hebert (New York: Macmillan, 1931), 98.

as evidence that something similar to substitutionary atonement existed long before Anselm.[38] Boersma does not deny the benefits of the "Christus Victor" approach, but he rightly refuses to periodize "atonement theories" in terms of Aulén's schema. Like many other theologians, he finds fault with a substitutionary atonement that became juridical and individualistic. Yet he claims that God's hospitality to us in the cross does necessitate violence. He sides in part with the philosopher Jacques Derrida, arguing that any return on a gift, any form of exchange, will necessitate a kind of violence.

This is the crucial question for atonement theory. Is it an economy of debt and repayment such that God simply is a participant in the cycle of violence that all such economies require? By siding with Derrida, Boersma would seem to say yes. Derrida argued that a gift could not really be given because every gift invited a return that will inevitably produce a closure in the gift relationship turning it into something other than what it was intended to be. Rather than a gift given in charity, it becomes an act of violence that excludes. He gives as an example the simple gift of feeding one's pet. Although it appears to be a gift, such a gratuitous act actually entails the violence done against every other pet, which likewise needed to be fed. For Derrida, then, a true gift could only be given eschatologically—in some possible future that never quite arrives where the gift does not invite violence. (More on this below.) Boersma affirms Derrida's analysis of hospitality: "There is simply no hospitality in our world without violence."[39] But while Derrida finds this lamentable, Boersma does not.[40] He then "affirms the paradox of redemptive violence" in order to demonstrate how the hospitality God shows to us in the cross does require violence and exclusion. It is necessary for the sake of hospitality. Hospitality has priority over violence. But the vindication of hospitality will only be demonstrated eschatologically.[41]

38. Hans Boersma, *Violence, Hospitality, and the Cross: Reappropriating the Atonement Tradition* (Grand Rapids: Baker Academic, 2004), 159.

39. Ibid., 18.

40. Ibid., 34–35.

41. "But it is theologically quite conceivable that this divine act of delivering Christ to the cross will one day prove to be an act justified by the eschatological hospitality that awaits us" (ibid., 37).

Our gestures toward hospitality are often empty because they overlook the price others will have to pay. In this limited sense, Boersma may be correct to state: "God needs to set boundaries precisely in the name of hospitality."[42] To participate in the Eucharist has always assumed some boundary condition, baptism, repentance, a willingness to live in peace with friends and enemies, humility. But the content of these conditions matters, and Boersma does not take that into account in this work. God's hospitality excludes not because God offers a conditional grace, but because we refuse to bring together the form and content of that hospitality. We cannot be included in God's formal offer of grace without a willingness to be transformed into the content that this grace is, for this content characterizes God's own being. If we are to participate in God's "rest," we must learn that content. There is no other way to it.

Boersma seems to see every act of hospitality as *inevitably* linked to violence, even that of God. Violence seems to get the better of God, as if this is how existence, or "ontology," must be. This is objectionable. In a more recent work, however, he calls for a "return to mystery" that would distance itself from Derrida's ontology in favor of a "sacramental ontology." This revises his intimate link between hospitality and death. Boersma gestures in this direction when he writes, "I regret not having done justice to the sacramental character of language in an earlier discussion on metaphors."[43] Here he retracts his earlier claim that we are ensconced in a debt economy where every act, including our use of language, comes at the expense of something else.

If Boersma incorporated his earlier defense of the atonement into his later "sacramental ontology," it would look much more like David Hart's intriguing defense of Anselm. As an Orthodox theologian, Hart would be one of the least likely defenders of Anselm and/or a "Western" theory of the Atonement. He too acknowledges that if Anselm's theory assumes a debt economy, it would be mistaken. "If the language of sacrifice in Christian thought did properly

42. Ibid., 53.
43. Hans Boersma, *Nouvelle Théologie and Sacramental Ontology: A Return to Mystery* (Oxford: Oxford University Press, 2009), 151 n. 8, where he cites his earlier *Violence, Hospitality, and the Cross.*

refer to an economy of exchange, such that God were *appeased* in the slaughter of a victim and his wrath were simply *averted* in the slaughter by way of a prudential violence of which he *approved* . . . , then indeed the Christian God would be a God of violence, and the Christian evangel of peace would simply dissemble another economy of violence and debt—one that, in fact (Nietzsche winning the field), has been monstrously magnified."[44] The economy would be "monstrously magnified" because now God would be implicated in it. Nietzsche would "win" because he claimed Christianity's proclamation of peace was just an act of resentment by which Christians performed a backhanded violence against their enemies; it never escaped the economy of debt and violence.

But unlike Aulén, Hart recognizes that Anselm's theology subverts such an economy for two reasons. First, his theology challenges any penitential system based on a cost-benefit ledger. Second, Anselm does not simply have Jesus as human fulfill some debt to God. Anselm subverts such a penitential system because every offense is "infinite," and thus no easy juridical equivalence can be provided for it. God does not become human so that as a mere human he could repay an infinite debt. This could not be done. *God* becomes human so that human creatures can participate in God's own economy of love whereby every exchange based on an easily calculated debt economy is called into question. This is why it is essential theologically to affirm that the cross does not effect any change in God. For Anselm, God was immutable and impassible. God does not gain anything through the cross. Hart states, "Christ's death does not even effect a change in God's attitude toward humanity; God's attitude never alters: he desires the salvation of his creatures, and will not abandon them even to their own cruelties."[45] Here is where he sees something many other theologians miss. For Anselm, like all the theologians prior to the modern era, the insistence on God's immutability and impassibility meant the atonement could not mean what it later came to mean to some fundamentalists and their objectors. God does not change. Therefore the crucifixion is

44. Hart, *Beauty of the Infinite*, 348–49.
45. Ibid., 371.

not an event that happens in the life of God. Only the philosopher Hegel suggested that, and it has had tremendous, malevolent influence on modern theology. But Hart correctly notes that for Anselm, "God is already always an infinite venturing forth and return, an action of reconciliation, response, and accord, in which any opposition of goods is already overcome by the work of deathless love."[46] The answer to Anselm's question, "Why the God-Man?" (*Cur Deus Homo?*), is because this is most fitting with who God is. Hart states it well: "the donation that Christ makes of himself draws creation into God's eternal 'offering' of himself in the life of the Trinity. . . . His gift remains gift to the end despite all our efforts to convert it into debt."[47]

Hart points out several mistakes made in the above critiques of Hebrews and Anselm. The first is that they teach God directly willed the death of the Son. This is neither the teaching of Hebrews nor the teaching of Anselm. For Hebrews Jesus' suffering and death are not first and foremost some offering to God, but his participation in our enslavement to death. It is what he does. He shares our humanity to the point of death. But he does so in such a way that he overcomes death (2:14–18). It is this "faithfulness" that overcomes fear and death that makes him high priest of a new covenant, and also allows for his own self-offering to God. He makes this offering in the "heavenly tabernacle." So the offering is not just his suffering and death on the cross, but his faithfulness that overcomes death by taking it upon himself, and thereby destroying the power of the devil, who for Hebrews is "the one who has the power of death." It is Jesus' completed work that he offers to God. But he offers it on our behalf, not on behalf of God.

God wills that this power be broken. Jesus accomplished that. Anselm, more than most theologians, recognized the beauty in Christ's sacrifice. He understood well Hebrews' argument. Far from making God a tyrant, Anselm saw that God is to be defined not in terms of arbitrary power, but by the beauty of God's creation. God's power is not the power to do whatever God wants to redeem us,

46. Ibid., 367.
47. Ibid., 372.

but to work consistently with the beauty, goodness, and justice God is. We can see this by revisiting Brown and Parker's quote from Anselm's *Cur Deus Homo?* and looking at it in its context.

Anselm offers a careful argument for what it means to say God willed the Son's death, an argument that many critiques ignore. He first responds to the question how God could will the death of an innocent man to redeem the world: "The will of God should be a good enough reason for us when he does anything." This could be the depiction of a tyrant. What God wills is its own reason. But Anselm then goes on, "For the will of God is never irrational."[48] In other words, God does not act irrationally by torturing and crucifying an innocent man. But nor does God act irrationally by simply acting as if creation does not bear the wounds of sin. God cannot simply wink at sin as if it has not damaged who we are. For God to act rationally is for God to repair the wound consistent with who God is. This is why the first theme Anselm develops in his so-called satisfaction theory is not the crucifixion but the incarnation. The debasement of God becomes the exaltation of humanity, but that debasement includes crucifixion. This fits well Hebrews' use of Psalm 8 (Heb. 2:5–9). God originally intended that humanity be "crowned with glory and honor." They could not accomplish this on their own because of the "power of death." Jesus becomes human, takes on all that it entails including suffering and death, and accomplishes God's original intention.[49]

For what justice is there in giving up the most just man of all to death on behalf of the sinner? What man would not be judged worthy of condemnation if he condemned the innocent in order to free the guilty? The whole thing seems to go back to the same incongruity that I mentioned before. For if he could not save sinners except by condemning the just, where is his omnipotence? But if he could, but would not, how are we to defend his wisdom and justice?

—Boso's question to Anselm

Cur Deus Homo? chapter 8.

48. Anselm, *Cur Deus Homo?* in *A Scholastic Miscellany: Anselm to Ockham,* ed. Eugene R. Fairweather, Library of Christian Classics 10 (1956; repr. Louisville: Westminster John Knox Press, 1982), 110.

49. See Schenck, *Understanding the Book of Hebrews,* 24–39, for the central role of Psalm 8 in Hebrews.

We seem caught in a dilemma: either affirming God's omnipotence but losing his wisdom and justice, or affirming his wisdom and justice but losing his omnipotence. If we say God could not redeem without finding himself caught in the horrible predicament of slaughtering the innocent, we lose his omnipotence. If we say God could have redeemed without this, but decided not to, then we lose his wisdom and justice. It is a perplexing question, one that obviously troubled Christians in the twelfth century as it does in the twenty-first. But unlike the latter, who tend to reject any notion of Christ's sacrifice, Anselm provided a response that helps us make sense of it. "God the Father did not treat that Man [Jesus] as you seem to think, or give up the innocent to death for the guilty. For he did not force him to die or to allow him to be slain against his will; on the contrary, he himself readily endured death in order to save men."[50] The first thing to notice is that God does not ask Jesus to die against his will. But the second is to note that God does not directly intend that he die at all. Jesus does not die because God's justice requires that the innocent should suffer and spill their blood. Instead, as Anselm puts it, "Therefore God did not compel Christ to die, when there was no sin in him, but Christ himself freely underwent death, not by yielding up his life as an act of obedience, but on account of his obedience in maintaining justice, because he so steadfastly persevered in it that he brought death on himself."[51] It is not the mere "yielding up his life" that is his "act of obedience," but his "maintaining justice." In other words, Jesus performs the complete human act that God intended for humanity even though he knew it would cost him his life. He did not let the fear of death deter him from performing God's wisdom and justice.

Who of us could ever say the same? I know many times in my life when I have failed to act in concert with what I knew to be true, or even said or did things I knew were untrue, because of the fear of violence or death. Let me give a trivial example. For years I have been a bicycle commuter. Once while riding on a street designated for cyclists in Philadelphia, a dump truck came so close to me that

50. Anselm, *Cur Deus Homo?* 111.
51. Ibid., 113.

I thought I would be sucked into its massive wheels. No oncoming cars required the driver to imperil my life, so I assumed he was indifferent to it. I looked in his mirror and shrugged my shoulders and raised my hand questioning, why? (I did not make any gestures for which Philly is famous.) The driver stopped the truck on a four-lane highway, jumped out of it, and this mountain of a man came running at me, all the while cursing and questioning my right both to ride on the road and to exist. My first thought was, "This is going to hurt." Before he fell upon me, I began to apologize for having offended him. Either my apology or the honking vehicles prevented him from acting on the curses he directed my way. He turned, went back to his truck, and drove away. I rode the rest of the way to work ashamed that I had said what I knew was not true, but glad that I had not been harmed. I knew my actions lacked goodness and justice; I had done him no wrong. The fear of violence and possible death held me fast. It caused me to be something other than I knew I should be. I did not tell the truth.

This example (I have of course greater failures of embodying who I should be that I share with confessors rather than readers) is meant to illustrate the point Anselm makes here. Jesus embodies the wisdom and justice of God. He is God's rational response to a creation held fast by the power of sin and death. Because the world is held such, Jesus knows, as does the Father, that he will die. But his death is an indirect effect of his directly willed embodiment of God's rational response to creation's wound. The death is secondary to the positively willed wisdom and justice. Anselm is saying that true obedience to God's goodness in a fallen world will bring about death not because God demands it but because the world does. Jesus is willing to undergo this. And that willingness is pleasing to God. It is in fact a sign of his omnipotence. Anselm states, "The fact is that the Son, with the Father and the Holy Spirit, had determined to show the loftiness of his omnipotence by no other means than death."[52] This is the work of the Holy Trinity; it is not a work of God against God's self, as if the first person sought the death of the second. It is a gift of God to the creation that discloses God's true omnipotence.

52. Ibid.

Hebrews does not state that Christ's suffering should have been ours; nor is Christ a substitute. If there is a "substitution" in Hebrews, it is the Levitical priesthood, its animal victims, and the earthly temple that stands in as a substitute for Christ's eternal priesthood, sacrifice, and heavenly temple. For Hebrews, Christ puts an end to the Levitical priesthood and animal sacrifices. The need for their repetition has now dissipated because of Christ's priesthood and where it is exercised (9:24–26). When the author gave us the "main point" in 8:1–2, he added to the exordium where Christ "sat down": he sat down "at the right hand *of the throne* of the Majesty *in the heavens.*" He then expands more fully on this location and its significance. Not only does Christ "sit down" in the heavenly temple, but he also does so as "minister" of *tōn hagiōn* (literally, "the holy"; NRSV "sanctuary") and *tēs skēnēs tēs alēthinēs* (literally, "of the true tent/tabernacle," 8:2). "The holy" usually refers to the first tent or tabernacle (*skēnē*) where the priests would regularly offer sacrifices. "The holy of holies" referred to the second or inner tent where only the high priest went once a year on the Day of Atonement. However, Leviticus also refers to "the holy" as the inner sanctuary.[53] Likewise, *skēnē* (tabernacle) refers either to the inner or outer tent, signifying that there are two "tabernacles." It can also refer to the tabernacle as a whole. The author of Hebrews uses these terms in both ways. In 9:1–5 and 6–7 he describes the overall tabernacle by noting a "first" and "second" *skēnē,* which he also refers to as the "holy" (*Hagia*) and the "holy of holies" (*Hagia Hagiōn*), respectively. However, in 8:2 and 9:11–12 the references to "the holy" and "the tabernacle" (*skēnē*) make best sense as a reference to the entire tabernacle.

All of this can be quite confusing. Hebrews does not seem to use the various terms with a rigorous consistency, but the argument seems straightforward enough. Hebrews is not comparing the heavenly temple/tabernacle as the inner, heavenly one to the outer, earthly one. Nor is the heavenly temple a literal edifice; it is after all not made by human hands. Nor is it some abstract, eternal archetype. As Kenneth Schenck notes, "events" take place in this heavenly temple. It is the place where Christ offers his sacrifice. So what is the

53. See Lev. 16:2. See also Schenck, *Cosmology and Eschatology in Hebrews,* 159.

heavenly temple? To understand that requires noting the comparisons Hebrews makes throughout chapter 9.

Hebrews compares the two temples by comparing two covenants. This follows upon the citation of the new covenant God will make according to Jeremiah (Heb. 8:8–13). There are similarities between the two covenants. Both have "regulations for worship" and a "sanctuary" (9:1, 15). But the place in which the two tabernacles or temples are found, and therefore the two covenants, markedly differs. In the first the "tent" is "constructed" (9:2), whereas the second, the heavenly temple, is "not made with hands" (9:11). The first was filled with Israel's sacred possessions. Hebrews places the golden altar of incense, the ark of the covenant (holding manna, Aaron's rod, and the tablets of the covenant), and the "cherubim of angels" over the mercy seat or "place of atonement" (*hilastērion*) in it. Only Christ appears in the eternal temple to offer himself at the place of atonement (9:26). Because the first covenant has an earthly, constructed temple, the sacrifices at the place of atonement must be repeated, which the high priest does once a year (9:7). But in the eternal temple Christ offers himself once and for all as a perfect offering. The first covenant and temple are temporal; their liturgies therefore must be repeated. Where Christ offers his sacrifice unites the eternal and the temporal. Christ enters into it, which is a temporal act, and performs an offering of his own blood, but he only does so once. Because his sacrifice is complete and perfect, lacking nothing, sacrifice is no longer necessary. It is this act that makes him "mediator of a new covenant" (9:15). Both covenants were ratified in blood because all such covenants require the death of the testator. But because Christ enters the eternal temple and is crowned with glory, his death never needs to be repeated again, even though it is also present "today." His body becomes the perfect offering (10:10). It is, as N. T. Wright suggests, a "temple substitute."

Wright argues this in defense of Jesus' self-understanding as "divine": "It is basic to New Testament Christology that the human Jesus discloses in himself the being and nature of the true God."[54]

54. N. T. Wright, "Jesus' Self-Understanding," in *The Incarnation: An Interdisciplinary Symposium on the Incarnation of the Son of God,* ed. Stephen T. David, Daniel Kendall, and Gerald O'Collins (Oxford: Oxford University Press, 2004), 50.

His historical argument is based on YHWH's expected return to the temple in Jerusalem, and Jesus' actions as a substitute for the temple.[55] This makes good sense of Hebrews' argument, but Wright questions if traditional Christian theology has taken it with sufficient seriousness: "What might it do to our systematic Christologies to make the Temple, rather than theories about natures, persons and substance, central to our reflection? I do not know. But I do know that if we were to try we might find all kinds of new themes opening up before us."[56] He poses a serious question to the Chalcedonian Definition, but does not answer it. The question suggests that the language of natures, persons, and substances has somehow set us off in a direction away from Scripture and the early church's recognition that Christ is the true temple. Perhaps. Wright's work makes possible a more faithful interpretation of Christ that recognizes the logic in Hebrews. What he has accomplished cannot be understood without attention to temple theology. But such theology has, and could once again, send us in a direction away from the canonical Scriptures.

FURTHER REFLECTIONS
Temple Theology

"Temple theology" offers several interesting insights into Hebrews and its Christology. This is a relatively new interpretation of the Old Testament that finds the origins of Christian mysticism present in an "older testament," the secrets of the priests in the First Temple transmitted primarily through apocalyptic texts such as *1 Enoch* and the *Apocalypse of Abraham*.[57] Margaret Barker has been central in promulgating it. She argues that we have the wrong canon to make sense of Christianity. The Synoptic Gospels' "tyranny" over us "has prevented unbiased access to extra-canonical sources." These sources set forth a more mystical gospel that was a residual element

55. Ibid., 55–57.
56. Ibid., 58.
57. The reference is to a book by Margaret Barker, *The Older Testament: The Survival of Themes from the Ancient Royal Cult in Sectarian Judaism and Early Christianity* (1987; repr. Sheffield: Sheffield Phoenix Press, 2005).

of the secrets from a priestly tradition of the First Temple. The theology of the First Temple assumed that the temple was part of an eternal covenant God(s) made with creation. This First Temple was not strictly monotheistic, but recognized that Yahweh had a wife, Asherah or Asheratah, who was also known as Wisdom. She had her own cult, the "cult of the Lady." We see glimpses of this in the current OT canon. According to Barker, "her cult must have involved a serpent and a tree symbol, the Asherah, the heavenly hosts (who were her sons), child sacrifice such as was forbidden by the story of Abraham and Isaac, a sun cult and linen garments."[58] Her cult was abandoned right before the First Temple was destroyed; some prophets proclaimed that this abandonment was the cause of the temple's destruction. Wisdom left the temple, and her cult migrated to Egypt.[59] The postexilic Deuteronomists then wrote her and the temple's secret knowledge out of the canon. The "reforms" of Josiah were a "disaster" according to this older testament, especially as it is recorded in *1 Enoch,* where the Deuteronomist's law plays little to no role.[60] Once we get the wrong OT canon, then the central theological significance of the temple gets lost. Its significance is the repair of the broken covenant with creation through the Day of Atonement when the high priest enters into the holy of holies, becomes an angel or divinized, and returns with the blood of the covenant to renew the created order.

The older testament remains primarily in early Christianity and residually in Gnosticism. At this point, Barker's work is both interesting and confusing. Who are the "gods" surrounding the God of the First Temple? Is this simply a way of affirming that the doctrine of the Trinity predates Christianity and was written out of the Jewish story by the Deuteronomists? Or is it more akin to other claims circling around Gnosticism in which its putative religious pluralism gets intentionally thwarted by legalist orthodoxy? Barker can be read both ways.

58. Margaret Barker, *The Great High Priest: The Temple Roots of Christian Liturgy* (London: T & T Clark, 2003), 236.
59. Barker finds evidence for this in *1 Enoch* 93:8 and Jer. 44:17–19 (ibid., 78).
60. Ibid., 235.

Barker offers fascinating insights into the temple, its veil, priestly vestments, sacrifices, and its concomitant theology even if her work sometimes reads like a Dan Brown novel with its conspiracies against the true, mystical temple theology. For instance, she notes, "Recent work on the transmission of the New Testament has shown convincingly that what is currently regarded as 'orthodoxy' was constructed and imposed on the text of the New Testament by later scribes 'clarifying' difficult points and resolving theological problems."[61] She refers to Bart Ehrman's work, who begins with a strong hermeneutics of suspicion in which every written history is the result of a power play accomplished by the victors.[62] Such a hermeneutics employs a vicious circular reasoning that begins with its conclusion. It dogmatically assumes that theological debates concerning God, despite their proponents' intentions, were not entered into or resolved based on the truth of the matter, since there is no such thing. Instead they are exercises in arbitrary power. Then it concludes that orthodoxy is nothing but an exercise in arbitrary power. The circle is vicious because it does not illumine anything; of necessity it must fit the "facts" to its hermeneutical lens. Ironically, the author's own historical narration somehow escapes the presupposition. Why is it not simply one more exercise of arbitrary power? A more important question is not whether judgments about right reading of Scripture are made, but on what basis they are made. Such judgments are inevitable. Barker and Ehrman clearly make them. If the cult of the Lady included child sacrifice, were not the Deuteronomists correct in their theological judgments?

Barker's "temple theology" might be one answer to Wright's call for Christology to take more seriously the role of the temple, but it has significant limitations, especially in that Jesus as high priest becomes one divinized creature among many. I doubt it provides the christological illumination Wright seeks, but he does suggest limitations in letting a historical-critical reading of texts become normative over against the dogmatic tradition. When Hebrews is read not within the Christian canon, but one that includes texts like

61. Ibid., 18.

62. Ehrman writes, without any qualification, "it is the winners who write history" (*Orthodox Corruption of Scripture*, 8).

1 Enoch and the *Apocalypse of Abraham*, Christology will swerve from conciliar consensus. This is inevitable. As Barker herself notes, "A new paradigm alters everything."[63] Should everything be altered? Should we read Hebrews not in the context of the canonical Old Testament, but one that replaces Deuteronomy with *1 Enoch*? This would require an explicit theological judgment for which Barker's "temple theology" has not yet provided an adequate foundation. Of course, such a judgment should not be made by theologians or biblical scholars but by the teaching office(s) of the church, none of which have replaced Deuteronomy with *1 Enoch*, although *1 Enoch* is in the Ethiopian Orthodox Church's canon.[64]

10:1–39

Christ as the Temple Who Brings Confident Speech, Faith, Hope, and Love

In chapter 9 Hebrews began a typological reading of the two covenants and two temples that continues into chapter 10. The Mosaic law and its correlative temple are a "shadow" of their "true form." Reading this in the context of Platonism would be largely to misread it. It is a typological reading of the Old Testament that Hebrews finds warranted in the Old Testament itself. To read Scripture as Hebrews does requires such typological readings. Two twentieth-century Catholic theologians, Yves M.-J. Congar and Jean Daniélou, give insight into Hebrews by their typological interpretation relating Hebrews 9 and 10 to the broader Christian canon and Christology. They found this in the church fathers, and not as an alternative to Chalcedon but as a basis for it.

Daniélou reads Hebrews 9 and 10 in the context of Scripture's seven temples: those of the cosmos, Moses, Christ, the church, the prophets, and then the mystical and heavenly temples. Congar adds to these a reflection on the "spiritual temple." The cosmos is the First Temple Scripture presents.

63. Barker, *Great High Priest*, 234.
64. Nickelsburg, *1 Enoch*, 104.

> **God's whole purpose is to make the human race, created in his image, a living spiritual temple in which he not only dwells but to which he communicates himself and in turn receives from it the worship of a wholly filial obedience.**
>
> **—Yves Congar**
>
> *The Mystery of the Temple, or, The Manner of God's Presence to His Creatures from Genesis to the Apocalypse*, trans. Reginald F. Trevett (Westminster, MD: Newman Press, 1962), ix.

For Daniélou and Congar the temple is a figure for the "presence of God," which is why the first and most basic temple is the cosmos. Heaven is God's tabernacle, the earth is God's footstool or the outer tabernacle, and the waters are the porch. This interprets Genesis, which presents creation and the garden as a temple where God dwells with creatures. This cosmic temple is "common to all," and yet God leaves it "in some way unfinished." It is present in all religious gestures, symbolized primarily by Melchizedek. Human creatures are to bring the cosmic temple to completion through "sacramental use."[65] The cosmic temple, however, is insufficient. Creation fails in its task. For this reason God gives Israel a mission, which is fundamentally defined by the "temple of Moses." Daniélou writes, "The establishment of the Tabernacle, whose ultimate form is the Temple, is the fundamental mission entrusted by God to Moses."[66] Now the temple becomes singular, a sign of God's oneness, a guard against polytheism, and a recognition of the "gulf that it fixes between God and man."[67] In some sense, God disappears behind the curtain and is no longer present as in the garden.

For Daniélou and Congar, like Hebrews, the cosmic and Mosaic temples find their completion in the "temple of Christ." Congar sees in the Mosaic temple more of a "Nestorian system." There is not yet "ontological union" between God's presence and the temple itself as there is with Christ's body.[68] As the Mosaic temple carries forth

65. Jean Daniélou, *The Presence of God*, trans. Walter Roberts (Baltimore: Helicon Press, 1960), 10–11. This theme is found in Josephus and Philo. See Josephus, *Antiquities* 3.180–81, quoted in Schenck, *Cosmology and Eschatology in Hebrews*, 151. See *The Works of Philo: Complete and Unabridged*, trans. C. D. Yonge, new ed. (1993; repr. Peabody, MA: Hendrickson, 2006), 540.

66. Daniélou, *Presence of God*, 15.

67. Ibid., 17.

68. Yves M.-J. Congar, *The Mystery of the Temple, or, The Manner of God's Presence to His Creatures from Genesis to the Apocalypse*, trans. Reginald F. Trevett (Westminster, MD: Newman Press, 1962), 17.

the cosmic temple, leading it toward its true end, now the temple of Christ replaces the Mosaic; it is no longer necessary, which is true for both Judaism and Christianity. This is a descriptive statement; both survive after its destruction. This is not to disparage the Mosaic temple; we could not have the temple of Christ without the "humility and perfection" the temple of Moses made possible. Yet once God is incarnate in Christ, he now becomes the true site of God's glory. According to Daniélou, "The Glory of the Lord dwelt in the Temple until the coming of the Incarnation. But from that day it began to dwell in Jesus."[69] Notice he writes "began"—the incarnation did not immediately replace the temple. Here we have a theologically significant reality that we must not ignore. For a brief time in history both the figure and reality exist side by side. Daniélou states that "the mystery of their connection, of their joint construction, was shown in a marvelous light," which is found in the presentation of Jesus to Simeon in the temple, the devil's temptation when he takes Jesus to the temple, and Jesus' bold claim to destroy the temple and rebuild it in three days.[70]

Jesus' flesh opens the curtain, making a "new and living way" into the inner court, but this is not merely a return to some cosmic temple. It is a "new and living way" that fulfills and exceeds all the temples prior to it. Daniélou draws on Hebrews 10:19–20 to explain this. He interprets those verses: "This is not simply a return to the cosmic Temple, but after the Mosaic purification, access to a higher Presence, entry by humanity into the Holy of holies, not simply the natural Presence of God in His creation."[71] Congar notes that Stephen's speech represents a decisive moment in the transition from the temple to Jesus' body as the decisive locus for God's presence. In Acts 7 Stephen renarrates the history of Israel. Toward the end of that important speech, in a passage Hebrews echoes, he states, "But it was Solomon who built a house for him. Yet the Most High does not dwell in houses made with human hands; as the prophet says, 'Heaven is my throne, and the earth is my footstool. What kind of house will you build for me, says the Lord, or what is the place of my

69. Daniélou, *Presence of God*, 20.
70. Ibid., 24.
71. Ibid., 27.

rest?'" (Acts 7:47–49). (The similarity between Stephen's speech and Hebrews' message is one reason some suggest Luke might be its author, or at least Paul's translator into Greek.) The answer assumed is Christ's body, which is the new temple.

In Christian tradition, perhaps beginning with Irenaeus, Christ's body is understood in a threefold form. The first form is the literal, historical body of Christ. The second is the Eucharist or Lord's Supper, which is also the body of Christ. The third is the church. It too is the "body of Christ." The incarnation does not end with the crucifixion; the tomb is empty. God's enfleshment continues, uniting heaven and earth. Christ's risen historical body is now mediated to us through Word and Sacrament such that we can become the body of Christ. This is referred to as the *totus Christus*, the "whole Christ." For Daniélou this constitutes the fourth temple.

The literal, historical body of Christ can be designated. We can point to it and say, "There it is." This is as true of his body prior to the resurrection as it is afterward. Christ's risen body was indeed odd; it is available within conditions of space and time and nevertheless exceeds them. Jesus appears in a locked room without using the door, and then asks for a fish. He walks with disciples who should know him, but they do not, until he breaks bread with them. Even Mary does not recognize him until he speaks her name. Yet all the Gospels depict the risen Jesus in continuity with the pre-Easter Jesus. In none of the Gospels is his identity so different that he has to let them in on the secret that he is Jesus, even when he reveals himself to them. It is his continuity in identity that makes Jesus the "new and living way" that is recognizable to us.

After telling us that Christ's flesh opens up the new and living way into the holy of holies, Hebrews repeats a version of the admonition we heard in 3:6: "we are his house if we hold firm the confidence and the pride that belong to hope." Hebrews recalls it by admonishing, "Let us hold fast to the confession of our hope without wavering, for he who has promised is faithful" (10:23). What is this confession (*homologia*) and confidence (*parrēsia,* 10:19) of hope we are to hold fast? It is that we have this "new and living way" into the holy of holies, or the house of God, because Christ is our high priest, who makes us into his house. Daniélou explains this well: "it is the Mystical Body in its entirety; this is the complete and final Temple. The dwelling of God is the Christian community whose Head is in heaven, and whose members are still making their earthly pilgrimage; it is the true Temple of which the Temple of stone was the figure."[72]

This brings us to the remaining three temples, the prophetic, mystical, and heavenly. If the cosmic temple represents the harmony and unity God intends for all of creation, the temple of the prophets reminds us that we cannot attain it without denunciation. The mysterious encounters between figure and reality in the presentation and cleansing of the temple signify the prophetic temple. Simeon's prophetic words to Mary remind us of this: "This child is destined for the falling and the rising of many in Israel, and to be a sign that will be opposed so that the inner thoughts of many will be revealed—and a sword will pierce your own soul too" (Luke 2:34–35). Likewise Jesus proclaims that the new temple of his body requires the destruction of the earthly. It is only on the cross that the temple veil is torn, making possible the new and living way. Many churches reenact this act liturgically each Sunday. A procession occurs in which the Bible and ministers follow the cross into the sanctuary. Most churches still have architectural similarities to the temple. The sanctuary proper or holy of holies is set apart by a chancel rail. The veil is not physically there because it was torn in two in the crucifixion. Nonetheless, the procession of the cross into the sanctuary is the repetition of the piercing of the veil. Our access to the presence of God comes through the way Christ's cross makes possible.

Hebrews draws on the prophetic denunciation of sacrifices and offerings when it places on Jesus' lips the words of Psalm 40: "Sacrifices and offerings you have not desired, but a body you have prepared for me" (10:5). This is a reference to Christ's body, but there is also in Jewish and Christian tradition a sense that every created body is itself a mystical temple. It has its outer court in the external senses and its inner one in the soul. Paul calls on this tradition when he admonishes us that our body is a temple of God (1 Cor. 3:16–17; 6:19; 2 Cor. 6:16). The Jewish exegete Philo drew upon this imagery and related it to Plato and Aristotle's tripartite rendering of the

72. Ibid., 29.

human person. Although we can see implicit and explicit references to the first five temples Daniélou mentions in Hebrews, this one is surprisingly scarce, albeit not completely absent. Perhaps the closest we come to this tradition is the admonition to "purify our conscience from dead works to worship the living God" (9:14). Likewise we saw earlier that Hebrews referred to Jesus as "a sure and steadfast anchor of the soul" who "enters the inner shrine behind the curtain" (6:19). But nowhere does Hebrews provide an extended allegory of the journey of the soul to the holy place separate from the "body," either individually or collectively. Although the tradition of the soul as a mystical temple is well established in Christian tradition and should be respected, Hebrews offers little support for it. As noted earlier, Origen interpreted Hebrews' temple imagery as the ascent of the soul to the heavenly temple, but this became a minor interpretation. He certainly draws on the tradition of the "heavenly temple," a tradition well attested in Jewish literature of all sorts (prophetic, wisdom, apocalyptic). The heavenly temple is God's presence. It has no outer sanctuary or porch other than creation itself to which God seeks to communicate God's presence. Hebrews' "main point" is that Jesus enters that "place." Jesus' flesh opens the way into that heavenly temple, uniting God and creation such that now God can shake creation and all that is not linked to that heavenly anchor will be "rolled up" like an old garment. This is not to say creation is destroyed and only bodiless souls remain. Instead, it offers us a profound theological politics, which we will examine in the commentary on chapter 10. Creaturely reality finds its permanent abode in the presence of God.

FURTHER REFLECTIONS
Turning Bodies into Stones

Janet Soskice sets forth Hebrews' theological politics by posing a question, "Which would you rather be, a stone or a chip?"[73] This

73. Janet Soskice, "Resurrection and the New Jerusalem," in *The Resurrection: An Interdisciplinary Symposium on the Resurrection of Jesus,* ed. Stephen T. Davis, Daniel Kendall, and Gerald O'Collins (Oxford: Oxford University Press, 1998), 41.

question comes in the context of a discussion of the "etiolated orthodoxy" found in popular Christian teaching on the resurrection. Soskice strongly affirms the bodily resurrection of Jesus, his empty tomb, and the Christian hope for resurrection. But her critique of an "etiolated orthodoxy" raises the question—to what end? What is the hope we have in resurrection? If all we desire is eternity, which could be a crass, hedonistic desire, then something like posthuman evolution would fit the bill as well as resurrection. Some posthuman evolutionists are working on the possibility of a kind of eternal life by learning how to download human consciousness into supercomputers that will then have the potential to keep our consciousness alive forever. It is very similar to the gnostic heresy. The problem with humanity, they suggest, is not the software (our consciousness) but the fragility of the hardware—the host in which the software resides (our bodies). If we can overcome the limitations of the "host," then we could have eternal life. Our consciousness could be compressed into a "chip," placed in a better host, and the end result could be something the church promised but never delivered—eternal life.

Soskice's question, a chip or a stone, questions if this is what Christianity means by resurrection and eternal life. She juxtaposes the Christian notion of a corporate body where each of us is a living stone making up the temple that is Christ's body to the posthuman notion of a "chip" where each of us contributes to the life of another as a chip in a virtual reality. If "Christian orthodoxy" is not to be "etiolated," then it will need to have something more substantive to offer than mere eternity. What is missing in this weak orthodoxy is a proper understanding of the "temple," or the "corporateness of the Christian conception of new life."[74] Jesus' body is the site for the new temple, which includes Gentile and Jewish believers in a project that does not happen only in the past or in the future, but even now. This emphasis on the temple gets lost when resurrection becomes primarily immortality. What also gets lost is "the central affirmation of Christian hope for the transformation of the universe."[75] We

74. Ibid., 45.
75. Ibid., 57.

> forget the importance of the prayer,"Thy kingdom come . . . on earth as it is in heaven." As Revelation puts it, whatever is worthy of glory and honor among all the nations is brought to this temple, who is Christ, in order to establish a new reign (Rev. 21:22–27). Perhaps burial practices could better reflect this hope. In a seminar on liturgy and loyalties, Creston Davis suggested to me that Christians change their burial customs, which we have lost to the funeral industry.[76] At his or her death, each believer's body should be cremated and literally turned into a brick. Churches would then include those bricks in their edifices so that our dead bodies would witness to the reality of being "living stones" in the body of Christ. This would be a witness to the confident hope that God will restore creation.

After setting forth Christ's priesthood in chapter 8 and offering a typological interpretation of the covenants and temples, the author of Hebrews admonishes his hearers to embody these important doctrinal teachings in 10:19–25. He once again offers his central admonitions: "Let us approach with a true heart in the full assurance of faith," and "let us hold fast to the confession of our hope." Because we can approach the holy of holies in the true temple, we can hold fast to faith and make a confession of hope. Chapter 10 explains what Christ's sacrifice brings, preparing us for the litany of witnesses who testify to it in chapter 11. We have already noted that the law as shadow with its sacrifices could not "make perfect"—only Christ accomplishes that. Likewise we saw that Hebrews 10:5–7 places the prophetic words of Psalm 40:6–8 on the lips of Jesus: God does not desire sacrifices, but "a body you have prepared for me."[77] Hebrews' statement, "a body you have prepared for me," finds its significance in the final words of that verse, "I have come to do your will, O God." The author explains his use of Psalm 40 at 10:10: "And it is by God's will that we have been sanctified through the offering of the body of Jesus Christ once for all." Jesus' single offering sanctifies or makes us holy. Hebrews directly relates it to our perfection (10:14).

76. D. Stephen Long and Michael Budde, "Liturgical Identities: Global, National, Ecclesial" (seminar, Calvin Institute for Christian Scholarship, Calvin College, Grand Rapids, Michigan, Summer, 2007).

77. That is, the LXX. The Hebrew of the Masoretic text has "ears you have dug for me."

The tense to the verb used in 10:14, "he has perfected," matters. It signifies that the action has already been completed. We do not wait for it. If we waited for it, it would be like the sacrifices in the earthly temple that need to be repeated. Christ's single sacrifice is eternal, perfect, fully accomplished. We do not expect any further sacrifice or any improvement on what he did. But we do nonetheless wait. In order to explain this, Hebrews returns again to Psalm 110:1, which we saw in the exordium and the catena. In the exordium the first part of Psalm 110:1 was an already accomplished fact—Christ is seated at God's right hand—but it made no reference to the second part, "until I make your enemies a footstool for your feet." This was a promise first raised in the catena (Heb. 1:13). It was not something yet accomplished, but on its way. This same gap between promise and accomplishment returns in the author's encouragement to his listeners in chapters 8 and 10. In 8:1 he restates the first part of Psalm 110:1, the already accomplished fact. This is repeated in 10:12, but with the addition in verse 13 of the second part of Psalm 110:1. Here, unlike the catena, where the verse is quoted without interruption, Hebrews interrupts the first and second parts of the verse with these important words: "and since then [he] has been waiting." Christ is waiting for the complete exercise of his political rule, for which Hebrews' listeners must also wait. Patient expectation is at the center of the message. Christ has already triumphed; his rule is assured, but it is not yet complete. Nonetheless, the second covenant is already present in that even now our sins are forgiven, which is the meaning given to Jeremiah 31. Hebrews cites a simplified version of the prophecy already noted in chapter 8 and expands on its significance: "Where there is forgiveness of these [sins and lawless deeds], there is no longer any offering for sin" (10:18).

So the covenant is established, Christ is enthroned, sins are forgiven, but his rule is not yet complete because all enemies are not yet subject to him. Until his rule is complete, we are called to "hold fast to the confession" (v. 23). Verses 19–25 provide a series of admonitions and encouragements delineating what it means to "hold fast." This section begins with that important inferential particle: "therefore." Here we find another instance where doctrine connects with its use. Given who Christ is and what he has done, we are admonished to hold fast to the theological virtues he makes possible—faith, hope, and charity. First Christ's work gives us "confidence" or *parrēsia*. We already saw this term in the first series of admonitions raised in chapter 3, which stated that we would be Christ's house (3:6). As noted earlier, the term *parrēsia* means the boldness of speech that a citizen would use in public. Once again Hebrews connects theology and ethics by insisting that Christ accomplished this kind of confidence and boldness for those who follow him. He reminds us again that Christ is the priest "over the house of God," and then offers three specific admonitions in the form of "let us. . . ." The three build on one another, bringing together nearly all the developed theological themes.

10:22 ***"Let us approach with a true heart in full assurance of faith, with our hearts sprinkled clean from an evil conscience and our bodies washed with pure water"***

This first admonition builds on the cultic imagery of 10:19–21. The admonition is to "approach" the true sanctuary. We can do this in faith, which is possible because we have a faithful and merciful high priest. His work makes our "approach" possible. It cleanses body and soul. We do not know if the latter is a reference to baptism or some specific cultic ritual practiced at that time. We do know this is the meaning the later tradition gives to this passage.

Aquinas sees in these admonitions three sets of concerns focused on "faith, hope, and love." Because the first concerns "faith," it naturally appeals to the "sacrament of faith"—"baptism." He notes Hebrews' allusion to "sprinkling" in the story of the red cow in Numbers 19: "By the sprinkling of the water of the red cow on the third day, the Passion of Christ was prefigured, for with faith in the Trinity we are cleansed from our sins in baptism."[78] If we limit meaning to the historical-critical method, then Aquinas's interpretation makes little sense. The doctrine of the Trinity has not yet been formulated, nor have those preparing for baptism been asked to give it back through the creed. All of this comes much later. Aquinas most certainly knew this as well. But he finds warrant for a retrospective

78. Aquinas, *Hebrews*, 212.

reading of Hebrews through its assertion of "fullness" of faith. It refers to both the "matter of faith" and its "form." Faith's matter is "all things proposed for belief," or its content, which are more clearly stated at a later date than that of the time of the biblical writing. For Aquinas these are specific teachings that must be affirmed, especially teachings about the heart of the mystery such as the Trinity. This is necessary but insufficient, for faith also has a "form." Faith must be "informed, which is by charity."[79] Right doctrine without charity is content without form. Charity without right doctrine would be form without content.

Aquinas's interpretation makes sense only if we allow that the matter of the fullness of faith gains expression over time. What gets established at Nicaea or Chalcedon is already present in form when Christians worship Jesus and also pray, "Hear, O Israel, the Lord our God is one." Hebrews admonishes us to worship Jesus (1:6). To confess with true hearts the fullness of the faith that makes our worship of Christ possible requires specific content such as the doctrines of the Trinity and incarnation. Hebrews *at the least* provides the seeds for those teachings. But faith always requires the other two theological virtues as well—hope and love. Hope orders faith toward its proper end. Hebrews' second admonition clarifies this.

Here we find another significant disagreement among Christian traditions as to how we understand faith and its relation to the other two virtues. Luther lectured on Hebrews between 1517 and 1518. As Kenneth Hagen notes, these lectures diverge from previous medieval exegesis, especially from Aquinas and his interpretation of faith. This will be more fully explored when we discuss Hebrews 11:1—"faith is the *hypostasis* [substance or assurance or possession] of things hoped for." For most medieval exegetes from Chrysostom to Aquinas, faith was understood as "substance." It was a foundation upon which the believer built through specific works of hope and charity. Hebrews 10:19–25 was read with that assumption. This was the basis for faith's "form" or the *fides formata*. Luther rejected this understanding of faith in favor of "faith as possession": "Therefore, since faith is nothing other than adherence to the Word of God, as

79. Ibid.

in Rom. 1, it follows that faith is at the same time the possession of the Word of God—of eternal goods—and the removal of all present goods, at least as far as one's devotion and adherence to them goes."[80] Faith is not a foundation that is formed by charity. It is a "possession." Hagen notes the difference: "In stark contrast then to medieval exegetes who define faith as the beginning of a process of adding love and hope to faith, faith as 'possession' means for Luther that salvation is complete and full to one who has faith."[81] This implies a distinct difference from Aquinas on the content of faith. Faith is less affirmation and assent to material teachings of the church and more an existential trust in God's promises.

These lectures represent the early Luther. In his 1517 preface to Hebrews he wrote, "We should note that Paul in this epistle exalts grace and contrasts it with the arrogance of legal and human righteousness. He shows that without Christ, neither the law nor the priesthood nor prophecy nor even finally the ministry of angels was sufficient for salvation." Eventually he will change his mind about Hebrews, setting it along with James, Jude, and Revelation as doubtful in canonicity.[82] Hebrews is doubtful because it teaches that there is no repentance after baptism. (Recall that Aquinas denied that it taught that, so here they would agree on theological content.) Luther also comes to question Pauline authorship. In his 1522 preface, after listing the twenty-three books he found canonical, he wrote, "Up to this point we have had [to do with] the true and certain chief books of the New Testament. The four which follow have from ancient times had a different reputation." Luther claims that Hebrews' different reputation arises because Paul's authorship was contested. Since Origen, Paul's authorship was contested without that being a convincing argument against its canonicity. For Luther canonicity was not based on apostolic witness anyway. It had to do with whether a book urged people toward Christ. Luther also had little place for interpreting Holy Scripture through the virtues: "It is a fact that all

80. Cited in Kenneth Hagen, *A Theology of Testament in the Young Luther: The Lectures on Hebrews* (Leiden: Brill, 1974), 86.

81. Ibid., 81.

82. Bruce Metzger, *The Canon of the New Testament* (Oxford: Clarendon Press, 1989), 243

the virtues of the philosophers, indeed of all men be they jurists or theologians, are virtues in appearance only, but vices in reality."[83]

10:23 ***"Let us hold fast to the confession of our hope without wavering, for he who has promised is faithful"***

So how should we read the references to faith, hope, and love in the important admonitory material of Hebrews 10:19–25? Should we with Luther be suspicious to read it as promoting virtue, even if infused through the Holy Spirit as the theological virtues of faith, hope, and love are?[84] Should we read them as temptations to vice, to trusting in our own merits rather than the promise of the Word that comes to us as an eternal possession searing all other temporal possessions? After first admonishing and encouraging us to approach the holy of holies through the blood of Christ "in full assurance of faith," Hebrews then adds that we "hold fast" to "hope." Faith comes first, but neither Aquinas nor Luther would disagree with that. Nor would they differ, I think, over this second admonition. The hope to which we unwaveringly cling is the Faithful One who promises. This would seem to side with Luther's early exegesis. What matters most is that the one who promises is faithful, and his faithfulness becomes our "possession." But then comes the third admonition:

10:24 ***"And let us consider how to provoke one another to love and good deeds, not neglecting to meet together, as is the habit of some, but encouraging one another, and all the more as you see the Day approaching"***

Luther's heading for this section omits the three words "and good deeds" (*kai kalōn ergōn*) and has only: "Let us consider how to provoke each other in charity."[85] He does not mention "good works" in his brief comments on this passage, but interprets it as a call to love even those who are "weak, impotent, imperfect, and sinful," for they have been "intermingled" in the church with others. This is at the

83. Hagen, *Theology of Testament*, 101.

84. They could not be acquired because they are forms of participation in Christ's own life.

85. *Consideremus invicem in provocationem charitatis*, in *D. Martin Luthers Werke: Kritische Gesamtausgabe* 57 (Weimar: Herman Böhlaus Nachfolger, 1939), 224. It is unclear if Luther or some editor provided this title. If it was an editor, however, he rightly understood Luther made no mention of the "and good deeds" anywhere in his lecture.

same time a call to those who consider themselves the opposite of this not to become "haughty," to "despise," and "to judge" others. For Luther, the call to "mutual love" is a call to avoid these divisions, which will culminate in schism and heresy. Instead we should love as Christ loves us: "This, therefore, is the Christian love that is shown to those who are contemptible and unworthy of love; this, in fact, is the kindness that is bestowed on those who are evil and ungrateful. For this is what Christ and God did for us; and we, too, are commanded to love as He did."[86]

Aquinas had a somewhat different reading of this passage. The "provocation" of love is to move our neighbor to good works through "emulation." He cites Paul in Romans 11:13–14, where he also seeks to "provoke to emulation" his fellow Jews. Aquinas then states, "This provocation proceeds from love, which is extended to exterior works." Aquinas will call these works the "fruit" of love, but he also seems to suggest that a jealous provocation that produces the "emulation" of works is something good; it even has a kind of merit. This would certainly be more "putting on" virtue than its infusion. I think Luther would find this "vice."

Jennifer Herdt offers an excellent account of "putting on virtue" in the Christian tradition, especially up until the Reformation. Virtue has a performative and theatrical character that involves emulation. We "assimilate" to that which we imitate. This is not hypocrisy, but a key component in human action. She notes the important role of the theater among some Jesuit theologians and how it sought, as Aquinas noted above, to provoke to the emulation of virtue. "Virtue is performative insofar as it is acquired through acting virtuously. It is also theatrical: persons are moved by observing virtue in action and thus inspired to emulate that virtue."[87] In other words, movement exists from the external emulation to an internal transformation. John Wesley recognized this point when he consented to Peter Bohler's admonition, "Preach faith until you have it, then, because you have it, you will preach faith."[88]

86. Martin Luther, *Lectures on Titus, Philemon, and Hebrews,* trans. Walter A. Hansen, ed. Jaroslav Pelikan, LW 29 (Saint Louis: Concordia Publishing House, 1968), 227.

87. Jennifer Herdt, *Putting on Virtue* (Chicago: University of Chicago Press, 2008), 175.

88. John Wesley, *Journal,* 4 Mar 1738, ed. Reginald Ward, "Works of John Wesley" vol. 23 (Nashville: Abingdon, 1988).

We often "put on" the virtues when they are not yet ours. Such striving for them was seldom viewed as inappropriate in Christian tradition. Hebrews advocates it, as do Paul and Aquinas. Luther, however, found it objectionable. Herdt notes, "For Luther . . . there is no route from 'external' practices to fundamental inner transformation." Grace opposes our natural power so thoroughly that our only hope for "growth in righteousness" is "a perfect recognition and acknowledgment of the bankruptcy of human agency."[89] She sees in both Luther and Calvin's theology a "shared instability" that requires a "relentless self-scrutiny so paralyzing that it could be expressed only through performative self-contradiction."[90] This allows for little progress in faith. Our attitude toward it is at best passive and receptive with little or no role for human agency. Neither Luther nor Calvin interpreted Hebrews 10 as did Aquinas, who concludes his commentary on this section by explicitly affirming a *natural* "progress in faith." For him, this is the significance behind the final statement, "and all the more as you see the Day approaching." What does it mean to say "all the more"? Aquinas writes. "For someone could say: Why do we have to progress in faith? Because the more a natural movement approaches its end, the stronger it becomes. The contrary is true in violent motion. Now, grace inclines in the manner of nature; therefore, for those who are in grace, the more they approach their end, the more they ought to grow in it."[91] The end, the Day of the Lord, attracts those who are graced like a magnet. The closer it gets, the stronger the attraction. The stronger the attraction, the more they "grow" in grace.

These verses certainly do not resolve the debate between Lutherans and others on the question of faith and works. However, the official spokespersons for the Catholics and the Lutheran World Federation did resolve this long-standing debate on October 31, 1999, when together they issued "The Joint Declaration on the Doctrine of Justification by the Lutheran World Federation and the Catholic Church." They both agreed with Luther that only Christ's saving word redeems us.

89. Herdt, *Putting on Virtue*, 174.
90. Ibid., 198.
91. Aquinas, *Hebrews*, 214.

For Hebrews, faith in Christ's work alone saves. It is that to which we hold fast. But this faith calls us "to good works," the chief of which is love. Lutherans recognize this is essential to their own tradition. Aquinas referred to these works as "fruit" as well; it is a biblical image, found in the horticultural metaphors in Hebrews (6:7–8). Catholics tried to assuage Lutherans that their emphasis on "work" was never intended to replace Jesus' meritorious work as that which brings our salvation. The "Joint Declaration" resolved one of the long-standing sources of division between Protestants and Catholics. Unfortunately, that seems to have made little difference to church unity. We still cannot "meet together" in the fullness of communion as Hebrews admonishes believers to do. "Mutual love" remains elusive. Can we hear Hebrews' message without it?

Together we confess: By grace alone, in faith in Christ's saving work and not because of any merit on our part, we are accepted by God and receive the Holy Spirit, who renews our hearts while equipping and calling us to good works.

We confess together that good works—a Christian life lived in faith, hope and love—follow justification and are its fruits.

When Catholics affirm the "meritorious" character of good works, they wish to say that, according to the biblical witness, a reward in heaven is promised to these works. Their intention is to emphasize the responsibility of persons for their actions, not to contest the character of those works as gifts, or far less to deny that justification always remains the unmerited gift of grace.

—"Joint Declaration" of Lutherans and Catholics, §§15, 37, 38

Reminiscent of the harsh judgment in 6:4, 10:26–32 returns to the theme of sin after receiving the truth of Christ. In that earlier judgment the author stated that no repentance was available to those who sinned after tasting God's goodness. Here he makes a similar claim—"there no longer remains a sacrifice for sins" to those who sin after they "received the knowledge of the truth." These passages are the primary reason Luther and others questioned the canonicity of Hebrews. It seemed to give shelter to heresies like Montanism that perhaps denied repentance after baptism and certainly was more rigorist in church discipline than the orthodox. This posed problems for the Christian tradition's reception of Hebrews. The common means of interpreting this text are found in Chrysostom. Luther cites him in his early lectures as the best defense he could provide for this passage. From Luther's comments we can see why this would pose a greater problem for Luther as his movement of protest unfolded: "Chrysostom says in opposition to the Novatians: 'Here those who take away repentance rise up again. . . . To them we shall say that here he excludes neither repentance nor the propitiation which comes about through repentance. . . . But he does exclude a second Baptism. For he did not say: "There is no further remission," but he says that "there is no further sacrifice," that is, there is no second cross.'" Luther then adds, "And this refutation of his can be strengthened from the preceding text, where the apostle spoke of 'not forsaking our assembly, etc.' Here he seems to be speaking about those who forsake the church, outside which there certainly is no repentance or remission."[92] Luther reads the earlier admonition to "meet together" as a refusal of church unity; it places one outside the church, and outside the church there is no repentance. It is a place to which he did not seek to go, but was forced to do so. It is a place Protestants should never accept. When we do, our tradition of "protest" becomes a tradition in itself and degenerates into unintelligibility.[93] We make sense only in so far as we are called to continue unsettling Catholicism for the sake of unity. We live from the fullness of an eschatological unity that we are called to embody "today."

For Hebrews, to "willfully persist in sin" after receiving "the knowledge of the truth" brings only "judgment." The emphasis here is not only on faith, hope, and love; it is also on "truth." But exactly what is "the knowledge of the truth"? Hebrews does not explicitly tell us. The author did refer to the truth in 9:24, and this points us in the right direction. Christ did not enter into a "copy of the true" tent, but into the true holy place itself. The "chief point" since 8:1 has been the contrast between a copy and the true. Human hands made the copy, but God commanded and directed those human hands to build sketches of the Eternal. The Eternal dwelt in those sketches until Christ's work. The contrast between Moses and Jesus

92. Luther, *Hebrews*, 227.

93. For a good discussion of this see Gerald W. Schlabach, *Unlearning Protestantism: Sustaining Christian Community in an Unstable Age* (Grand Rapids: Brazos, 2010).

repeats in 10:28–31, a contrast differentiating the sketch, shadow, or copy from the true. The former had its own covenant, and it too was not to be violated, especially by worshiping other gods. Moses' proposed penalty was harsh: "you shall bring out to your gates that man or that woman who has committed this crime and you shall stone the man or woman to death. On the evidence of two or three witnesses the death sentence shall be executed; a person must not be put to death on the evidence of only one witness" (Deut. 17:5–6). If violation of the sketch of the true covenant brought such a horrifying judgment, how much more will a violation of "the knowledge of the truth." The contrast here helps us understand what the truth is: the blood of the covenant the Son of God offers and to which the Spirit of grace "testifies" in order to bring perfection and sanctification. This had repeatedly been established in this main section and now the consequences of falling away from the new covenant are brought before the sermon's hearers. Hebrews desires nothing less for them than that they share in perfection and sanctification. They are not promised wealth; Hebrews is as far from any "prosperity gospel" as one can possibly get. They are not promised improved self-esteem. They are not promised that Jesus will make everything all right in their lives. They are promised sanctification, perfection, and rest. But this comes from a frightening encounter: "It is a fearful thing to fall into the hands of the living God" (10:31).

The frightening image of a "fury of fire" (10:27), which is a reference to the searing grace of God's glory and presence throughout Holy Scripture, gives way to a more consoling image of enlightenment (10:32). Both use the metaphor of light, but to different ends. Having taken us into the place only the high priest dared to go, the place of God's judgment in the holy of holies (9:19), Hebrews poses two possibilities: we can hold fast or we can shrink away. We can be bold and confident (*parrēsia,* 10:35) or we can be timid (*hypostolē,* 10:39). Either way we find ourselves falling into the hands of the living God. The former entails approaching in faith, holding fast to hope, and inciting one another to charity and being illumined. The latter turns away in retreat, fearful, lacking faith, hope, or charity, and being consumed by a fury of fire. After setting up this juxtaposition, Hebrews reminds his hearers who they are. He expresses utter confidence in them because of the works he witnessed. They did not fall into the hands of the living God only to find the judgment of a fury of fire, but to have that blinding light bring illumination. What was the result? Here we are given some historical insight into what this community faced.

What Hebrews listeners already encountered:

- **Enduring many contests (*athlēsin*) or struggles of suffering**
- **Being made a public spectacle (*theatrizomenoi*) in insults and persecution**
- **Or having become sharers or partners (*koinōnoi*) with those who were made such a spectacle**
- **Being compassionate toward those imprisoned**
- **Accepting the plundering of their property with joy**

Whatever precisely these Christians faced, and we will most likely never know exactly, it could not have been good. Who would blame them for grumbling, wanting to shrink away and neglect the boldness Hebrews encourages? Nonetheless, the author of Hebrews does not stop to understand their situation and express sympathy. Instead he reminds them of their previous boldness in order to encourage them to endure until Christ returns. The purpose is to "receive what was promised," and he reminds them of God's word to the prophet Habakkuk, which is now God's word to them: "my righteous one will live by faith. My soul takes no pleasure in anyone who shrinks back" (10:38). The contrast between proceeding in faith or shrinking back in fear captures well the choice before them; it is the choice between having God's searing glory illumine one's being or looking away and finding it the source of judgment. The author repeatedly asks his listeners: will you have the boldness, the *parrēsia*, faith brings, or will you remain enslaved to the fear of death and the devil? (2:14–15). But the question is only asked in light of what Christ has accomplished. This is why faith matters so much. If the power of death and the devil have not been defeated, boldness would be mere bravado. But because they have been defeated, because we have a merciful and faithful high priest who purifies and perfects, faith has a "substance" that makes such boldness something more. Hebrews then offers these consoling and transitional words: "we are not among those who shrink back and so are lost, but among those who have faith and so are saved" (10:39).

11:1–12:13

Finding Yourself among the Saved: Faith and Endurance

Because Hebrews' audience consists of "those who have faith," they will not "shrink back" but endure. The closing words of chapter 10 lead into the next two sections: the litany of faithful witnesses (11:1–40) and a call to endurance (12:1–13). Endurance flows from faithfulness. Witness demonstrates faith's substantial reality. As Luke Timothy Johnson puts it, "Since faith defines a life based on what is not seen rather than what is seen, it thereby also becomes a 'proof'—in the very lives of the humans who live by it—of the reality of the unseen."[1] This proof is apocalyptic. It is based on the vision faith brings that gives hope that life will be other than what it is, which requires at the same time dissatisfaction with life as it is. If faith endures in the face of contests, struggles, insults, persecution, imprisonment, and loss of property, then the reality of that for which such loss must be surrendered is first established, which Hebrews does in a powerful litany of the faithful in 11:1–40 that culminates in the "pioneer and perfecter" of our faith to whom all the litany of the faithful are witnesses, Jesus (12:1–2). Only then can the admonition to endure in 12:1–11 be heard as something reasonable rather than masochistic.

1. Johnson, *Hebrews*, 280.

11:1–12:2

Faith: The Substance of Hope

The concluding admonition to the "main point" was a call to persevere in faith. We were told in 10:22 to "approach" the sanctuary or holy of holies "in full assurance of faith." This emphasis on faith was repeated in 10:39. That we are the ones who have faith marks something of a turn. To this point in Hebrews, "faith" is primarily an attribute of Jesus or a description of his performance in obedience to God. It notes his faithfulness. The first time we encountered the term *pistos*, "faith(ful)," it was Christ's (2:17). In one of the very first admonitions, we were told to "consider that Jesus . . . was faithful to the one who appointed him" (3:1–2). Until 10:22, Hebrews primarily explains the faithfulness of Jesus and why it offers a better sacrifice than that of the Levitical priesthood. His faithful obedience gains entrance into the holy of holies. The emphasis was never on our faith, but on Christ's. This does not imply that our faith is irrelevant, nor has it been neglected. We were given a preview of its significance in 6:12 when we were told to be "imitators of those who through faith and patience inherit the promises." But this was just a preview of chapter 11. Our author did not yet take the time to set before us what our "faith" and "patience" look like. He first established who Christ is as a faithful and merciful high priest (2:17). But now it is established, and in chapters 11 and 12 the emphasis shifts from Christ's faithfulness to ours, but always with attention to his. As 12:2 reminds us, only Jesus "pioneers" and "perfects" our faith. Our exercise of faith is only possible as we enter the sanctuary through his flesh. In chapter 11 Hebrews shows us what faith is for us, what it pioneers.

Faith is a fullness related to "perfection." In 8:1–9:28 the author depicted Jesus as a priest who saves through purification and perfection. Purification is a cleansing, a removal of something that does not belong, whereas perfection is a fulfilling, a completion of something that should be. Hebrews sees Christ as effecting both simultaneously. Christ is made perfect through his obedient suffering, and by this he is the cause of perfecting believers. Hebrews 12:2 develops this theme more fully. We proceed by "looking to Jesus the pioneer and perfecter of our faith." Here again we find familiar words. Jesus is "pioneer" (*archēgon*) and "perfecter" (*teleiōtēn*). His faith leads the way, making the new way, bringing our faith to the fullness of completion necessary to endure. This is the background to make sense of the "definition" of faith in 11:1: "Faith is a *hypostasis* of things hoped for, a conviction of things not seen," the third use of that difficult term *hypostasis*.

Ancient, medieval, and contemporary exegetes argue over this term and its relation to faith. It is primarily interpreted as "foundation," "substance," "confidence," or "possession." Luther interpreted it as "possession." Most patristic and medieval exegetes understood it as a "foundation," to which was added "hope and charity." Luther did not. Attridge divides interpretations between the subjective and objective. The latter he finds in "architectural images" such as "foundation." It also connotes a "title deed" or "guarantee." The term may also have an ethical meaning through a "subtle wordplay" between "shrinking back" (*hypostolēs*) and faith as a *hypostasis*. Faith is the courage to move forward rather than retreat in cowardice. Attridge also interprets it in a more ontological sense as the "reality" of things hoped for.[2] He finds Erasmus and Luther interpreting it as the "subjective, psychological sense of 'assurance' or 'confidence.'"[3] But that does not bring out adequately Luther's interpretation as "possession." Which is the correct meaning? There is no such thing. Luke Timothy Johnson acknowledges "the possible meanings of *hypostasis* make precise interpretation difficult."[4]

Ancient exegetes seem less interested in giving precise definitions to terms like *hypostasis* than their medieval and modern counterparts. This is not to say that they overlooked the significance of the term *hypostasis*. Augustine, like Luther, interprets it as wealth or possession and relates it to hope: "When you hope, you do not yet have what you are hoping for, but, by believing it, you resemble someone who does possess it."[5] Faith renders hope substantial. Chrysostom offers a similar interpretation. Faith is the "substance" of "hope,"

2. Attridge, *Hebrews*, 308–9.
3. Ibid., 308.
4. Johnson, *Hebrews*, 276–77.
5. Cited in Heen and Krey, eds., *Hebrews*, 174.

which is unsubstantial.[6] Hope is what we do not yet possess. Faith is the present, substantial possession of that which we do not yet have in full.

Many ancient exegetes interpret 11:1 through other important theological themes in Hebrews. For instance, the Syrian bishop Theodoret (393–457) interpreted this verse through what Hebrews teaches about resurrection. "Faith depicts for us in advance the resurrection of those still lying dead in their tombs and causes the immortality of the dust of our bodies to become evident."[7] He expresses less concern about a formal definition, and more the narrative content in the sermon that fills out the "substance" of hope. This makes good sense in that we are told throughout chapter 11 that all the faithful who exemplify the *hypostasis* died without receiving the promise, but they died in hope largely because of resurrection. The meaning of faith as a *hypostasis* is best discovered by its use in the context of the litany of the faithful and the apocalyptic vision that functions as an interlude in the middle of that litany (11:13–16). The theme of resurrection from death runs through nearly all the characters mentioned, explicitly and implicitly in Hebrews 11. These references demonstrate how decisive the resurrection is for Hebrews' argument. Abel still speaks even though Cain killed him. Enoch never tasted death but still lives. From Abraham and Sarah, even though they are "as good as dead," the promise is fulfilled. Abraham was willing to offer Isaac as a sacrifice because "God is able even to raise someone from the dead." Examples continue until we are told that some women "received their dead by resurrection." Others found no resurrection but were willing to be tortured "in order to obtain a better resurrection." Theodoret wisely sees the substance of faith in the context of the promised resurrection. This finds fulfillment in 12:1–3, which once again admonishes Hebrews' listeners to "look" to Jesus, to *see* him. He is the substance of "faith" because he "endured the cross," was raised, and now "has taken his seat at the right hand of the throne of God" (12:2). That all-important theme already noted in 1:3 and in the "main point" at 8:1 returns.

6. Chrysostom, "Homily 21," http://www.newadvent.org/fathers/240221.htm.
7. Cited in Heen and Krey, eds., *Hebrews,* 172.

Pope Leo the Great (400–461) interprets faith in terms of the broader theme of the relation between the two testaments in Hebrews. Faith is the fulfillment of the figures that "came first so that their fulfillment could follow."[8] All the figures are a type of Christ, who is their fulfillment. Christ, then, would be the substance of faith. Cyril of Jerusalem (313–386) interprets it through the doctrine of creation noted in 11:3, where we are told that what is seen was made from what is not seen. For him all of life requires faith; it is intrinsic in all good activities: "all things that are accomplished in the world, even by those who are strangers to the church, are accomplished by faith." He offers farming as an example. "By faith, farmers are also sustained for the one who does not believe that he shall receive a harvest is not going to endure the work."[9] In a similar vein Rufinus (345–411) defends Christianity against the charge of fideism not by denying the important role of faith but by acknowledging all reason assumes an element of it: "the pagans are wont to object to us that our religion, because it lacks reasons, rests solely on belief. We have shown, therefore, that nothing can possibly be done or remain stable unless it is preceded by belief." He gives examples of bearing children and teaching. We enter into those activities without knowing for certain their outcome. Faith is then necessary to do them well.[10] Faith seeks reason, but reason presumes faith.

Medieval, Reformation, and modern exegetes did not always preserve the rich theological context within which faith as *hypostasis* was used. They seem more concerned with precise definition. Aquinas interprets it in two ways. It means "substance" and "essence." "Sub-stance" literally means "to stand under." It is "making the things hoped for to stand under us," which is accomplished in two ways. The first is through "meriting." We do not actually see what we hope for but through faith we merit it by acting as if we possessed it when we do not. The second is through possession: "as it were by its own property, faith may bring it about that that which is believed to come in the future in reality is in some way already possessed." Here we see an interpretation similar to Luther's. Faith as "essence" is the fullness

8. Ibid.
9. Ibid., 174.
10. Ibid., 180.

of the thing hoped for, which is the vision of God. Aquinas writes, "Therefore, the full vision of God is itself the essence of beatitude." This essence is contained in the "articles of faith" that we receive. Aquinas then offers a definition of faith. It is "the habit of mind by which eternal life is begun in us making the intellect to assent to things which are not apparent."[11] He relates this to Christ's two natures. Faith is found in the example of Thomas, who saw Christ after the resurrection. What he saw was the humanity. What he believed was the divinity.[12]

Luther examines three interpretations of the word "substance." It can be "cause" or "foundation"; he disagrees that this definition defines faith adequately. He also rejects connecting the "*substance* of things hoped for" with the "*conviction* of things not seen" when the latter is understood as "argument" that supposedly "proves" the existence of invisible things. Interestingly, Luther sees this as a kind of fideism: "For this way faith would be nothing else than one person's credulity that has been established and proved by means of the credulity of another person; and thus the apostle would be speaking, not about the faith of all but only about a persuasion, and the proof would be passive, not active."[13] For Luther, the litany of the faithful is not a "demonstration" that in any sense proves faith. His more "active" sense of faith interprets substance as "possessions." He finds Hebrews comparing the "substance" (*hypostasis*) of 11:1 with the "substance" (*hyparchontōn*) of 10:34. The latter term, which is usually translated "possession," has the sense of the "substance" of everyday life—the material possessions that constitute it. Hebrews' listeners were once willing to have such goods plundered, but now they are tempted to cling to them. Luther sees chapter 11 as reminding them of a different kind of possession. The point is to "divest them of their affection for temporal things and transfer them to heavenly things." Faith is a possession, but it is "of the Word of God, that is, of the everlasting goods."[14]

Both Luther and Aquinas find in 11:1 a "definition" of faith. Aquinas states, "it is evident that the Apostle completely defines faith,

11. Aquinas, *Hebrews,* 229–30.
12. Ibid., 231.
13. Luther, *Hebrews,* 229.
14. Ibid., 230–31.

albeit obscurely."[15] Luther's lectures on Hebrews appear to agree with him in that he engages the various definitions put forward by medieval exegetes (although we have no evidence Luther read Aquinas's commentary). Not every theologian agrees. Calvin rejects the idea that it gives us a definition at all. For him 11:1 should not be read as beginning a new section in Hebrews' argument. The chapter-and-verse divisions mislead us into seeing it as a definition. Instead, it is the conclusion to a syllogism that began with the "testimony of Habakkuk" in 10:37–38. Therefore 11:1 is limited in its scope. It does not tell us much about faith, but only the minor point that faith requires patience. The major proposition of the syllogism is "the righteous shall live by faith." The minor proposition is "faith is the substance of things hoped for."[16] The conclusion is that faith entails patience. This is not, then, contra the vast majority of Christian tradition, a definition of faith. We should not look to Hebrews 11 for a theological treatise on faith, but only as a specific, contextualized argument employed by its author to encourage patience.

It is clear from this that those who think that an exact definition of faith is being given here are greatly mistaken. The apostle is not discussing the nature of faith as a whole but he selects that part which fits his purpose, namely that it is always joined to patience.

—John Calvin

Hebrews, 157.

Calvin, in opposition to Christian tradition, downplays Hebrews 11 as a treatise on faith, but rightly connects it to the prophecy from Habakkuk 2:3–4 in Hebrews 10:38. Much as we should not "interpret" faith as *hypostasis* without seeing it in the context of the litany of the faithful and the apocalyptic vision that follows, so we should not overlook the importance of Hebrews' earlier reference to Habakkuk.

Habakkuk 2:4 was central for the church fathers, other biblical authors, and especially Paul for understanding faith. As Richard Hays argues, Paul interpreted it as "unmistakably messianic."[17] The "coming one" refers to the Messiah. A similar argument for Hebrews'

15. Aquinas, *Hebrews*, 231.
16. Calvin, *Hebrews*, 157.
17. Richard Hays, *The Faith of Jesus Christ: The Narrative Substructure of Galatians 3:1–4:11*, 2nd ed. (Grand Rapids: Eerdmans, 2002), 135.

use of it should be uncontroversial. Like Paul, it clearly understands faith in terms of a "representative Christology." Hays explains this by relating Paul's teaching to Ephesians 3:11–12 and Hebrews 12:2. "Christ is here, as in Hebrews, portrayed as the *archēgos,* the representative figure in whom the drama of salvation is enacted, in whose destiny the destiny of all is carried."[18] Christ then is less the object of our faith than its subject. His faithfulness makes possible our entrance into God's presence. Hays relates Paul's teaching in Galatians to Hebrews repeatedly: "Our investigation has identified as the basis for Paul's argumentation a Christ-story which bears significant affinities to certain christological statements in Hebrews: Jesus Christ is the archetypical (or prototypical) hero (*archēgos*) who, through faithfulness unto death on the cross, wins deliverance and access to God for his people."[19] Hebrews' litany of the faithful is intentionally sandwiched between Habakkuk 2:3–4 as a statement about the "coming one" (Messiah) who lives by faithfulness, and the culmination of faithfulness in Christ in 12:1–3. The flow of the litany is interrupted, however, by the very important claim in 11:6 that "without faith" God cannot be rightly known or approached. The interruption of "by faith" with this discordant "without faith" requires some theological reflection to see well the important relations between faith and knowledge of God.

11:6 *That God Is*

Calvin is correct to bring our attention back to Habakkuk, even though he downplays Hebrews 11 as a treatise on faith. The traditional understanding of faith divided it into three parts. First was to believe "that God is," which in Latin is *credere Deum*. Second was that God rewards those who seek him, *credere Deo*. Third is to believe in, or into, God, *credere in Deum*. All three aspects are necessary for faith, and are found at least implicitly in Hebrews, but how they are interpreted remains contested. The status of the first aspect, "that God is," could be a statement about the divine name, God is the One Who Is, so that Hebrews 11:6 could be a reference to Exodus 3:14. This is

18. Ibid., 151.
19. Ibid., 217.

Aquinas's argument. It could also be statement about a more generic theism; faith first requires one to be convinced that a God exists. Aquinas's argument assumes God's existence is primarily a matter of faith. The second position, which has been the official position of the Roman Catholic Church since the Counter-Reformation, assumes reason alone can account for God's existence. Hebrews clearly teaches "that God is" must be affirmed through faith—"for whoever would approach him must believe that he exists." Whatever is meant by this interesting expression, "that he exists," it alone is insufficient for faith. One must also believe what God has said, that God will reward those who seek him—"and that he rewards those who seek him" (11:6). Although both these aspects of faith were necessary, a third was still important. This third aspect not only believes that God is, and what God says, but also requires that persons will their lives over to God, that they believe *into* God. The litany of the saints in chapter 11 depicts this aspect of faith.

Catholics and Protestants, often drawing on Hebrews 11:6, largely agreed that there were three aspects of faith. The Lutheran theologian Heinrich Schmid (1811–1885) affirmed a version of them. He did not make explicit the first aspect, the need to believe "that God is," but it is assumed in his threefold account.

Faith, considered with reference to its individual elements, consists accordingly of —

1. ***Knowledge, and that explicit*, of things to be believed, especially concerning Christ and His merit, concerning the grace of God, or the remission of sins, and concerning the salvation to be obtained thereby from God.**
2. ***Assent, i.e.*, an approving judgment of the intellect, by which we believe that those things which the Scriptures say concerning Christ and His merit and atonement for our sins, and concerning the grace of God and the promises of the free forgiveness of our sins for Christ's sake, are certainly and indubitably true, and by which we absolutely acquiesce in them.**
3. ***Confidence*, an act by which the will rests in Christ, the Mediator, both as our present good and as the cause of another good, namely, the remission of sins and the attainment of eternal life.**

—Heinrich Schmid

http://www.ccel.org/ccel/schmid/theology.vi.iii.iii.html

The division between the Catholics and Protestants was more which of these were to be emphasized. Was it the content of faith and assent to it as perhaps Catholics emphasized? Or was it the confident trust in the promises Protestants emphasized? Calvin sees a temptation here in that faith is first turned into a definition; it is given a nature. Then it is turned into a work and our confidence is in our own "merits" to trust in a definition. He speaks of those who "falsely pervert this clause [Heb. 11:6] and induce from it the merits of work and trust in what they deserve. They reason this way: if we please God by faith because we believe Him to be the Rewarder it follows that faith has regard to the merit of work."[20] This will not do because it takes away the sole source of grace, who is Christ. Only those bewitched could think this about faith. "No one will have confidence that God will be the Rewarder of his merits unless he is blinded by pride and bewitched by depraved self-love." Rather than trusting in our own merits, Calvin states, "This trust that we speak of lies therefore not in works, nor in man's own worthiness, but in the favour of God alone. Since the grace of God is found only in Christ He is the one to whom faith should have regard."[21] I do not know if this is the reason Calvin objected to the more common interpretation that found in 11:1 a definition and explication of the nature of faith, but for whatever reason he did not want us to take 11:1 and 6 as such.

Catholics maintain that faith has the three components of *credere Deum, credere Deo,* and *credere in Deum,* but to know that God is is not to be determined solely by faith. For many Catholics, this is the problem with Protestants. They have an irrational, fideistic faith. They lose the reason present in God's good creation that makes it *possible* to know "that God is" by reason alone. For some this is only a possibility, not something ever actualized. For others it is necessary, a rational proof for the existence of God that does not depend on faith, but is a condition for faith. Indeed, in 1910 Pius XI required all Catholic clergy to take an oath against what he perceived to be the modern rejection that a rational proof for God's

20. Calvin, *Hebrews,* 163.
21. Ibid., 164.

existence was possible. The irony of instituting a "confession" that required a willful submission to the proposition that God's existence was demonstrable solely by reason was not lost on many within and outside Catholicism. That confession was not rescinded until 1967 at Vatican II. Catholic theologians concerned that a sharp distinction between reason and faith had misled Catholic theology were largely responsible for undoing the antimodernist oath.

For Hebrews, "that God is" (*credere Deum*) is a matter of faith. Aquinas is often thought to have taught something different than this, and the Roman Catholic neoscholastic tradition has argued to this day "that God is" is known through a reason independent of faith. Faith and reason are two distinct orders of knowledge. That faith and reason lead us to the knowledge of God should be uncontroversial. What is controversial is whether the two distinct orders of knowledge we call "faith" and "reason" are autonomous and independent from each other, or whether they are related. That they are related would assume that faith always seeks understanding, and yet reason does not operate without some sense of faith. This is the position of the Fathers, Augustine, Anselm, and some versions of Thomism. Hebrews' knowledge of God with its beginning definition of what faith is followed by its exemplification in historical characters from Israel's history would suggest an intimate relation between them. Both Chrysostom and Augustine would agree with Hebrews that faith and reason are related. Indeed, they both used Hebrews 11 to argue for a necessary relation between them. Knowledge of God's existence is itself a matter of faith. To believe "that God is" was not a result of some pure reason; neither was it irrational. They refused any sharp distinction between faith and reason as if they worked in two separate realms, autonomous from each other.

Chrysostom interprets Hebrews 11 as follows: "It is necessary to *'believe that He is,'* not 'what He is.' If *'that He is'* needs faith, and not reasonings, it is impossible to comprehend by reasoning 'what He is.' If that *'He is a rewarder'* needs faith and not reasonings, how is it possible by reasoning to compass His essence? For what reasoning can reach this? For some persons say that the things that exist are self-caused. Do you see that unless we have faith in regard to all things, not only in regard to retribution, but also in regard to the very being of God, all is lost to us?"[22] Like many ancient exegetes Chrysostom sees "faith" as a necessary feature of "all things." Without it, reasoning itself gets lost. This has been the dominant tradition of Christian thought: faith seeks understanding.

Augustine received and perpetuated this dominant tradition. In his *Enchiridion* he answers a series of questions put to him by Laurentius about the relation between faith and reason as well as the true starting point and goal of religion. Augustine's answer is interesting in that he does not provide an argument per se for God's existence. The only God he expresses interest in is the triune God. His short answer to Laurentius is that this "God should be worshipped with faith, hope, and love." In these he will "know the answers to all these questions."[23] When Augustine explains why this is so, he attends carefully to Hebrews, which he says "is used by the enlightened defenders of the catholic rule of faith." Hebrews defines faith in relation to hope, and for this reason to the good, for we hope for that which is good. For Augustine this is inevitable; it is intrinsic to the practice of everyday life even among those who reject it.

Like Hebrews, he draws on Habakkuk 2:4 to make his argument.

And assuredly it was necessary at the very outset to remove this utter despair of reaching truth, which seems to be strengthened by the arguments of these [skeptic] philosophers. Now in their eyes every error is regarded as a sin, and they think that error can only be avoided by entirely suspending belief. For they say that the man who assents to what is uncertain falls into error; and they strive by the most acute, but most audacious arguments, to show that, even though a man's opinion should by chance be true, yet that there is no certainty of its truth, owing to the impossibility of distinguishing truth from falsehood. But with us, "the just shall live by faith." . . . And there are truths, whether we know them or not, which must be believed if we would attain to a happy life, that is, to eternal life. But I am not sure whether one ought to argue with men who not only do not know that there is an eternal life before them, but do not know whether they are living at the present moment; nay, say that they do not know what it is impossible they can be ignorant of. For it is impossible that any one should be ignorant that he is alive, seeing that if he be not alive it is impossible for him to be ignorant.

—Augustine

The Enchiridion on Faith, Hope and Love, 26–27.

22. Chrysostom, "Homily 22.5," http://www.newadvent.org/fathers/240222.htm.
23. Augustine, *The Enchiridion on Faith, Hope and Love* (1961; repr. Washington, DC: Regnery Gateway, 1987), 3–4.

Certain truths are necessary for our existence. If we do not expressly assent to them, we at least tacitly do so. Only philosophers get themselves in irrational binds by trying to find a level of certitude that requires they bracket out all faith and only assent to that which is indubitable. But in so doing they miss what is most obvious—their own existence.

Here we have two different approaches to knowledge. The first finds faith as reasonable, as a necessary beginning from which reason can then emerge. Without faith, without a first principle received as a gift that is the condition for the possibility of thought and not thereby possible to be the object of critical doubt, reasoning does not get going. The second way always finds this immature. It either seeks a reason void of all faith or privatizes faith to an arational realm. This is the illusion of a "pure reason," a reason that always begins in doubt rather than a basic trust. It can be found in expressions like "always keep an open mind," "doubt everything," or "question authority." It assumes that no one should ever make a commitment to a first principle that she or he would not be willing to call into question. The willingness to "suspend belief" and "doubt everything" is the only method for indubitable knowledge.

Are truth and goodness found by suspending belief via a pure reason? Or is the command to do so a policing that refuses to ask certain questions simply on the assumption that mature, educated persons should not ask such questions? Perhaps truth and goodness are best found by affirming faith, hope, and love. Aquinas, like Augustine, takes the latter path, especially in his interpretation of Hebrews 11:6. Aquinas acknowledges that some philosophers, without faith, knew some things about God, such that God is and that God is one. But this does not rise to the level of true knowledge of God because it "does not fall under faith." Hebrews tells us "that God is" must be known by faith or it is not properly known. Aquinas has an interesting biblical insight into 11:6. It is not an argument about the need for a mere theism, a claim that faith requires a rational conviction that there is a God. Instead, Hebrews is specifying which God; it is the "God Who Is." Aquinas writes, "Therefore he says, for he that cometh to God must believe that He is, which he says because of His eternity. Ex. 3:14 HE WHO IS, hath sent me."[24]

24. Aquinas, *Hebrews,* 237.

"That God Is" is the name given to us in the revelation to Moses. This is an intriguing interpretation of Hebrews 11:6. It means that Hebrews does not simply make a philosophical point—to have faith first requires acknowledging God's existence, some bare theism. Instead, Hebrews makes a profound theological claim. To have faith requires knowing the "God Who Is." Given the context within which Hebrews narrates faith, Aquinas's interpretation is convincing. God is the God of Abel, Enoch, Noah, Abraham, Sarah, Isaac, and Jacob. If we are to know "That God Is," then we will also need to know these characters; for the "God Who Is" is the God of their history.

FURTHER REFLECTIONS
Faith, Reason, and "That God Is"

One of the more interesting controversies before the church today is how we arrive at the knowledge "that God is." The official Roman Catholic position affirms a twofold order of knowledge in which either order allows us to arrive at the truth that God is. Vatican I stated this in 1870 in its decree *Dei Filius*.

> **The perpetual agreement of the catholic church has maintained and *maintains* this too: that there is a twofold order of knowledge, distinct not only as regards its source, but also as regards its object. With regard to the source, we know at the one level by natural reason, at the other level by divine faith. With regard to the object, besides those things to which natural reason can attain, there are proposed for our belief mysteries hidden in God which, unless they are divinely revealed, are incapable of being known.**
>
> —***Dei Filius*, Vatican I**

What this natural reason accomplishes continues to foster debate. For some, it does not mean that we have any specific rational proof available to all right-thinking persons demonstrating God's existence with certainty, but that such is possible. For others, this is exactly what it means. The council suggested the latter, making the bold claim: "that God, the beginning and end of all things, may be known for certain by the natural light of human reason, by means of created things." "That God is" can be known with certainty by unaided human reason. This statement became the first proposition to be affirmed in the antimodernist oath. It suggests a specific kind of knowledge of God. First, it is knowledge "by means of created things." Human creatures do not have an immediate intuition of God; knowledge "that God is" comes by way of analogy from sensible, creaturely things. We know God by examining them and abstracting what is unfitting to God. Moreover, this knowledge by the "natural light of reason" does not let us know the mysteries of the faith, such as that God is triune or incarnate in Jesus. It lets us know God as "beginning" and "end" of creatures, and from that we can deduce other of God's "attributes." The Vatican decree claims this is "certain" knowledge. Anyone who taught otherwise was to be anathematized.

The Dominican Réginald Garrigou-Lagrange argued that such knowledge is necessary to avoid a number of modern errors, which he describes as "atheism, positivism, traditionalism, fideism and Kantian criticism."[25] The atheists and positivists claim we have no way to arrive at knowledge of God because our knowledge is limited to sensible, finite, historical realities. We cannot abstract from them and analogize to God's existence. The traditionalists and fideists argue "we can know God only through revelation or by some positive teaching received by tradition."[26] Kant was the major target that the council had in mind. He participated in both errors, arguing that our knowledge was incapable of any "intellectual intuition" and thus we could not move from sensible, creaturely realities to a true knowledge of God.

For Garrigou-Lagrange the Catholic Church teaches that God can be known based on the specific proof of causality, and this is directed against Kant. This is a contested interpretation of the decree. Gerald McCool gives a different reading: "although the constitution declared that natural reason had the ability to know God's existence and attributes, it did not determine whether, in point of fact, natural reason ever did so. . . . Nor did *Dei Filius* specify any definite argument through which the existence and nature of God

25. See Réginald Garrigou-Lagrange, *God: His Existence and His Nature,* trans. Dom Bede Rose, 2 vols. (St. Louis: B. Herder, 1939–1941), 1:8.
26. Ibid., 8–9.

could be established."[27] Garrigou-Lagrange appears to see in the decree the defense of a specific proof. It was an a posteriori proof, grounded in causality, that did not need any authority to support it, neither the "testimony" of God nor the consensus of "tradition" nor even that of the whole human race.

Garrigou-Lagrange's articulation and defense of this proof is brilliant, and to my mind convincing. It shows the weakness in Kant's critique of a rational knowledge of God. Nonetheless, for Garrigou-Lagrange "that God is" is known primarily from rational arguments outlined in Aristotle's *Posterior Analytic* and this *necessarily* precedes knowledge of God that comes from faith; the latter is based on the former. Reason and faith are divided into two discrete, even "pure" realms, and here, despite all his protest against Kant, he shares an understanding of the relation between faith and reason with him. Reason works from a source within "pure nature"; faith works elsewhere: "Reason is placed in contrast with supernatural faith." This reason is not historically mediated, for "whatever we know with certainty to be true, is due to the intrinsic evidence of things."[28] For Garrigou-Lagrange it was essential that the "natural knowledge of God . . . precedes supernatural faith."[29] The latter builds on the former like a foundation. We cannot know God if we do not first have Aristotle. If Aristotle is the necessary basis for faith, then how is this not a return to "paganism"?

Contemporary Roman Catholic theologians Steven A. Long and Thomas White (O.P.) share much with Garrigou-Lagrange. Both identify Barth as the cause of great error in contemporary theology because he called such insights into question, refusing to ground revelation in an a priori natural theology. For them, Barth had too much influence in Catholic theology; they seek a return to Vatican I's decree of the twofold order of knowledge where faith and reason are independent sources. At the end of a long critique of Henri de Lubac and Hans Urs von Balthasar that assumes Barth's undue influence on them, Long writes, "Perhaps it all resolves to this: St. Thomas

27. Gerald McCool, *Nineteenth-Century Scholasticism: The Search for a Unitary Method* (New York: Fordham University Press, 1977), 219.
28. Garrigou-Lagrange, *God*, 1:17.
29. Ibid., 54.

Aquinas remains, at the end, a richer and more profound dialogical partner and teacher than Karl Barth."[30]

Likewise White begins his masterful book, *Wisdom in the Face of Modernity*, with a critique of Kierkegaard and Barth. For them, "natural knowledge of God is not an authentic foundation for understanding human life with God, that philosophical interest in such a natural inspiration is in fact morally problematic, and that more basically, such knowledge is not possible."[31] Barth's insistence on revelation as the only locus for the knowledge of God is, for White, not antimodern but another version of Kant's stricture against natural theology, a stricture against the possibility of moving from creation to an authentic knowledge of God. The problem is Barth remains Kantian in his epistemology.[32] Although some Barthians unfortunately affirm and present Barth exactly as White fears, that is, as a Kantian fideist who thinks knowledge of God can only come through faith, this is a misinterpretation. Barth is more like Chrysostom, Augustine, and Aquinas. Faith requires reason, but unlike the view of Kant and the neoscholastics, they are not two separate realms independent of each other. Indeed, Barth confessed that under the proper situation he could sign the antimodernist oath! He could do so

Barth notes how central the natural knowledge of God has been to Catholics since the first Vatican Council, and he does not find it at odds with Protestant orthodoxy, which he affirmed. He explains it quite well and then states, "Our older Protestant predecessors took no offense at such statements. Quite the contrary. Nor need we do so, even if I say so with tongue in cheek. The decisive point is that on the Roman Catholic view the claiming of reason for the knowledge of God is an article of faith, an assertion of the church that thinks in terms of revelation. The older Orthodox were thinking along the same lines. . . . Revelation does not exclude but includes natural religion, as a major includes a minor."

Karl Barth, *Göttingen Dogmatics*, 344.

30. Steven A. Long, *Natura Pura* (New York: Fordham University Press, 2010), 108. See Thomas Joseph White, O.P., *Wisdom in the Face of Modernity: A Study in Thomistic Natural Theology* (Ave Maria, FL: Sapientia Press of Ave Maria University, 2009), xvii–xviii.
31. White, *Wisdom in the Face of Modernity*, xxi.
32. Ibid.

> only if he emphasized the Vatican's sense of human creatures *"being able* to know or demonstrate." Barth said he would have to repeat this "*being able*" three times in order to take the oath.[33] This is not a vow Kant or a good Kantian could consider taking. Kantians are convinced Kant destroyed all these proofs for good.
>
> Barth interpreted the oath as many Catholics do and did. It does not say that we have a proof for God's existence in natural theology, but it says that since we know God has spoken to us, it is quite possible for such to be included under the articles of faith. In other words, because we know "That God Is" from the revelation to Moses—it is after all first and foremost the divine name—we should not be surprised if someone, someday, comes up with a proof within natural theology that confirms faith. Barth was much less sanguine about this possibility than Garrigou-Lagrange, Steven A. Long, or Thomas Joseph White, but he did not rule it out. If it is a necessary condition for knowledge of mysteries such as the Trinity or incarnation, however, then Aristotle has a primacy in our theology over Holy Scripture. Barth rightly saw how that contributed to theology's modern secular misery.

"That God Is" is first and foremost the divine name revealed to us. Because the world has no fixed, secure ground in itself, because it comes from what cannot be seen (11:3), from a Word God speaks before it is (1:3), no one can finally understand it by some secure "reason" that would be foundational to creation itself, from some putative pure nature. For Aquinas the Word is how God even understands God's self: "the Word of God is the very concept of God, by which He understands Himself and other things." For this reason he finds in 11:3 an affirmation of creation out of nothing: "from the invisible rational ideas in the Word of God, through Whom all things were made, the visible things were produced."[34]

Hebrews already told his listeners that they do not yet see all things subordinated to humans as God intends, but only to the one human Jesus. In 11:3 we are reminded that "the worlds were prepared by

33. Karl Barth, *Göttingen Dogmatics: Instruction in the Christian Religion,* ed. Hannelotte Reiffen, trans. Geoffrey Bromiley, vol. 1 (Grand Rapids: Eerdmans, 1991), 346.

34. Aquinas, *Hebrews*, 233.

the word of God [*rhēmati theou*]," just as we were told in 1:3. What is seen, which does not appear all that beneficial to Hebrews' listeners at the present time, is made from what is invisible. The purpose of all this is to hold fast the confession, endure in faith, because by faith they see Jesus' triumph. They are encouraged to hold fast by being reminded of those who came before them and did this very thing without having seen Jesus. Some did not see it as clearly as they, and yet they hoped for its fullness. Because of it, they were able to withstand the very opposite of that fullness in their "visible" existence. Hebrews reminds us of their history. By faith the elders were "approved" or "well spoken of." The verb used here is the verb for witness or testify, *martyreō*. It conveys the sense that their lives were "attested" or "approved." It connects 11:2, 4, 5, and 39 with 12:1. The faithful who were "attested" or "approved" are now a "cloud of witnesses." The litany of witness in chapter 11 has a lyrical and confessional character to it. The best commentary on it is to sing with all the saints that great hymn of the church, which explicitly drew on Hebrews 11, "For All the Saints."

> **For all the saints, who from their labors rest, who thee by faith before the world confessed, thy name, O Jesus, be forever blest, Alleluia, Alleluia. Thou wast their rock, their fortress, and their might; thou, Lord, their captain in the well-fought fight; thou, in the darkness drear, their one true light. Alleluia, Alleluia.**
>
> William W. How, "For All the Saints," *United Methodist Hymnal*, #711.

Hebrews admonished us to approach the holy of holies in the "fullness of faith" (10:22); now we see what this fullness looked like in the fathers and mothers of the faith. "By faith" gets repeated eighteen times. In each case we are given examples of the faithful who did not see what they were promised, but still acted in faith. All these exemplars participate in a hidden fullness whose origin and perfection is Christ. The common thread throughout this beautiful litany is a fullness that overcomes lack, death, and sin. Faith is a "greater wealth" (11:26). Yet we must remember that the faithful in Hebrews 11 are not explicit Christians. They did not know him. Nonetheless Hebrews find Christ to be the "pioneer" and "perfecter" of faith, including theirs. How is this possible? Only because a relation exists between the two covenants where the second is the fulfillment of the first. Because a priesthood such as Melchizedek's existed, Hebrews can find Christ to be the origin even of the faith of the OT patriarchs and matriarchs. Christ is the high priest whose faithfulness inherits the promise, which is entrance into the holy of holies. In him we see the glory of God, and he shares his fullness, his perfection, with us by allowing us to glimpse the apocalyptic vision only he sees clearly.

11:4–5, 7–40 *That God Is the God of Abel, Noah, Abraham, Sarah*

God cannot be known without faith. Hebrews 11:6 makes this important negative judgment, but it is sandwiched between the positive accounts of faith's fullness found in the ancestors and prophets through whom God spoke in the past. The fullness of faith is found in Abel, who made a "more ample sacrifice" (my trans.). It is found in Enoch, who lived from such abundance that he did not taste death. Noah was given instructions about the things not yet seen and saved his entire house, whereas Abraham waited patiently for a city built by God, refusing to be satisfied with anything less. Sarah's barrenness was overcome by faith, and she and Abraham received a concrete sign of the promise—a child. Abraham was willing to offer Isaac as a sacrifice in obedience to God. Hebrews gives an interesting interpretation of this troubling episode in the biblical narrative: God would raise him up from the dead. In other words, Abraham's potential sacrifice was not the ultimate "gift" of death, since we know a gift can finally be given only because there is no return and therefore no interested desire on the part of the giver (as one finds more or less in the philosophies of Kant, Levinas, and Derrida). Abraham can offer up the child of promise because he knows it is secure in the fullness of faith. He will receive a return; bodily life is affirmed, not death. It is this hope that makes faith reasonable. From this hope come blessings: Isaac blessed Jacob and Esau; Jacob blessed the sons of Joseph.

Moses is "hidden" because of his great "beauty." This draws on Exodus 2:2, but also fits well Hebrews' understanding of faith. The beauty of Moses was for a time veiled by his parents' faith. They made invisible what was visible so that it might one day be made visible. They did this because they had no fear of Pharaoh. The implication for those hearing is obvious: be like Moses' parents. Be ready to make visible that which is not yet fully seen in spite of any authority's threat. Moses himself did the same when he left Egypt with its riches because he lived out of hope in a "greater wealth" in Christ. This connects back to the reminder that at one time Hebrews' audience was also willing to forgo their wealth (10:34), and forward to the admonition "keep your lives free from the love of money" (13:5). Perhaps it is also the "weight" that keeps them from running the race in 12:1? For Hebrews, material possessions are a temptation to let go of the possession (*hypostasis*) that truly matters—faith in Christ as the triumphant priest-king. This faith has had its triumphs—the people passed through the Red Sea, the walls of Jericho tumbled, Rahab was saved. In the middle of this litany, we find a statement that lends support to Aquinas's interpretation that the divine name is "that God is." We are told, "Therefore God is not ashamed to be called their God" (11:16). Who could this "God that is" be except the God who is named from the history of Abel, Enoch, Abraham, Sarah, Isaac, and Moses? To know this God requires knowing their stories and living out of the same fullness of faith.

The litany of the triumphs continues in 11:32–35a. The author says that more could be said about Gideon, Barak, Samson, Jephthah, David, Samuel, the prophets, and their accomplishments as well as the unnamed women who "received their dead by resurrection" (11:35a). One wished the author had said something more here. The list of the faithful includes people who did scandalous things. For instance, what are we to do with Jephthah? His inclusion has troubled commentators throughout Christian tradition. Chrysostom recognized this: "Some find fault with Paul, because he puts Barak, and Samson, and Jephthah in these places. What do you say? After having introduced the harlot, shall he not introduce these? For do not tell me of the rest of their life, but only whether they did not believe and shine in faith."[35] Notice he does not defend the entirety of their actions but only their faith. Aquinas stated, "it must be known that some of these did evil deeds, and some good, wherefore they are not numbered here except regarding the good which

35. "27th Homily on Hebrews," http://www.newadvent.org/fathers/240227.htm.

they did or received." He states that Jephhtah "sinned" in his actions, citing Jerome as witness.[36] Calvin likewise said that the inclusion of Jephthah means: "In every saint there is always to be found something reprehensible. Nevertheless although faith may be imperfect and incomplete it does not cease to be approved by God. There is no reason, therefore, why the fault from which we labour should break us or discourage us provided we go on by faith in the race of our calling."[37] These answers as to Jephthah's inclusion may not be that convincing, but they do recognize that Christian tradition did not simply affirm evil because it was in the Bible. It had to be explained.

The story of Jephthah can be found in Judges 11–12. He was the son of a prostitute who was told by his stepbrothers he would not inherit anything. So here we see the theme of inheritance once again. He lived as an exile and outlaw, but when the Ammonites sought the return of their land, the elders of Gilead sought him out and placed him over the Gileadites in order to seek peace with the Ammonites. They were unwilling to consent to Jephthah's requests. He prayed that God would deliver them into their hands, and vowed he would sacrifice the first person or thing that met him coming out of his own house if God granted them the victory. The first person who met him was his only daughter. She consented to his vow, only asking to mourn her virginity for two months before being sacrificed. Jephthah's sacrifice of his unnamed daughter bears similarities to Abraham's offering of Isaac, but this time the victim was not spared. Why is it that the male heir finds a reprieve from sacrifice, but Jephthah's unnamed daughter does not? This sacrifice puts an end to her and to Jephthah's biological line. Why would such a horrendous sacrifice be placed in Hebrews' litany of the saints? We do not know because the author of Hebrews tells us he does not have time to say more. Given what he said about Abraham's potential sacrifice of Isaac, the same may be implied here. Jephthah's "faith" was his willingness to sacrifice biological descent in hopes that through resurrection he would still inherit the promise. This does not excuse his rash vow of actions, which were uniformly condemned in Christian tradition, even labeled as "sin." Nor should it cause us to turn

36. Aquinas, *Hebrews*, 257–58.
37. Calvin, *Hebrews*, 182.

away from the obvious sexism present in these biblical stories. The named male heir escapes death; the unnamed female one does not.

Sarah and Rahab do get named in the litany, but the women who received their dead do not (Heb. 11:35). Perhaps this is a reference to Elisha and the Shunammite's son in 2 Kings 4:17–37, but the verse uses the plural, suggesting others received "resurrection" as well. Resurrection is the theme uniting the characters. It signifies the hope from which they lived, which allowed them to overcome the fear of death. Yet this is no gospel of prosperity, for Hebrews is clear that their act of faith, their movement toward and from this fullness, often came only under the "appearance," albeit actual, of a genuine loss: taunts, whips, chains, prison, stoning, cutting up, burning, slaughtering by sword, wandering upon the earth. In the explanation of the litany, Hebrews presents a symmetry between resurrection fulfilled and unfulfilled. After delineating what the faithful were able to accomplish through faith, a stark and ominous turn begins with verse 34b, contrasting what had been accomplished with what had not yet been accomplished; a symmetry exists between the fulfilled and unfulfilled promises.

Resurrection Fulfilled:	**Resurrection Not Yet Fulfilled:**
conquered kingdoms	tortured
obtained promises	suffered mocking and flogging, chains and imprisonment
shut lions' mouths	stoned to death
quenched fire	sawn in two
escaped the sword	killed by the sword
won strength out of weakness	went about in skin of sheep and goats, destitute, persecuted, tormented
mighty in war, putting foreign armies to flight	the world did not consider them worthy
culminating in: already received resurrection	culminating in: wandering

Why this symmetry? Once again the important theme of perfection helps us. The reason they still wandered was because "God had provided something better so that they would not, apart from us, be made perfect [*teleiōthōsin*]" [11:40]. The fullness of resurrection can only be seen from a distance both by the faithful described here and by Hebrews' own listeners. In other words, a gap exists between the fullness from which we are to live in faith, hope, and charity and its present realization. This creates an apocalyptic reserve that produces dissatisfaction with the current political order. Hebrews names this dissatisfaction first with Abraham, who "set out for a place" God promised. "For he looked forward to the city that has foundations, whose architect and builder is God" (11:10).

Hebrews has this twofold message. First, Jesus' body is the new city, house, or temple, and we already see the priest-king who rules while he awaits all things to be placed under his feet. Second, like the promise to the patriarchs and matriarchs, the fullness of that promise from which we are called to live is not yet realized. We are called, like them, to live lives of patient expectation not being content with our current dwellings. Hebrews says this explicitly in the closing admonitions: "here we have no lasting city, but we are looking for the city that is to come" (13:14).

An important pause in the narrative occurs again in the midst of the litany of the faithful, and we are told that even though they all received the fullness of faith, nonetheless they died not having received the promise (11:13). Instead they confessed they were foreigners and wanderers on the earth; their desire is not yet fulfilled. They still seek a "better country," a "city prepared for them" by God. Here we find the apocalyptic element in Hebrews. We cannot do justice to Hebrews without discussing this element and its theological and political significance.

FURTHER REFLECTIONS
Apocalyptic

The term "apocalyptic" is notoriously difficult to define. On the one hand, it is a biblical genre, defining those texts where God radically breaks into human history to bring to an end one political and cultural era and establish another. On the other, it is a "tone," "style," "sensibility," or "space" in contemporary theology, philosophy, politics, and culture. As a biblical genre, apocalyptic has sometimes been distinguished from wisdom, priestly, or prophetic material, but such distinctions are no longer credible. Those texts we designate as "apocalyptic," such as *1 Enoch*, Daniel, Revelation, and *Apocalypse of Abraham,* draw upon all these genres. Some suggest that apocalyptic literature emerges from a priestly tradition in which the "revelation" was given to the priest in the holy of holies as he was transported into the presence of God. This is certainly how it occurs in *1 Enoch*. Apocalyptic is also often claimed to originate from an oppressed people. George Nickelsburg argues that the "apocalyptic eschatology" in *1 Enoch* originated from a people "that look to another world and hope for a better day" because of the "dismal state of affairs here and now. The hope that God and the angels will intervene derives from the frustration of impotent people unable to change their circumstances, and its corollary is the belief that one's oppressors are personifications or operatives of demonic power."[38] Apocalyptic belongs to the marginalized and oppressed, as a source either for liberation or for resentment.

Apocalyptic is not found only on the margins of Christianity in texts such as the Enochic literature. Nor is it only in Revelation. It is also present in the Gospels, Paul's Epistles, and Hebrews. Albert Schweitzer's work had tremendous influence in our understanding of Paul by challenging Wilhelm Bousset's thesis that Paul's work makes best sense in terms of Hellenistic mystery religions. Instead, Schweitzer argued, it can only rightly be understood against the backdrop of Jewish apocalyptic. J. Louis Martyn, Richard Hays, and others have recognized how central this is for our understanding of Paul. Hays affirms Schweitzer for recognizing the importance of "apocalyptic" in Paul, but he critiques him for reducing the specificity of Paul's apocalyptic thought to a general framework distilled from "the eschatological worldview of 'late Judaism.'"[39] Rather than offering a critique of the history of religions school, Hays notes Schweitzer places Paul's thought in a different history of religions' "explanatory context," which is "late Judaism" rather than the "Hellenistic redeemer myths." Apocalyptic then functions as a generic

38. Nickelsburg, *1 Enoch*, 5.
39. Hays, *Faith of Jesus Christ*, 43.

account of religion that seeks to explain Christianity within it just as Bousset did with his now defunct universal, hellenized "redeemer myth." When this happens, "apocalyptic" becomes an alternative canon within which Scripture gets read.

Apocalyptic is much more than a biblical genre; it is also a theological and philosophical "tone" or "sensibility" that characterizes diverse ways of life. Throughout much of the nineteenth and early twentieth century apocalyptic discourses were an embarrassment to those both within and without the church. It was a sign of an apolitical theology, or a form of resentment. Ernst Troeltsch (1865–1923), an influential German Protestant theologian, set apocalyptic against ethics and political responsibility. As Nate Kerr recognizes, Troeltsch's theology represents the "eclipse of apocalyptic."[40]

Troeltsch's analysis of apocalyptic would fit with a crass Marxism in which the religious longing for "another city," one built by God, is viewed on the one hand as positive in that it signifies people's alienation from the everyday conditions of their own existence; they recognize something is not right. But on the other it is viewed as a form of "ideology" because it prevents people from recognizing the true source of their alienation. But a number of philosophers now argue that modern politics cannot be understood well without seeing its similarities to apocalyptic.

The political scientist Michael Gillespie traces the apocalyptic moment in modernity back to Descartes and Hobbes. "Like Descartes, Hobbes believes philosophy must begin with epistemological destruction. In Descartes this is his famous path of doubt by which he thinks away the material world, leaving only the bare *cogito ergo sum*. Hobbes too begins by imagining the world to be annihilated. Both thinkers in this respect build on the nominalist method for eliminating reified universals by asking what would still exist if the rest of the world were destroyed."[41] Here we find the origins for our flat world; such origins are apocalyptic and nominalist.

40. Nathan R. Kerr, *Christ, History and Apocalyptic: The Politics of Christian Mission* (Eugene, OR: Cascade Books, 2009), 19.

41. Michael Gillespie, *The Theological Origins of Modernity* (Chicago: University of Chicago Press, 2008), 233.

They deny all universality and continuity for a radical singularity that calls into existence everything that came before. The world that previously existed, the Dark Ages, with its realist understanding of existence, gives way to the scorching light that must destroy it all in order to begin again, and again, . . . on new foundations.

The realist understanding assumed existence was complex, filled with overlapping layers of reality such that no singular entity could be understood without seeing it situated among those layers. The nominalists cut through those layers to make everything a singularity that can now be mapped by its coordinates on a grid. In order to do this, they had to bring down every mountain and raise every valley, which was largely accomplished through modern technology. No one can gainsay the advantages this produced for our existence, but nor should we be naive about its disadvantages, especially the change in our understanding per se.

Although once the province of fringe elements expressing their dissatisfaction, apocalyptic became "mainstream" in theology and philosophy during the modern era. Indeed, the modern era itself is best understood as apocalyptic (if not gnostic—the two are related). It thrives on crises (just watch CNN), and it always waits for the "new and improved" product, which when it comes will render obsolete everything that came before. An apocalyptic turn can be found not only in philosophy and politics, but also in contemporary culture. Movies such as *I Am Legend, The Children of Men*, and *The Book of Eli* have strong apocalyptic themes, as do television series like *24*, *Heroes*, and *Lost*. We seem fixated on impending catastrophes, whether it is an ecological disaster, human bioengineering gone awry, or the invasion of space aliens. Of course, we experience such catastrophes: tsunamis, hurricanes, earthquakes, the collapse of the banking industry, the BP debacle in the Gulf of Mexico.

Likewise the postmodern strikes an apocalyptic tone. In 1980 the philosopher Jacques Derrida spoke of "a newly arisen apocalyptic tone in philosophy." This was a commentary on Kant's 1796 essay, "On a Newly Arisen Superior Tone in Philosophy," in which he polemically attacks, and then seeks a peace treaty with, *Schwärmerei* (enthusiasts), who were passing themselves off as philosophers. These "philosophers," suggests Kant, have reduced philosophy to a "mode whereby secrets are revealed."[42] They do this through a supposed "intellectual intuition" of the supersensible realm that bypasses the hard labor of the philosophical enterprise. For Kant, Plato himself, with his doctrine of participation in the divine Ideas, is the "father" of all *Schwärmerei*. It is a common pejorative term against mystical illumination as apocalyptic theology would propose. Kant opposed all such claims to illumination as if such persons had some oracle from God, an apocalyptic knowledge of the secret that has been veiled for all eternity. No mystical illumination, no spiritual communication is necessary. This means that for Kant we can have no theoretical knowledge of God. However, a practical knowledge is possible because we all stand before the "veiled goddess" of the "moral law in us, in its inviolable majesty."[43] This veiled goddess is Isis. She is veiled because she reminds us no one can really know her and her wisdom. There is "no passage to the supersensible."[44] But there is the moral law, and for it we must have the "inner Idea of freedom." The moral law may "come from man" or it may come from an "other." It might come from God, but who knows? "At bottom," he writes, "we would perhaps do better to rise above and thus spare ourselves research into this matter."[45] All the apocalyptic *Schwärmerei* "must necessarily promise a surrogate of cognition, supernatural communication (mystical illumination), which is the death of all philosophy."[46]

For Kant, then, we are at the end of apocalyptic just as we are at the end of metaphysics. Derrida responds to Kant's supposed rejection of apocalyptic after he himself was accused or questioned about his apocalyptic tone, rightly noting that Kant himself did not reject apocalyptic, for he too has his secret, his mystery.[47] Indeed, Derrida notes, "the West has been dominated by a powerful

42. Immanuel Kant, "On a Newly Arisen Superior Tone in Philosophy," in *Raising the Tone of Philosophy: Late Essays by Immanuel Kant, Transformative Critique by Jacques Derrida*, ed. Peter Fenves (Baltimore: Johns Hopkins University Press, 1993), 51.

43. Ibid., 71.

44. Ibid., 70.

45. Ibid., 71.

46. Ibid., 62.

47. Jacques Derrida, "On a Newly Arisen Apocalyptic Tone in Philosophy," in *Raising the Tone of Philosophy*, 132–33.

program that was an untransgressable contract among discourses of the end."[48] Proclaiming we are at the "end" of something has become permanently fashionable, whether it be the end of metaphysics, history, class struggle, philosophy, God, religion, Christianity, morals, the subject, man, the West, the earth, and so on. Although what is pronounced as coming to an end differs, Derrida claims, "Haven't all the differences taken the form of a going-one-better in eschatological eloquence, each newcomer more lucid than the other, more vigilant and more prodigal too, coming to add more to it: I tell you this in truth; this is not only the end of this here but also and first of that there."[49]

In response Derrida proclaims his own apocalypse—the end of the end, an apocalypse without apocalypse. This attempts to take what is revolutionary in apocalypticism without adding to it any determinate content. Apocalyptic is inevitable for us. Kant did not abandon it any more than any other Western philosopher; there is always a "secret" that one assumes. But for Derrida apocalyptic must be dispossessed; it must say nothing determinate that can be identified as actually existing. It must be permanently diasporic. It only prays, "Come." It would never say, "Next year in Jerusalem," or "Christ has come, Christ has died, Christ will come again." It would never read the book of Revelation (or Hebrews) and say, "The Word of the Lord. Amen." As Derrida's faithful defender John Caputo asserts, the latter biblical books constitute a determinate apocalyptic that is the source of violence, bigotry, and destruction.

Derrida's philosophy goes by the name of "deconstruction." Caputo has not only defended this philosophy but argues it bears strong similarities to the Jewish and Christian prophetic tradition: "Deconstruction . . . repeats dogmatically the religious structure of experience . . . *sans* the concrete messianisms of the positive religions that wage endless war and spill the blood of the other, and that, anointing themselves God's chosen people, are consummately dangerous to everyone else who is not so chosen."[50] For Derrida and

48. Ibid., 145.
49. Ibid.
50. John Caputo, *The Prayers and Tears of Jacques Derrida: Religion without Religion* (Bloomington: Indiana University Press, 1997), xxi.

Caputo, apocalyptic designates the "wholly other" as always coming but never arriving. Caputo writes, "He must always function as a breach of the present, opening up the present to something new to something impossible." Caputo confesses that this apocalyptic requires a "nominalism and a generalized *ignorantia* about what is coming, that cultivates the possible not *as possible*, but as *the* impossible."[51] The impossible is "justice," the one thing that cannot be deconstructed, but also never arrives.[52]

Deconstruction knows the secret of apocalyptic—there is no secret. Caputo announces this "secret without secret" definitively and deterministically: "the revelation that nobody has the Apocalyptic Word from On High means that no one can lord it over the rest of us and keep us all in line."[53] Nobody has the word Hebrews proclaims. The result of deconstruction is to throw the message of Hebrews with its determinate proclamations such as "you are his house" or "Jesus Christ is the same yesterday, today, and forever" into crisis. Like modernity, deconstruction thrives on irresolvable crises, on diaspora.

Christianity assumes that the crisis will be resolved, and indeed in Christ it already has. Modern-postmodern apocalyptic thrives on the irresoluble character of the crisis. Take, for instance, the atheist, Marxist philosopher Slavoj Žižek, who wrote *Living in the End Times*. Picking this book off the shelf at a local bookstore could prompt one to think of something like Hal Lindsey's *Late Great Planet Earth*. Lindsey's work represents "apocalyptic gone bad." His book was a best seller in the 1970s and was made into a movie narrated by Orson Welles. I remember seeing it in my local theater and being frightened that somehow he had unlocked the secret knowledge to a catastrophe right around the corner. This kind of apocalyptic did not bring hope but fear. It truly was a form of resentment. Lindsey's work was gnostic. It claimed to have the "code" by which present events could be interpreted through the book of Revelation.

Žižek's confused, often rambling, but nonetheless insightful work is much more interesting than Lindsey or Derrida. He critiques

51. Ibid., 56.
52. Ibid., 71.
53. Ibid., 102.

Derrida and Caputo's apocalyptic, calling Caputo's apocalypticism "Derridean deconstructive messianism." He states, "Caputo is horrified at the very idea of a religious dogma, i.e. the notion of a God who decided to address a particular group of people at a particular moment, according them privileged access to absolute Truth. Religion is thus reduced to its pure desubstantialized form: a belief that our miserable reality is not all there is, the ultimate truth; that 'there is another world possible,' a promise/hope of redemption-to-come betrayed by an ontological positivization."[54] This is an interesting critique. An avowed atheist, Žižek, challenges a philosopher whose own position on God is characterized by an ambivalence similar to Kant's take on Isis,[55] for refusing to affirm any concrete, determinate dogma. Žižek chides him for failing to see that the Jewish and Christian God speaks a definitive word. In one sense, Žižek at least knows which God not to believe in! But Caputo's Derridean deconstructive messianism eschews any "ontological positivization" that would imply a determinate content to theology.

Žižek allows for the possibility of "ontological positivization," but only through a strong doctrine of kenosis whereby Jesus is crucified without his body being resurrected. He only has a "Jesusology," no Trinity, no Christology, no ecclesiology. In the end, it is difficult to see how his apocalyptic is anything but a form without content. The only material Christian dogma he can affirm is the crucifixion: "The crucified Jesus is the apocalyptic Jesus: it stands for the end of the world as we know it, the end of time when God himself dies, empties himself; at this point of apocalypse, opposites coincide, the lone Jesus is Satan himself, his death is the death of Evil, so that crucifixion and resurrection are one event."[56] This "determinate" apocalyptic is no more preferable to Derrida and Caputo's "indeterminate" view. What he finds useful in Christianity is this sense of the "new."

Particular communities are not redemptive; they are often the source of oppression. But Christianity is one of three great

54. Slavoj Žižek and Milbank, *The Monstrosity of Christ: Paradox or Dialectic?* (Cambridge: MIT Press, 2009), 256.
55. Caputo confesses, "Is God an example of justice, or justice of God? Does it matter?" (*Prayers and Tears*, 54).
56. Žižek and Milbank, *Monstrosity of Christ*, 261.

movements that overcome particular communities toward a universal humanity. The first was the movement from mythos to logos in Greek philosophy; the second was the movement from the Greek polis to an abstract Christian universality; and the third was the disenchantment of creation with Descartes.[57] The universal tendencies in the above three movements drew together people alienated from such particular communities. What we need is a universal humanity capable of bonds of solidarity based in goodness and truth. Žižek rightly recognizes that Christianity could be an ally in that cause.

Žižek uses and affirms elements of Christianity, which might strike folks as odd given that he is an atheist. He addresses the accusation that he uses it "without acknowledging its content," and answers, "The reply is that this 'emptying the form of its content' already takes place within Christianity itself, at its very core—the name for this emptying is *kenosis*: God dies and is resurrected as the Holy Ghost, as the *form* of collective belief. It is a fetishistic mistake to search for the material support of this form (the resurrected Christ)—the Holy Ghost is the very collective of believers, what they search for outside is already here in the guise of the love that binds them."[58] His theology is almost identical to that of Jennings cited earlier except Žižek confesses it is atheism. Žižek shows that the logical result of what passes for much of modern theology, especially Protestant theology, is best represented by atheism. Perhaps for employment reasons, most Protestant theologians simply do not follow the logic of their position.

Žižek strongly favors Protestant Christianity over Catholicism and Orthodoxy because it, more so than the other two, "universalizes" the "excremental status to the whole of humanity": "Martin Luther directly proposed just such an excremental identity for man; man is like divine shit, he fell out of God's anus—and effectively, it is only within this Protestant logic of man's excremental identity that the true meaning of Incarnation can be formulated." What does the Protestant doctrine of incarnation have that others do not? *God* suffers and dies. Unlike many theologians who play with this idea not

57. Slavoj Žižek, *Living in the End Times* (London: Verso, 2010), 278.
58. Ibid., 118.

truly intending what it says, Žižek follows out its logic. If God suffers, God dies. If God dies, Christianity is the source for atheism. This is its promise and political usefulness. The Divine is thoroughly emptied out into new immanent possibilities.

He concludes his work by urging the radical left to embrace theology. "This is the kind of God needed by the radical Left today: a God who has fully 'become a man,' a comrade amongst us, crucified together with two social outcasts, who not only 'does not exist,' but also *knows this himself,* accepts his own erasure, passing over entirely into the love that binds all members of the 'Holy Ghost,' that is, of the Party or emancipatory collective."[59] As so often with Žižek, this evocative quote needs careful parsing (something he seldom does). What does it mean to say that the God who empties himself, who suffers and dies and therefore erases himself, "knows this himself"? In part, this means that God does not seek to establish a particular people who live according to his will. Žižek would, like Caputo, find the Jewish eschatological proclamation, "Next year in Jerusalem," to be a serious problem. Christianity is affirmed because in the end it is nothing but a universal form without content. He affirms Christianity as permanent diaspora.[60] Christianity is not about the establishment of a people, formed around a common practice of worship and liturgy in and through the church. He loses any relationship between ecclesiology and apocalyptic, a position that is radically different from Hebrews. Indeed, both Derrida and Žižek's apocalyptic is more like Gnosticism than the determinate content of a scandalous particular people that constitutes Christian apocalyptic.

This version of apocalyptic is making a return in contemporary theology. Something very similar to it can be seen in some elements of the "missional church." Some ardently Protestant theologians have latched on to apocalyptic in order to challenge an "ecclesiocentric" theology. The "house" Jesus builds is not the church, and it should not be in any sense visibly identified with the kingdom. Instead, Jesus interrupts all continuity of history and authority.

59. Ibid., 402.
60. Ibid., 143 n. 6.

Nathan Kerr has developed such a line of apocalyptic thought. He calls for a "new form of ecclesial political life," where the church is "a mode of dynamic and dispossessive *liturgical action*, which action occurs as a *work of exile*, via the reimagining of Jesus and the church through the medium of Jewish diasporic existence."[61] Kerr draws on Hebrews 13 for his reimagined ecclesiology.[62] Although this apocalyptic return bears strong similarities to the "tone" present in postmodern philosophy and uses similar expressions, it seeks to distance itself from them. It arises more from strong trajectories in modern theology's apocalyptic turn.

Cyril O'Regan traces the turn to apocalyptic in modern theology. Rather than calling it a "tone," he speaks of it as a "space": "it indicates fields of force that attract some discourses and repel others. A space of apocalyptic suggests a constellation of discourses that bear close family resemblances to each other."[63] Like a magnet drawing other fields into its pull, apocalyptic functions more like a force field than a distinct genre. Its pull can be salutary or negative. It can show us a vision of what God is doing and how it relates to questions of Christian identity and ethics, or it can lead us off into speculative irrationalities such as those found in Umberto Eco's novel *Foucault's Pendulum*. In it three characters invent a secret "Plan" and get trapped by their own apocalyptic-gnostic speculation. Although their "Plan" was a joke, they nonetheless find themselves caught up in a supposed secret conspiracy of the Knights Templar to take over the world, complete with a secret code that lets them read the hidden meaning in texts.

For good reason apocalyptic has often been marginalized in theology. Much heretical or heterodox Christianity emerges from apocalyptic speculation. O'Regan acknowledges: "Throughout its long history, theology has developed largely in non-apocalyptic directions that variously featured doctrine, institutions, spiritual and moral disciplines and practices. Even with those inclined to a dose of nostalgia for the early church, there is a general recognition that

61. Kerr, *Christ, History and Apocalyptic*, 21.
62. Ibid., 190.
63. Cyril O'Regan, *Theology and the Spaces of Apocalyptic* (Milwaukee: Marquette University Press, 2009), 26.

the emergence of catholic Christianity seriously debilitated, even if it did not sign the death warrant of, biblical apocalyptic, already riven by disappointment regarding the parousia."[64] While heresy and heterodoxy are always a temptation in theology that adopts an apocalyptic tone, they are not its only consequence. Apocalyptic need not be set against orthodoxy. Largely inspired by Karl Barth's explosive commentary on Romans, the Orthodox theologian Sergius Bulgakov, and the Roman Catholic Hans Urs von Balthasar, twentieth-century theology made an unexpected "apocalyptic turn" that cannot be dismissed as heterodox.

O'Regan describes the kind of apocalyptic that has a strong "determinable content" as can be seen in Hebrews as "pleromatic."[66] *Plērōma* means fullness. He contrasts this with a "kenomatic" apocalyptic, from *kenōsis*, which means emptying.[66] The kenomatic envisions the future possibility of a different form of existence as necessary for an ethical critique of contemporary injustices, but because injustice emerges from a too determinate content that creates division and hierarchy, it must limit if not eschew determinate content. The pleromatic assumes we must have a fullness present to us in order to hold fast and endure.

Pleromatic and kenomatic apocalyptic spaces will have very different understandings of the place for "church." The pleromatic sees it as participating in the fullness Christ is. Christ brings an "end to exile." He is the odd return of God's glory to the temple, which is now mediated through the fullness of his body, which is present to the church. It has a political, or public, role in the world as a transnational reality with a determinate, visible content. Because Christ redeemed the world, it is the holy habitation of God, as found in the Eucharist. The church is the firstfruits of that redemption, which will occur when Christ returns. We exist now in the fullness of Christ's body, which stands unshaken after his triumph over the cross. For this reason, the church's existence is not simply "diasporic," although the "eschatological reserve" reminds us that all things are not yet subject to him.

64. Ibid., 12.
65. Ibid., 59.
66. He also suggests a third, metaxic space, in between pleromatic and kenomatic.

For the kenomatic, the church occupies a less important, even a problematic "space." For instance, Nathan Kerr develops an "altogether different conception of *ecclesia*" in this kenomatic space. Undoubtedly, Kerr seeks a distinctly Christian apocalyptic that finds its meaning in Christ. But he rejects any sense that the church mediates Christ's body through its material practices. He has a pleromatic christological apocalyptic with a kenomatic ecclesiology: "If we are to go on speaking of *ecclesia* at all, it will have to be in terms of an 'exile,' a 'diaspora'—terms which are distinctively Jewish and, perhaps especially for that reason, irreducibly political."[67] Notice he questions *if* we can still speak of ecclesiology. It has become problematic. The only way that we can speak of the church is in terms of exile. Kerr notes that "diaspora" as "normal Jewish existence" is controversial. Exile was to come to an end. It was not permanent. He nonetheless asserts, "whatever one might finally decide regarding the status and identity of 'Israel,' as both a 'people' and a 'land,' it remains the case that the 'Jewishness' of Christianity, as oriented by and towards the historicity of Jesus of Nazareth, can only truly be conceived according to the terms of a 'diasporic' peoplehood."[68] But why is this? Was there no "restoration" in Christ's body? Was creation not shaken and yet because of Christ's triumph certain things remained?

Kerr concludes his call for a "diasporic" ecclesiology by drawing on Hebrews 13:12–13. He comments, "This 'worldly' site of inbreaking itself becomes the site of 'calling out' and 'gathering,' a site that is politically a nonsite, always 'outside the city gate.'"[69] Earlier he stated that diasporic existence is political, but now it is not. It is unclear what he means by "political." By calling the church "politically" a nonsite, he seems to be referring to those accounts of politics that assume clear and defensible boundaries. We are called outside of them. But if this is the meaning, then he has no "public" church.[70]

67. Kerr, *Christ, History and Apocalyptic,* 181–82.
68. Ibid., 182.
69. Ibid., 190.
70. For an important alternative to Kerr see Reinhard Hütter, "The Church as Public: Doctrine, Practice and the Holy Spirit," in *Bound to Be Free: Evangelical Catholic Engagements in Ecclesiology, Ethics, and Ecumenism* (Grand Rapids: Eerdmans, 2004), 19–42.

A site that is a nonsite is rhetoric similar to that of Derrida and Caputo, religion without religion, apocalypse without apocalypse. It is intended to be indeterminate. Kerr distances his apocalyptic from theirs, but it does bear a family resemblance through its development of an ecclesiology within a kenomatic space.[71] Christ does not gain a "people," who are found in the visible church as a public witness. His sovereign freedom stands over and against the church, bringing the kingdom. I fear that the result of this Protestant anti-ecclesiocentric apocalyptic is that the space within which Christians exercise their discipleship will be conceded to the secular.[72]

The apocalyptic "space" in Hebrews is clearly "pleromatic." It is filled with Christ's perfection accomplished through his obedient sacrifice, which includes his "house." The author does not say we "will be" that house, but "we are the house if we hold firm the confidence" (3:6). Holding firm assumes Christ's perfection is available even now for those who are attentive, even if it is not yet what it will be. For this reason, the next section encourages Christians to be willing to suffer discipline for God disciplines those whom God loves.

12:3–13

Endurance in the Face of What We Do See

This is one of the most difficult and demanding sections in Hebrews. We are not only told that we too might be called to resist to the point of shedding blood, but also that such trials are God's "discipline," making us his children. The unmistakable point here is that just as Christ was called to suffer in obedience, "enduring the cross" (12:2), so we too are made God's children by "enduring trials for the sake of discipline" (12:7). God is the agent behind these trials who treats us as beloved children by exposing us to such trials. They

71. The family resemblance may stem from their common use of Walter Benjamin.

72. Of course I could be wrong. Much of the development of this theology has only taken place so far within the blogosphere. We are yet to see how it will develop. Its emphasis on the "singularity" of Jesus does not seem to need a robust doctrine of the Trinity as well as the church. Perhaps once those committed to it develop it more fully, such judgments will be proven incorrect.

are our "training." We can only make sense of this by recalling the christological teaching of Hebrews, especially the insistence on the ascension.

We find in this section yet another inclusion based on strengthening ourselves for an athletic contest (12:1, 11–13). The beautiful litany of the faithful culminated in the proclamation in 12:1–2 of the one for whom they waited—the pioneer and perfecter of their faith, Jesus. The author of Hebrews encourages his listeners both not to "grow weary" (12:3) and to "lift drooping hands and strengthen weak knees" (12:12). To strengthen our knees is to run the race set before us, the race Christ successfully ran. The admonitions in these verses are connected to what comes before through the metaphor of an athletic contest, but they are tied into the sermon as a whole by the repetition yet again of the statement of Christ's ascension. Now Hebrews add a third variation on this theme:

1:3: *ekathisen en dechsia tēs megalōsynēs en hypsēlois*
(he sat down at the right hand of the Majesty on high)

8:1: *ekathisen en dechsia tou thronou tēs megalōsynēs en hypsēlois en tois ouranois*
(one who is seated at the right hand of the throne of the Majesty in the heavens)

12:2: *en dechsia te tou thronou tou theou kekathiken*
(at the right hand of the throne of God has taken his seat)

In this third version, Hebrews uses a synthesis of the terms in the earlier two, omitting the periphrasis for God in the exordium. Now we have a reference to "the throne" as in the second version, but rather than "of the Majesty on high," Hebrews simply states "of God." The throne of God is the ark of the covenant in the holy of holies. It is where we look to see Jesus, for here he brings an end to exile. God's presence returns to the temple. In this third version the emphasis is on Jesus' action: *He has taken his seat, he sat down.* In other words, he inherits the promised rest. This was something he achieved by enduring the cross. Now he not only rests but he also brings rest. This rest came through struggle. Christ *endured* the "hostility" (*antilogian*) of sinners (12:3) to the point of the cross, but the point is not simply to struggle. Permanent diaspora would only know struggle; it becomes an end in itself, like a "Protestantism" that only knows protest without any hope for reconciliation. Hebrews has no such unending dialectic; hostility and conflict are endured for the sake of *rest*. Christ's ascension is that rest. The image of Christ sitting at the right hand is one of peace, not struggle or conflict.

Whatever persecution his audience faced, the author of Hebrews tells us that they have not yet had to shed their own blood (12:4). This suggests that they might have to do so, and the author prepares them for such a possibility. He reminds them of the "exhortation" found in Proverbs 3:11–12: the Lord disciplines and chastises the child whom he loves. The "child" here has a reference both backward and forward. It points backward to Christ and what he endured. It points forward to Hebrews' listeners and what they are called to endure. Only because Christ as the Son of God is the "pioneer and perfecter" of faith can they themselves endure and become his brothers and sisters, the children of God. But this most likely will not take place without enduring some kind of "discipline" as he himself did.

Is this abusive? Is it another example of a scolding father lashing out at a child, telling her that it is for her own good? Is this not morally objectionable? If Hebrews suggests that God wills evil in order to bring about good, then certainly it is morally objectionable and this exhortation should be ignored. God cannot will evil. Where then does evil come from? The author of Hebrews neither raises nor addresses this question. His listeners face and have faced something evil. Like the faithful recalled in Hebrews 11, they were not delivered from it the first time, and Hebrews offers no guarantee they will be delivered this time. What the author does suggest is that whatever they face should be thought of as something more than the bare act of aggression brought against them by their oppressors. The Father uses it to discipline them just as Christ's cross was the means for his obedience.

One way the Christian tradition makes sense of this inevitable feature of our redemption in Christ is to divide his righteousness in terms of an active and passive aspect. His active righteousness is the good he performs; it is his perfection. As the fullness of being, it would be complete, lacking nothing. However, when performed in the context of a sinful and rebellious creation, this perfection incites resistance. Christ's perfection exists without this resistance in heaven but not in a fallen creation. Thus to will the former, his active righteousness, requires at the same time willing the latter, the passive righteousness that endures trials in the face of hostility. The hostility, however, can be endured because it contains something more than bare resistance. God is present even in it, willing the perfection that can endure and obtain the rest. This helps make sense of the striking results that Hebrews proclaims such endurance produces: "it yields the peaceful fruit of righteousness" (12:11). Struggle is not an end in itself; it is only the means that can be redeemed and taken up because of this "peaceful fruit." Far from advocating a resentment that only seeks the demise of enemies, the author of Hebrews calls his listeners to endure for the sake of peace. This also helps us make sense of the surprising concluding admonitions that flank either side of Hebrews' theophanic vision. On the face of it they are anything but radical or revolutionary. Hebrews concludes by calling for endurance and faithfulness in the most ordinary, mundane activities.

12:14–13:25

Concluding Paraklēsis *and Theophanic Vision: Pursue Peace and Holiness*

After telling us the story of the saints in chapter 11, and correlating their faith to our need for patience in chapter 12, Hebrews turns once again to admonition: "Pursue peace with everyone, and the holiness without which no one will see the Lord." Peace and holiness are gifts from God, who brought them out of even the most violent of situations, such as Abraham's willingness to sacrifice Isaac. Peace and holiness define the politics of Jesus. Hebrews returns to these themes in its closing benediction. In what Harold Attridge defines as a "rare, Jewish expression,"[1] it sums up the entire letter poignantly in terms of peace and holiness: "Now may the God of peace, who brought back from the dead our Lord Jesus, the great shepherd of the sheep, by the blood of the eternal covenant, make you complete in everything good so that you may do his will, working among us that which is pleasing in his sight, through Jesus Christ, to whom be the glory forever and ever. Amen" (13:20–21). Holiness is being made complete in everything good the God of peace provides through Jesus' resurrection.

What is the God of peace "working among us"? Surely it is his own peace, which we are to pursue with all, including our enemies. Now we see again the significance of Hebrews' neglecting Psalm 110:2, 3. Nowhere does this letter call on its audience to form a people's militia and protect one another's lives and property. Instead they are called to "go to him outside the camp [*parembolēs*] and bear the

1. Attridge, *Hebrews*, 405.

abuse he endured" (Heb. 13:13). The term *parembolē* means a fortified camp. It can also mean "army." It was the term used to describe the location of the Levites in Numbers 1:50. They "camp" around the tabernacle. Unlike the other twelve tribes, the Levites are not part of the census of those "able to go to war" (Num. 1:2–3).[2] But each of those tribes then camps around the Levites, who perform "guard duty" over the tabernacle. Given Hebrews' preoccupation with the tabernacle and the Levitical priesthood, the author may be thinking of this construction of sacred space when he calls us to go "outside the camp." Perhaps he calls us out of this fortified camp in order to meet Jesus?

The "space" in which God revealed God's glory to Israel was that of the tabernacle/temple, which we have already noted. It is a space where transcendence and immanence meet without either collapsing into the other. This space was overseen by the Levitical priesthood, which was in turn guarded by the camps of the twelve tribes. The author of Hebrews takes up this same sense of a complex space. However, he finds the meeting of transcendence and immanence to be present now in Christ's body. This makes it more reliable, firm, and eternal than the previous space. When God shakes the creation and all the nations, they will not be able to stand. But the city the priest-king Christ builds will withstand such shaking because he rules and exercises his office from the heavenly temple, which like his body is immutable and eternal. The architecture of many churches demonstrates Christ's triumph and the kind of king he is. When you enter the church, which if properly constructed would be facing east in the direction of the rising sun, you see the crucified Christ, who is according to Hebrews both priest and victim. But when you leave the church, you see an image of Christ as the risen, ascended king. You cannot see the king if you do not first gaze upon the priest who is victim.

2. Nickelsburg, *1 Enoch*, 382.

FURTHER REFLECTIONS
The Politics of the Priest-King

Plato posed a question about politics that any generation forgets only to its peril. In its simplest form the question is, Who guards the guardians? Politics often assumes that we set aside certain persons to rule over us. Those persons are our guardians, and they are entrusted with the means of violence that is supposed to protect us. In other words, they are given brute power. But to what end is this power to be used? If it is an end in itself, as occurs when national security becomes the overriding preoccupation of any politics, then the power knows no limits. Christian tradition has always *in theory* set limits to the exercise of this power, either through its opposition to war or through the limits it places upon it. Power must be used for well-stated purposes. But who knows those purposes? For Plato, only the philosophers truly know those purposes, for they alone know "the good." A just city only arises when the use of power is subordinate to the good. This would require a "philosopher-king." The king would not only be someone of practical skill who knows how to match means to ends, but he would also be a contemplative who has the theoretical wisdom to know the good such practical skills should serve. But for Plato the king must also tell the "noble lie," and here is where the religious cult, and perhaps religious ideology, finds its place. Religion serves the civic interest by keeping people in their proper stations so that the guardians do not exceed their authority.

Plato recognized that most people who chase after political authority seldom pursue a life contemplating the good, but without this no just city is possible. Plato begins his account of the just city by having Thrasymachus cynically challenge Socrates by saying that justice is nothing but "the advantage of the stronger."[3] If that constitutes justice, then it would be power without the good. The philosopher-king is his answer to Thrasymachus's statement. The question Plato posed prompted responses from Jewish and Christian sources. Augustine's *City of God* is one of the most eloquent

3. Plato, *The Republic of Plato,* trans. Allan Bloom (New York: Basic Books, 1968), 15 (338c).

Christian responses. Augustine argues that without the proper worship of the true God, there can be no truly just city. Rather than the contemplation of the good, it is contemplation of God in worship that properly limits power. Hebrews, I suggest, offers another such response. That may seem unwarranted. Hebrews nowhere mentions Plato's *Republic*, but I think this suggestion is defensible. This defense requires a discussion of Philo's two books on the life of Moses, for Philo did see in Moses an explicit answer to Plato's question. If the author of Hebrews knew Philo, which seems likely, then it would be hard to read Hebrews as not offering a similar argument in its depiction of Jesus as the priest-king. But even if the author of Hebrews did not know Philo, he offers us an excellent response to Plato's all-important question.

Philo offers two books on the life of Moses. The first discusses his "kingly power," and the second his powers as chief priest, lawgiver, and prophet.[4] Philo begins his second book by acknowledging the truth in Plato's philosopher-king. "For some persons say, and not without some reason and propriety, that this is the only way by which cities can be expected to advance in improvement, if either the kings cultivate philosophy, or if philosophers exercise the kingly power." Yet Philo recognizes that more than a philosopher-king is needed. For a truly just city or nation there is also need for a priest and prophet who give inspired legislation. Only Moses unites these powers; no one else has ever done so. As lawgiver he unites "humility, the love of justice, the love of virtue, and the hatred of iniquity." Philo argues that he is the "only one" who unites these four, and this is why his laws are fit for people who are truly free.[5] His laws have an "allure" rather than a "drive" to virtue.[6] Likewise in his exercise of the "priesthood" his piety perfects all the "fruits of virtue." Philo then discusses the "moveable temple" using expressions similar to, and yet significantly different from, Hebrews. Like Hebrews, it is "made by hands." It has a temporality that points to something eternal. But unlike Hebrews, Philo's eternal temple has more to do with what Daniélou called the "mystical temple." Moses builds the

4. Philo, *On the Life of Moses* 1.60.334; 2.1.1 (in *Works of Philo*, 490–91).
5. Ibid., 2.2.8, 10 (in *Works of Philo*, 491, 492).
6. Ibid., 2.9.51 (in *Works of Philo*, 495).

temple taking into account the "essences" by which God created the world. Moses builds it "contemplating with his soul the incorporeal patterns of bodies which were about to be made perfect."[7] It is an "emblem of the soul."[8] Philo also adds Moses' prophetic office to his most excellent ability to craft a just city. Moses embodies the prophetic power because of his inspired prediction of future events that save his people—the crossing of the Red Sea, the manna from heaven, the commands to hallow God's name and honor the Sabbath. For Philo, Moses' legislation is adopted by all the nations, for it is unlike other laws that are only for this or that nation. Moses' legislation is fit for all of creation because it is eternal.

Hebrews interprets Jesus as priest and king, and only indirectly as prophet. It does put prophetic words in his mouth at 10:5b–7, but it does not see any tension between priest and prophet. Hebrews' focus is on Christ as king and priest. The exordium began with his royal enthronement (1:3), and the catena that follows speaks of his "throne" (1:8). He is then "crowned" (2:7), and all things are placed in subjection to him (2:8). But his is an odd kingship, for it is won by his activity as a "faithful and merciful high priest" (2:17). Jesus then gets compared to Moses (3:1–6), but unlike Philo's defense of Moses as the true philosopher-king-priest, Hebrews emphasizes that those who followed Moses never entered into the promised rest. Not even his successor Joshua provided it. Instead, "A sabbath rest still remains for the people of God" (4:9). Hebrews, like Philo, is willing to claim that only one person truly answers Plato's question, but it is not Moses—it is Jesus the high priest (4:14). His priesthood is as odd as his kingship. Jesus is not from the tribe of the Levites. His priesthood comes from Melchizedek. But it even exceeds that of Melchizedek by its once-and-for-all sacrifice in which Jesus is both priest and victim. It is offered not in the temporal temple made by hands, but in the eternal temple where the king-priest reigns. His reign is not yet fully apparent, but it is nonetheless accomplished and unshakable. Hebrews will conclude chapter 12 with this important admonition: "Therefore, since we are receiving a kingdom that

7. Ibid., 2.15.74 (in *Works of Philo*, 497).
8. Ibid., 2.34.183 (in *Works of Philo*, 507).

> cannot be shaken, let us give thanks, by which we offer to God an acceptable worship with reverence and awe; for indeed our God is a consuming fire" (12:28–29). Cult and polis (or "kingdom," *basileia*) come together. The just city comes not from a philosopher-king who must tell a "noble lie" to keep people in order, but from a priest-king who makes himself a sacrifice, making possible a confession of "hope, faith, and love" (10:22–25). As Augustine said, the truly just city requires proper worship.

Hebrews concludes with a series of admonitions that are in many ways anticlimactic. Given what the author has called his listeners to endure, claims such as "pursue peace with everyone" or "let marriage be held in honor by all" are downright odd when faced with persecution. But Hebrews' admonitions make sense because of what the author has seen, and what his words show us—the "mountain" to which we have arrived. This theophanic vision in 12:18–24 renders the admonitions that come before and after it intelligible.

12:14–17

Pursue Peace and Holiness

Three admonitions come prior to this vision, although only the first is an imperative—"Pursue." The Greek structure is important in understanding this first important admonition. Verses 14–16 are one sentence, which begins with this admonition in the structure of a command: "Pursue peace with everyone, and the holiness without which no one will see the Lord." Everything that follows is best understood as explicating this command. The next word is a participle, *episkopountes* ("taking care"; NRSV "See to it"), which is followed by the repetition of three phrases, each beginning with a negation and indefinite pronoun: "not any" (*mē tis*). So the structure of the sentence is like this (my trans.):

1. Pursue peace with everyone, and the holiness without which no one shall see the Lord, taking care that
   a. no one (*mē tis*) falls short of the grace of God,

b. not any (*mē tis*) root of bitterness grows up causing trouble and through it defiling many,
c. no one (*mē tis*) is immoral (or a fornicator—*pornos*) or profane like Esau, who. . . .

Once we see the structure of this initial sentence it becomes clearer that it is a single admonition, "pursue peace . . . and holiness," that then gets filled out by the qualifications found in the phrases repeating the indefinite pronouns. They tell us how we "pursue peace and holiness." This is first accomplished by not falling short of God's grace. Here Hebrews repeats its central admonition, "hold fast the confession," through the variation, "do not fall short of God's grace." The second means of pursuing peace and holiness anticipates Nietzsche's critique: do not become bitter. In other words, do not let resentment arise because things did not go as planned. Such resentment is defiling; it causes persons to be reactive, knowing what they oppose rather than what they hold fast. It would keep us from peace and holiness. The novelist Graham Greene tells the story of a group of nuns who had dedicated their lives to taking care of lepers, and are then disappointed when a cure for leprosy is found. Their identity became so consumed with standing against the disease that they had secretly colluded with it, needing it for their sense of purpose. They lost sight of what they should have held fast, the wholeness of their patients, and now resented that wholeness when it should have been a cause for rejoicing. The lepers' wholeness took away their mission. How often is this played out in peoples' vocation to tend to the poor, fight the enemy, stand against the forces opposing revolution, or a myriad of other causes to which we give ourselves? If we begin to need what we oppose for the sake of who we are, then a root of bitterness arises when what we oppose gets taken away. Bitterness also arises when we think we have not been given what we deserve. This is the deadly vice of envy, which is the inability to rejoice when good things come to others because we think they should have come to us.

If the first two means by which we fail in the pursuit of peace and holiness are primarily negatives—we fail to obtain grace, we allow resentment and bitterness to take the place of the fullness from which we should live—the third is a positive, something we take on in exchange for peace and holiness. Our lives get filled with immorality and profanity. The first is most likely a reference to sexual immorality and the second to an irreligiousness or worldliness. Once again Esau is the witness to this, for he sold his inheritance to satisfy his hunger. Given how important holding fast to the inheritance is for Hebrews, it is easy to see that Esau's sin represents the preeminent threat his listeners face. Harking back to the rigorous teaching found in 6:4, the author tells his listeners that having betrayed the blessing Esau could not retrieve it even though he sought to do so with tears.

12:18–24

The City of the Living God

Hebrews interrupts the flow of admonitions by a theophanic temple vision. Verses 18–24 might seem out of place. They lack the imperative structure that characterizes this section. Nor do they fit with the string of practical counsel that flanks both sides of this section. Yet because the author just told his audience to "pursue peace . . . and the holiness without which no one will see the Lord," this interlude makes perfect sense. It follows upon the rigorous word about Esau as a word of comfort about the access they now have to God's presence. Zion fulfills Sinai. It does not do away with it. The serious call to holiness demanded by Sinai remains in effect. The author will follow up on these contrasting theophanies by reminding his listeners that "God is a consuming fire" (12:29). The serious call remains, but it has a mediator who is enthroned in a "festal gathering," who accomplished that holiness and is now the source and perfection of its fulfillment for others, some of whom are now "made perfect."

The author of Hebrews contrasts covenants, the one made at Mount Sinai with Moses and the other at Mount Zion with Jesus. An explicit mention of Sinai is not present, but it is clearly what the author has in mind. If Sinai represents the Mosaic covenant, Zion represents the Davidic. Hebrews has not rejected the former. Moses was "faithful in all God's house as a servant" (3:5). Yet the emphasis on the temple, the cult, the "house," and the "heavenly Jerusalem" offer a different window into the Old Testament than the Mosaic covenant alone would have provided. The holiness demanded by it incited an unendurable awe. The mountain they were called to approach was so holy that an animal was to be stoned if it touched it. (People were to be stoned as well, but Hebrews does not mention that.) In Exodus 19:10–11 Moses was commanded to "consecrate" the people by washing them and preparing them to receive the Torah.[9] In Exodus 20, once the people were prepared, God gave them the Ten Commandments. In order to make these preparations God told Moses, "Set limits around the mountain and keep it holy" (Exod. 19:23). This was a material, concrete holiness. What one did and did not touch mattered.

Hebrews suggests a shift in holiness. This shift would be misconstrued if we interpret it as material versus immaterial, as earthly versus heavenly. The shift is better assessed if we examine carefully the relationship between these two mountains as Hebrews presents them.

Mt. Sinai: You have not approached . . .	Mt. Zion: You have approached . . .
something that can be touched	the city of the living God
a blazing fire . . .	the heavenly Jerusalem
a tempest	innumerable angels in festal gathering
the sound of a trumpet enrolled in heaven	the assembly of the firstborn
a voice whose words the hearers . . . could not endure	to God the judge of all
	to spirits of the righteous made perfect
	to Jesus, the mediator of a new covenant
	to the sprinkled blood that speaks a better word than the blood of Abel

9. See Attridge, *Hebrews*, 373.

Hebrews contrasts what they have not approached to what they have. This emphasizes the liturgical setting. To approach is to go toward God's presence; it is the act of gathering for worship. Exodus 19 emphasized the preparation necessary for such gathering given God's holiness and perfection. It required material, concrete commands about what could and could not be touched. When God appears on the holy mountain no one but the priest Aaron along with Moses can go on the mountain (Exod. 19:24). Like the high priest in the holy of holies, the presence of God is to be entered into with fear and trepidation. The first contrast between "something that can be touched" and "the city of the living God, the heavenly Jerusalem," suggests a contrast between something material and something immaterial. In part this is undeniable. This city is not locatable in the same way Sinai was. Zion is still to come even though it is already present in heaven. Angels, the firstborn, and the perfected spirits of the righteous inhabit it, but we cannot yet go to it and designate it by pointing. It cannot be "touched." But it is a reality through the "sprinkled blood." In that sense it is as material as Jesus himself. It is a liturgical site where people can gather in order to live in communion with "innumerable angels," and those who have gone before us, ordering their lives to God, Jesus, the spirit of the righteous, and the new covenant. So what then are they to do?

12:25–13:25

*Do Not Refuse the One Who Is Speaking. . . .
Let Mutual Love Continue*

With the "better word" that Jesus' blood speaks, and the admonition to "not refuse the one who is speaking [*ton lalounta*]," Hebrews' argument comes full circle with its concluding admonitions. It began by telling us "God has spoken" (*elalēsen*) in the Son (1:2). Now we are told the Son's blood is speaking (*lalounta*) a better word. We are told this by someone who wrote it in order for someone else to speak it. So when we are given the admonition, "do not refuse the one who is speaking," we are confused as to which one is meant: God, Jesus, the author of Hebrews, the leader of the community reading this sermon to its hearers? Given the admonitions that follow, the answer would seem to be, "yes, all of them." Now this is complicated further, for the church throughout the ages continues to read Hebrews as canonical Scripture, admonishing the people of faith, "do not refuse the one who is speaking." The "one" who is speaking has become so multiplied that his or her identity has layer upon layer of "authorship." Of course, the one who speaks in these concluding admonitions is first and foremost the one who spoke in Jesus Christ—it is God, whose voice shakes heaven and earth. He speaks for a purpose—that what can be shaken is removed and what cannot remains. The key admonitions leading up to chapter 13, then, are these four:

1. Lift your drooping hands and strengthen your weak knees (12:12) to run and endure what is before you!
2. Pursue peace with everyone, and the holiness without which no one will see the Lord (12:14)!
3. Do not refuse the one who is speaking (12:25)!
4. Let us give thanks, by which we offer to God an acceptable worship with reverence and awe (12:28)!

These are the ethical results of the doctrinal teaching to which the author asks us to hold fast. These four admonitions and the ones that follow in chapter 13 only make sense in the light of Hebrews' presentation of who Christ is and what he has done. Lose hold of that central point and it all comes tumbling down. The third admonition is the foundation for all the others. It is a variation on the first admonition that followed upon the exordium and catena: "pay attention!" (2:1). Before examining the concluding admonitions, we should consider what it means not to refuse the one speaking. We can do so by returning once again to the all-important exordium and examining more fully the two crucial claims that begin and conclude Hebrews. First, *in these last days God has spoken to us by a Son;* second, *do not refuse the one who is speaking*. These two passages should be read together. To understand and hear God speak in the Son is not to refuse the one who is speaking and vice versa.

Now that we come to the concluding chapter of Hebrews we are in a much better place to understand what it meant to say, "God has spoken to us by a Son." God's speaking in the Son communicates such that it draws those who hear it into a unity, a unity that should characterize their worship, doctrine, and ethics. God's communication, in other words, creates communion, a common unity affecting all those means that allow us to communicate with one another—including language, sex, and economics. How we think and speak about one of these will necessarily affect how we think and speak about the others; for all of these are means of communion God has given to us in order to communicate God's own being to us. Such a communication is also an invitation to communicate in the lives of one another. This rich communion challenges any "flat" world that can be laid out on a grid because our lives are implicated in each other's through our common confession, worship, and ethics. There is no such thing as a "bare" exchange whether it comes to language, sex, or economics. What we confess, how we worship, relates to our sexual and economic practices. The Word Hebrews communicates draws us into a communion that requires attention to all these matters. Indeed, once the words are read and heard, they already communicated something. From "*in these last days God has spoken to us by a Son*" to "*do not refuse the one who is speaking*" a common unity that furthers that communion is being formed among Hebrews' hearers. To take the time to listen to it has already accomplished communion through communication.

God speaks in a specific time, but one that does not come to an end. God speaks "*in* these last days" (1:2) and "yet once more" (12:27). God also speaks through a specific means. Hebrews emphasizes that God speaks in and through the flesh, the concrete materiality of the Son. This is why it says that for God to speak in the Son, he "had to become like his brothers and sisters in every respect" (2:17). This fleshes out for us (pun intended) the common meaning of the statement, "God has spoken to us by a Son." There is a beauty to God's speech that must be seen before it can be heard, an indestructible beauty. If God communicates, then the places and times of that communication will possess a beauty we are obliged to honor. It is a "festal gathering." Such spaces cannot be reduced to the hideous, even when they are destroyed, for they are God's communication to us. Was this not true of the tabernacle, the ark of the covenant, the temple, its liturgy and priesthood, and even the flesh of Christ? Although they are destroyed, they continue to speak throughout Hebrews' message just like Abel's sacrifice.

The materiality of God's Word, through creation, is beautiful. When God speaks it is unlike all other speaking. The Jewish exegete Philo offers some help here: "God is not like a man, in need of a mouth, and of a tongue, and of a windpipe, but as it seems to me, he at that time wrought a most conspicuous and evidently holy miracle, commanding an invisible sound to be created in the air, more marvelous than all the instruments that ever existed, attuned to perfect harmonies; and that not an inanimate one." For Philo God's Word is not inanimate but animate. It creates, and creation is material. The embodied character of God's miraculous Word is found in the flaming fire.[10] It is the creaturely means of God's communication, and that communication can be seen as readily as it can be heard. Philo says it must be seen before it is heard.

> **For the truth is that the voice of men is calculated to be heard; but that of God to be really and truly seen. Why is this? Because all that God says are not words, but actions which the eyes determine on before the ears.**
>
> **—Philo**
>
> *The Decalogue* 9.33; 11.44-49 in *Works of Philo*, 520

Philo draws on the story of the burning bush that first catches Moses' eye before he can hear God speak. The church fathers loved this. It is one of the reasons they drew so heavily on Philo—because of his emphasis on the materiality of the Word. Was this not fulfilled in the Son? "God has spoken to us by a Son" who is "the same yesterday and today and forever." In that speaking we not only hear, but we also see. God's Word is so substantial that it not only can be heard, but it must be seen. God's Word is the most substantial thing in all of creation; everything else is insubstantial in comparison. It is the "cornerstone" on which it is all constructed. As Hebrews reminds us, "But we do see Jesus."

10. Philo, *The Decalogue* 9.33; 11.44–49 (in *Works of Philo,* 520–22).

FURTHER REFLECTIONS

The God Who Speaks

God speaks in the *Son*. But it is *God* who speaks in the Son. To not refuse the one who is speaking requires that we can locate the subject who speaks—God. We must share in common a language about God. This is not prescriptive; it is descriptive. It is what has to be for Hebrews' communication to take place. We find our common language of God in Scripture, and especially the first three commandments given to Moses. To understand the God who spoke in the Son and whom we must not refuse, we have to receive who God is through the canonical witness of Holy Scripture, not Gnosticism, *1 Enoch*, or Philo—as illuminating as they may be. For the author of Hebrews the Mosaic and Davidic covenants are not forgotten. He assumes them and draws on them to make sense of Jesus. Jesus is not some radical singularity who comes like a bolt out of the blue. Those other covenants render his life intelligible even as he fulfills them. Although the author of Hebrews does not state the commandments, clearly his argument assumes them, especially as they allow us to locate the God who speaks.

Exodus 20:2–4, 7

1. **I am the Lord your God, who brought you out of the land of Egypt; . . . you shall have no other gods before me.**
2. **You shall not make for yourself an idol, whether in the form of anything that is in heaven above, or that is on the earth beneath, or that is in the water under the earth.**
3. **You shall not make wrongful use of the name of the Lord your God, for the Lord will not acquit anyone who misuses his name.**

The beauty of these commandments is that they instruct us in what can and cannot be said about God. The first commandment tells us that God acts, the second that God is not a creature, and the third that God's name must not be used to express vain and empty things. They help us recognize what it does and does not mean to say, "God has spoken to us by a Son." For instance, if having heard this read, someone sincerely asked, "Does God then have a mouth?" we would know that we have miscommunicated, that we do not share in communion; we lack a common language that binds us together in the worship of God who is not a creature. This violates the second commandment. It should not keep us from speaking about God. We know it is permissible to say (metaphorically), "God is a rock" or "God is a friend." We would all recognize, I trust, that it would be impermissible to say, "God is that rock," or "God is my friend Bob."

The first commandment *requires* that we speak of God. God acts in history. To know the God who communicates in the Son is to meet God in this history. It is to receive God's name as one of our greatest gifts. This name is a "sacred possession" entrusted to Israel. It is the same name that is given to Jesus in the exordium—"I AM WHAT I AM" (Hebrew: *'ehyeh 'asher 'ehyeh*). God is "to be" the great I AM, the fullness of being, lacking nothing. We stand in a tradition that has developed these divine names so that we might know when we speak we are properly communicating God.

The fathers and mothers of the church articulated what these commandments mean for proper speech about God: God is simple (without parts) and therefore lacking nothing. God is not a potentiality yet to be realized, but a pure activity, the fullness of goodness. In other words, God is perfect. Because God has no potentiality and is perfect, God is immutable and impassible. God cannot be affected by creation, which does not mean God is aloof or does not sorrow or is incapable of love or emotion. As Herbert McCabe notes, God's nearness is more intimate to us than the term "suffering" permits.[11] God is also infinite, eternal, and one. What this language provides is, as David Burrell states, more a regulative grammar about how we speak of God than some kind of ontological description of who God is.[12] This grammar reminds us of the second commandment—God is not a creature who can be given the "form of anything that is in heaven above, or that is on the earth beneath, or that is in the water under the earth." But this only makes our effort to understand what it means to say "*God* speaks" all the more difficult. We already noted that a basic condition for our ability to communicate is that

11. See Herbert McCabe, "The Involvement of God," in *God Matters* (Springfield, IL: Templegate Publishers, 1991), 44–45.
12. See David Burrell, *Aquinas: God and Action* (London: Routledge & Kegan Paul, 1979), 16–17.

we are creatures. We speak because we are creatures. So how is it possible to say that God, who is not a creature, "speaks"? How does God speak without being changed into a creature like us? We could easily miscommunicate at this point, restricting our speaking about God to the status of the conditions necessary for speech, an all too common pitfall in modern theology that demands a logical univocity between God and us for our language to be meaningful.

Here we must remember the first three commandments together: First, I am the Lord God who acts. Second, do not attribute to me any creaturely form. Third, do not misuse my name. The first tells us God does act. The second reminds us that when we speak of God's acting, we must always recognize the difference between God's activity and that of creatures, even when we necessarily use creaturely means to speak of God. And the third tells us that when we use God's name we must not misuse it. God commands that we not *misuse* God's name, not that we avoid using it altogether. The commandments require that we speak of God's actions. We are commanded to use God's name, but must do so in such a way that we do not attribute creaturely form to God. This helps us know what we are not to say and how we are not to speak, so we can say what must be said well.

I think it teaches us to avoid two temptations, temptations especially prominent in contemporary preaching and theology. The first temptation is to treat God as the sublime about which nothing can be said, because if God exists, no one could know it given that we (supposedly) know the limits of our knowledge. For those of a philosophical bent, this is our Kantian inheritance; it is the epistemological policing some philosophers and theologians set up. This is a real temptation because this policing makes sense. It has plausibility. It even obeys the second commandment—we do not give God any creaturely form. Let me give an example. I once participated in an interfaith event that opened with a Unitarian Universalist pastor offering this prayer: "We pray to you, the Unnameable God, not knowing how to address you, for we know that all the names we give you are only names we have come up with ourselves. Forgive us and remind us that you are beyond all our language." At this point I was no longer praying but doing philosophy because I wondered how she could know that—how could she know that God is unnameable, beyond our language? Only if she claims to know more about God than what the revealed names imply could she also know that those names never fit.

This reminds me of that very bad, supposedly Indian proverb about the elephant and the blind men, which was made famous in the English-speaking world by the nineteenth-century American poet (raised as a Methodist) John Godfrey Saxe. He used it to claim God was a sublime about whom nothing reasonable could be said. The parable has six blind men come upon an elephant and touch it, misconstruing what it is—a wall, a spear, a snake, a tree, a fan, and a rope. The moral of the story, Saxe noted, is this: "So oft in theologic wars, the disputants, I ween, rail on in utter ignorance of what each other mean, *and prate about an Elephant not one of them has seen!*" If you find yourself either using or agreeing with this parable, you may very well have fallen prey to this first temptation, which is not consistent with reason or faith. It is inconsistent with reason because the parable only works because you already know what an elephant is. It would not work if Saxe used it to speak about a zigwobjubilisk.

In other words, it is only because you tacitly claim to know more than you admit that this parable and the Unitarian Universalist's prayer works. It is because they claim to know who God is that they then tell us who God is not. It is inconsistent with faith because the first commandment and Hebrews commands that we speak and speak well of God's activities. "God has spoken to us by a Son. . . . do not refuse the one who is speaking." To fall prey to this epistemological policing is to ignore the basic message Hebrews conveys. It tells us to speak with "bold confidence"—act as if you are free citizens of God's city, living stones in the heavenly temple, and not sniveling creatures policed by insecurities.

If we fall prey to this first temptation to treat God only as the sublime about which nothing can be said, then every use of God's name by definition can only be a misuse. Then we will be reduced either to silence in order to keep the third commandment, or we will neglect keeping it altogether and capitulate to a second temptation. This also assumes a priori that we know our language about God is a naive effort to name the unnameable and all we are really

> doing is projecting language about ourselves onto God. There is no difference between saying "God is a friend" or "God is my friend Bob." All our language about God is really language about ourselves or about our own context. This second temptation is also a temptation because it seems so reasonable. If the first temptation treats God only as the wholly other who is never actually present to us, the second treats God as fully immanent—only found in history. God is reduced to an immanent divine force acting in history to accomplish God's own being, or "God" is the term we use to make sense of our own agency. Here everything can be said about God because "theology is [nothing but] anthropology.'"[13] For those of a philosophical bent, this would be the Hegelian-Feuerbachian inheritance. If we are to proclaim God's speaking, as we must, then either of these ways of speaking must be avoided. They can be avoided because Hebrews communicates God's speech, drawing us into a communion. God's communication is always, as Philo recognized, material. It produces material conditions of a common life; doctrine and ethics are inseparable.

After a stirring sermon on who Jesus is, how he is a faithful and merciful high priest who calls us to endurance even in the face of persecution, and summons us to boldness in our speech, Hebrews ends with some admonitions that might seem anticlimactic. Indeed, they caused some biblical scholars to wonder if chapter 13 was original. Here is a distillation of the basic thirteen admonitions found in this closing chapter.

1. Let mutual love continue.
2. Do not neglect to show hospitality to strangers.
3. Remember those who are in prison.
4. Let marriage be held in honor by all.
5. Keep your lives free from the love of money.
6. Remember your leaders, those who spoke the word of God to you; consider the outcome of their way of life.
7. Do not be carried away by all kinds of strange teachings.

13. Ludwig Feuerbach, *The Essence of Christianity* (N. Charleston, SC: Createspace Publishing, 2011), 123.

8. Let us then go to Jesus outside the camp and bear the abuse he endured.
9. Through him, then, let us continually offer a sacrifice of praise to God, that is, the fruit of lips that confess his name.
10. Do not neglect to do good and share what you have.
11. Obey your leaders and submit to them.
12. Pray for us.
13. Bear with my word of exhortation.

Although these thirteen concluding admonitions might appear mundane, they are a profound testimony to what it means to hear God definitively speak "by a Son." That speaking created a communion, which is obviously already present among Hebrews' audience. These admonitions do not call for something new, but to hold fast to what they were once doing. To say, "Let mutual love continue," suggests that it was once present. The author of Hebrews repeats what he called his listeners to in 10:25: mutual love entails not "neglecting to meet together." A similar exhortation is found in the second and tenth admonitions. They are called not to "neglect" certain things, which it is assumed they have been doing.[14] Do not neglect showing hospitality to strangers or sharing your goods. The two are related. The *koinōnia* (communion) called for is not only internal to the community but also open to the stranger. Indeed, the stranger may well be one of God's messengers. In welcoming strangers, we welcome God.

This should not be neglected in any Christian approach to immigration. I have a good friend who took her law degree from Yale University to work for migrant farmworkers. One day she brought a young Guatemalan woman, who had just had a baby, to our house because she needed a place to hide. She was fifteen years old and had been raped by the overseer at the work site. She came from the highlands in Guatemala where soldiers were sent to fight "communist rebels," and the local population was caught in the cross fire. She gave birth to her baby in the fields on a day she was picking

14. The verb used in 13:2 and 16, *epilanthanomai,* is not the same as that used in 10:25, *enkataleipō*.

sweet potatoes. The boss threatened to kidnap her baby, and she was scared. What would any Christian be called to do in this situation? If we refuse to show hospitality to strangers, then we have not heard the Word. Indeed, we need to show such hospitality in order to hear the Word. Likewise, we need to visit those in prison. Jesus himself "suffered outside the city," outside those places in which we find comfort and security, and we cannot know him if we do not join him there.

I have another friend who has always embodied the holiness for which Hebrews calls. He has spent his life living and ministering in gang territory. Once he was driving across country and consented to give a stranger a ride. He stopped for gas and returned to find that the stranger had disappeared. At first he thought, "At last I entertained an angel unaware!" Living with such an expectation means that he does not live in a flat world; it is a world still enchanted by God. But then he noticed that $10 of the $20 that was sitting on the car's console had also disappeared, and he did not figure that was the kind of thing an angel would do. When he called me to tell me this story, he rejoiced that he had made sufficient witness to this stranger that he only took half the money. To live by the exhortation to find in the stranger God's messenger is to move out of the flat metaphysics with which we have become comfortable. This is troubling because it is dangerous. It is to live by the reality that "here we have no lasting city." Thus we do not need to cling tightly to the cities that would call for our loyalty.

Not to cling to those cities allows us to use our money differently. Money often represents our attempt to secure our own existence. We live with the indeterminate apocalyptic reality that at any moment our world resources will run out and we will not have sufficient means to sustain our own lives. Against such an indeterminate apocalyptic, Hebrews advocates a determinate one: "The Lord is my helper: I will not be afraid. What can anyone do to me?" This is not mere sentimental rhetoric. Hebrews already told us what can happen in chapter 11. You might be stoned, sawn in two, persecuted, tormented, reduced to wandering as a stranger on the earth. Only because you hold fast to the confession that Christ will bring you to perfection would you dare to live without this kind of security.

Perhaps most odd in these admonitions is Hebrews' exhortation about sex. Given all that his community faces, why take the time to tell them to avoid fornication and adultery? Something more revolutionary would seem to be in order, such as "Fight the powers!" or "Long live the revolution!" Instead Hebrews takes the time to instruct its hearers not only about the use of money, obeying leaders, and living peacefully with others but also about sexuality. Contrast these admonitions with that given by Slavoj Žižek in his affirmation of the approach to sexual relationship found among the Bolshevik revolutionaries: "From what we know about love among the Bolshevik revolutionaries, something unique took place there, a new form of amorous couple emerged: a couple living in a permanent state of emergency, totally dedicated to the revolutionary Cause, ready to sacrifice all personal sexual fulfillment to it, even ready to abandon and betray each other if the Revolution demanded it, but simultaneously totally dedicated to each other, enjoying rare moments of extreme intensity together."[15] Living in an apocalyptic state of emergency requires a willingness to sacrifice everything for the cause, including fidelity to one's partner. Hebrews' listeners certainly lived in such a state of emergency.

These concluding admonitions offer a very different vision of life together than that of the Bolshevik revolutionaries. Rather than a willingness to betray one another in confronting one's enemies, Hebrews admonishes them to fidelity and peace, to communion. To avoid fornication and adultery is to live peacefully with one's neighbors. It is to share the goods of communal life without indulging in excess. Learning to share economic goods in common and at the same time being content with sexual "goods" go hand in hand. Isn't this why a bourgeois, capitalist society so often advocates sex without consequences? Does it not demand that we live in a state of apocalyptic emergency, one fabricated crisis after another that says, "If I don't get mine today I won't get it at all"?

What does it mean to "remember," "obey," and "submit" to leaders? These admonitions should make us nervous. There is a kind of

15. Žižek, *Living in the End Times,* 114.

obedience that is faithless, a blind obedience based solely on willfulness rather than anything reasonable. But there are also improper reasons why we find obedience problematic. We assume we are autonomous individuals who think for ourselves and must never obey another. This characterizes the Enlightenment. The eighteenth-century philosopher Immanuel Kant put it succinctly in his famous newspaper editorial answering the question, "What is Enlightenment?" It is "man's emergence from his self-imposed immaturity. Immaturity is the inability to use one's understanding without guidance from another. This immaturity is self-imposed when its cause lies not in lack of understanding, but in lack of resolve and courage to use it without guidance from another. *Sapere Aude* [dare to know]! 'Have courage to use your own understanding!'—that is the motto of enlightenment." In other words, Kant issued a command, "Think for yourself!" and many Westerners responded, "Okay." The irony of this should not be lost on us. Why is it a sign of immaturity to be guided by another in those aspects of life that matter most? Isn't this inevitable? But nearly every Westerner is a trained Kantian. It probably happened in kindergarten. A student came home from school with a note from the teacher that he did something inappropriate—put gum in Cindy's hair, or ate Jimmy's paste. His parents asked why, and his innocent answer was, "Billy did it." We all know the proper refrain, "If Billy jumped off a cliff, would you do that too?" In saying this we are, and we teach our children to be, obedient Kantians.

Imagine a different scenario. The son of Hebrews' author comes home to his father with a similar note. He asks him why and he says, "Ajax did it." His father's response might be, "Is Ajax worthy of emulation? Is his character sufficiently formed such that following him will allow you to discern good from evil and embody a virtuous life?" Of course, this could only be a rhetorical question for his father. His son does not yet have the trained ability himself to know whom he should emulate. (Perhaps he would read to him chap. 11.) That is his and the community leaders' responsibility. But he would never use language so poorly as to communicate that the answer is, "Think for yourself." Obedience to those worthy of imitation matters, but notice it is not every leader they are called to obey. They are called to obey those who spoke God's Word to them and whose manner of life authenticates it. Obedience is not a matter of blind will, but of truthful speech and life. Without the latter, no proper obedience is possible.

Herbert McCabe explains this well. Reminding us that the word "obedience" comes from the Latin *ob-audire,* "whether to listen," he writes, "Obedience is first of all an act of *learning,* though not learning an abstract or speculative truth, as when you learn biology or physics, but learning a practical truth, what is to be done, learning how to live. . . . Obedience only becomes perfect when the one who commands and the one who obeys come to share one mind. The notion of blind obedience makes no more sense in our tradition than would blind learning. It would be like the pupil who simply learns his lecture notes off by heart and parrots them in the exam."[16] Obedience cannot be had without a proper telling that produces a shared communion. Not to refuse the one who is speaking, not being carried away by strange teachings, and bearing the word of exhortation are conditions for obedience because they live from and produce communion.

Are not all these admonitions further expressions of that call Hebrews issued in beginning this closing section: "Pursue peace with everyone, and the holiness without which no one will see the Lord" (12:14)? What do that peace and holiness look like? The thirteen admonitions show us their shape. The author puts before us the beauty of holiness both in the famous litany of the faithful in chapter 11 and here in the encouragement to have our bodies exude that beauty. While much of this does not seem revolutionary or even extraordinary given the potential persecution his listeners face and what he is calling them to endure, attention to these admonitions provides insight into the theological politics he advocates throughout the letter. He attends to those forms of communication that matter most in everyday life. He does not tell the community to abandon everyday life, take to the hills, and wait for the Lord to return. His apocalyptic vision requires all the more attention to those basic forms of communication that constitute everyday life: language, sex, economics, worship, and the distribution and exercise of power.

16. McCabe, *God Matters,* 228–29.

That Hebrews is about language and communication should have been well established by now. From the exordium to the final admonition, "bear with my word of exhortation" (13:22), Hebrews invites its listeners to hear a word and by that be drawn into the communion God establishes in God's communication with us. Hebrews admonishes us to remember that we do not possess some right to use whatever language we want about God. Scripture and our forebears in faith must discipline our language about God through right doctrine ("Do not be carried away by all kinds of strange teachings") and right worship ("Through Jesus, then, let us continually offer a sacrifice of praise to God, that is, the fruit of lips that confess his name"). Such language matters because it will either communicate or miscommunicate. Just as we do not have some private language because communication would be impossible, so we must not have a private or individual theology. Language in common is what allows us to communicate with one another.

Nor must we consider our sexual or economic communication as somehow "private," as immune from public accountability. How we use language will influence our economics and sex. How we exchange with one another in economics will influence language and sex. And how we go about sexual activity influences our use of language and economics. These are all inextricably linked because they are forms of *communication*. If they are privatized they will be distorted. Recently I came across an essay on sex and family that was considered "radical." The author wrote, "I support the fight for everyone to make choices regarding how they wish to author their own lives [in their sexuality] and the meaning they seek for themselves and those they wish to define as 'family.'" This statement is unreasonable because it hides the truth of what everyone at some level agrees upon. Language cannot be used this way to talk about sex, any more than it can be used to discuss economics or language itself without concealing what must be communicated. Everyone says no to some choices and definitions of family, so this does not speak truthfully, and language is meant to communicate truth. Therefore the statement miscommunicates. If we replace "sex" and "family" with "economics" and "theology," notice how a similar form of miscommunication occurs. "I support the fight for everyone to make choices regarding how they wish to author their own lives [in their use of money] and the meaning they seek for themselves and those they wish to define as 'trading partners.'" Or: "I support the fight for everyone to make choices regarding how they wish to author their own lives [in doctrine and worship] and the meaning they seek for themselves and those they wish to define as 'church.'"

Such admonitions are not radical; they are the commands that bombard us every day through the market, the university, and unfortunately the church. They provide the basic contours to modern political life. The theological politics of Hebrews differs. It calls for a "communion," a "sharing in common" (*koinōnias,* Heb. 13:16) in doctrine, worship, and ethics.

This communion begins and ends with God speaking. Those of us who have received the bold witness that God has spoken in the Son already find God communicating with us before we arrived to hear it read to us. God's communication to us is always material. It is seen before it is heard. It produces a communion that is spiritual and yet always visible, requiring that we hold the material conditions for everyday life—ethics, worship, doctrine—in common. Our task is to pay attention.

Conclusion

"In these last days he [God] has spoken to us by a Son." Hebrews begins and ends here; it is a repetition of God's unique speech in Christ, a material word that must be seen and heard in order to infuse its hearers with the confidence and endurance that arise from faith and hope. What it means for God to speak "by a Son" initiates the letter and then gets fleshed out in thirteen chapters, which the author(s) intend to be read and heard attentively. The purpose of such attentiveness is that we will "bear with" its "word of exhortation." Such a "bearing with" requires patience that calls us to "hold fast the confession" even in the midst of temptations to drift away. Those temptations differ in each generation of Christians, and among them in their various geographical and historical contexts. Perhaps the temptation is to cowardice in the face of persecution, or ambition through the potential loss of status? It might be sloth through complacency or settledness. Perhaps it is despair over the church's own failings. Whatever it might be, Hebrews still speaks: hold fast, be patient, be bold.

The power to hold fast the confession is not some ethical agency we have solely through our own resources. It is only possible because "God speaks." The sermon began there, showing how God spoke through the Son and how that speech is found in the Old Testament. This required admonition ("pay attention") and encouragement ("hold fast"). Behind both this admonition and encouragement is an unshakable hope. God seeks to share God's glory with us just as God did with the Son. Hebrews does not call its readers out of creation. It presents us with a vivid, theophanic image of creation, a creation filled with God's glory. If Jesus can bear God's name and make it holy, then God can share that glory with all creation. The shadowy, flat creation we inhabit will be infused with a "festal gathering" that perfects it, a richness that we see in Jesus even if it is not yet complete. This is nothing less than the City of God, the city for which we wait. It is a city that puts in question any final allegiance to all other cities that are constructed solely by immanent, human power. Jesus produces the firstfruits of this glorious city, which fruits are found in his house. If we are attentive, we are that house, the first shoots breaking forth out of dry ground. This is a scandalous, provocative claim that requires boldness and faith to sustain, but without which we cannot hear or see well God's glory.

The glory of that house is found in Jesus' person and mission, and his ability to share that mission with others. He does this because of his unique priesthood, which unlike that of the Levites is permanent—one sacrifice alone suffices. He is a priest according to the order of Melchizedek. The heart of the sermon is that we have a faithful and merciful high priest who held fast, and holds fast, even when he was tempted in all things as we are. It is by looking to him that we can hold fast because the confession we hold is that he is our unshakable high priest who offers a sufficient sacrifice on our behalf. The first half of the sermon establishes his faithfulness before Hebrews turns to its significance for us, and calls us to share in his faithfulness.

Christ's sacrifice accomplishes at least two things for us. First it cleanses, then it purifies or perfects. It cleanses by removing what cannot be held fast in God's glorious presence: fear, death, sin, and demonic evil. But Hebrews' message is not primarily negative. It does not tell us what we are not to be, but focuses on what we are and shall be. It is in the light of that glorious image that these other things fall away. Hebrews offers an anthropology that soars far above the giddiest Enlightenment account of what humans could accomplish. We are called to perfection, to a fullness that allows for God and creatures to live together—as it is in heaven so it will be on earth. Holding fast, then, is not a bare endurance, as if we were merely to hang on with all our might and muddle through as best we can. It is something much more than that; it is a boldness in speech and action, in doctrine and ethics that can only make sense if we believe, like Abraham, in resurrection. Its concluding benediction emphasizes this. The God of peace can perfect or complete creation because he has brought Christ back from the dead.

Hebrews boldly proclaims that we do know something about who God is and what God has done on our behalf, and we are not to have some false humility about it. But Hebrews also boldly admonishes that because we do know something about who God is and what God has done for us, we are to witness consistent with what God has done. The admonitions and the doctrines work together; both show us who God is and what God does. This is what makes fidelity, obedience, and hospitality possible. We follow a faithful and merciful high priest who does not seek revenge or cling to hope solely out of resentment. We do not fight some lack that we long for and can never attain, but live out of the fullness Christ himself is, the source of our perfection. It allows us to take the time to be faithful in a world where such faithfulness will most likely not be rewarded. In so doing we find ourselves among the saved, among those whose lives were so filled with faith and endurance that they persisted in their perfection despite success or failure. They were drawn by a vision of God's rest that gave hope and provoked them to love. We are admonished to be and do likewise.

I began this commentary suggesting that Hebrews assists us in negotiating troubled times, that it troubles us in the complacency of our own flat metaphysics, and that it teaches us how to read Scripture after God has definitively spoken in the Son. These three concerns relate to one another. Hebrews helps us negotiate troubled times by drawing us into a communion, where our lives are mystically linked to one another and to God, and all God's entourage of creaturely beings—a festal gathering. Hebrews admonishes all Christians "to provoke one another to love and good deeds, not neglecting to meet together." Since the Great Schism of the eleventh century, followed by the numerous divisions besetting Christ's body since the sixteenth, we have not been able to attend to this admonition. We cannot yet meet together. Hebrews suggests that such a situation will bring upon it a "fearful prospect of judgment." Perhaps the divisions and their consequences are themselves judgment? This means we can never be content with the divisions among us in our life together, whether they are doctrinal, liturgical, or ethical. We are called to communion. That does not mean homogeneity, but it does mean we hold things in common, for God is building a house or temple, and we are to be its stones. Stones do not determine the architectural plan; they inherit it by being formed together through the Architect's work.

Here is where Hebrews also challenges our modern flat metaphysics. Our lives cannot be rendered intelligible by the bare exchange of goods and services, as if all that matters is fulfilling the minimum obligations of a contract and then walking apart from one another. The communion Hebrews creates seeks more than that. How we use our money, our goods, our sexuality, and our language are all matters that affect one another's ability to be faithful, which is what it means to be brought into a communion. We are not our own; we belong to Christ. What we do is what he now does in part, and what he does is what we are called to do. Once anyone has heard and attended to Hebrews' sermon, she or he can no longer be a mere individual whose doctrine and ethics are left to her or his own devices. We are members of one another, and Christ is our priest-king who forms us into his body.

The importance of Christ's body as our temple also teaches us how to read Scripture well. The sources within which we hear its message will inevitably function as canons that produce normative content for doctrine and ethics. Hebrews insists that we understand Jesus in the context of God's call to Israel and its sacred places and times. If we lose that context, we will lose the ability to hear well. Far from being supersessionist, Hebrews demands that we be attentive readers of God's call upon Israel's life if we are to recognize how we now share in that call. If we do not recognize how God's glory was manifest in the name, the temple, and its liturgy, we will not understand what it means for Christ to bear that name and perfect the temple and its liturgy. The call of Israel is a call to make God's name holy and share in his glory, a call for the richest possible form of communion. Jesus does not reject that call for some other; consistent with the words of the prophets, he brings it to completion.

That we must continue to read Hebrews reminds us as well that our communion is not yet perfect or complete. We have also all miscommunicated—with our language, our worship, our doctrine, and our ethics. I do not want to leave the reader with some unrealizable ideal of communion. I continually wonder why the author of Hebrews continued to write after his first sentence. He tells us God has definitively spoken in the Son such that no more needs to be said, and then goes on to say a great deal more for thirteen chapters. That we all miscommunicate reminds us that we all stand in the same situation as those who have not yet seen or heard as they should. Most of us are the immature, seeing only in part. One hopes that this keeps us from improper judgments, which are always a source for disunity. When we wrongly judge one another, the result is further division because we miscommunicate. Nonetheless, that we miscommunicate should provide no solace. We are called to discern good and evil. We cannot receive the glory of God's communion by a laissez-faire approach to doctrine and ethics that lets each one decide for her- or himself. Instead, Hebrews reminds us we are to "hold fast the confession" and trust in the priest-king who gathers us in order to train our character to distinguish good from evil, the true from the false, the beautiful from the hideous, so that we might see and hear rightly as we go on toward perfection. That is obviously not easy, as the nearly two thousand years of church history since Hebrews was penned amply demonstrate. It is nonetheless a necessary practice of the Christian life—to give and receive counsel in terms of doctrine and ethics until we are perfect. If we had already heard the message of Hebrews perfectly, we would not need it repeated. We will need to repeat it until Christ returns. Until that time Hebrews' benediction sustains us in hope as we hold fast the confession:

> Now may the God of peace, who brought back from the dead our Lord Jesus, the great shepherd of the sheep, by the blood of the eternal covenant, make you complete in everything good so that you may do his will, working among us that which is pleasing in his sight, through Jesus Christ, to whom be the glory forever and ever. Amen.
>
> Hebrews 13:20–21

For Further Reading

Aquinas, Thomas. *Commentary on the Epistle to the Hebrews*. Trans. and ed. Chrysostom Baer, O. Praem. South Bend, IN: St. Augustine's Press, 2006.

Attridge, Harold W. *The Epistle to the Hebrews*. Hermeneia. Philadelphia: Fortress Press, 1989.

Barker, Margaret. *The Great High Priest: The Temple Roots of Christian Liturgy*. London: T & T Clark, 2003.

Bauckham, Richard, Daniel R. Driver, Trevor A. Hart, and Nathan MacDonald, eds. *The Epistle to the Hebrews and Christian Theology*. Grand Rapids: Eerdmans, 2009.

Bruce, F. F. *The Epistle to the Hebrews*. Rev. ed. New International Commentary on the New Testament. Grand Rapids: Eerdmans, 1990.

Calvin, John. *The Epistle of Paul the Apostle to the Hebrews*. Trans. William B. Johnston. Calvin's Commentaries. Grand Rapids: Eerdmans, 1963.

Congar, Yves M.-J. *The Mystery of the Temple, or, The Manner of God's Presence to His Creatures from Genesis to the Apocalypse*. Trans. Reginald F. Trevett. Westminster, MD: Newman Press, 1962.

Demarest, Bruce. *A History of Interpretation of Hebrews 7, 1-10 from the Reformation to the Present*. BGBE 19. Tübingen: Mohr (Siebeck), 1976.

deSilva, David A. *Perseverance in Gratitude: A Socio-Rhetorical Commentary on the Epistle "to the Hebrews."* Grand Rapids: Eerdmans, 2000.

Dunn, James D. G. *Christology in the Making: A New Testament Inquiry into the Origins of the Doctrine of the Incarnation.* 2nd ed. Grand Rapids: Eerdmans, 1996.

Ellingworth, Paul. *The Epistle to the Hebrews: A Commentary on the Greek Text.* New International Greek Testament Commentary. Grand Rapids: Eerdmans, 1993.

Hay, David M. *Glory at the Right Hand: Psalm 110 in Early Christianity.* Society of Biblical Literature Monograph Series 18. Nashville: Abingdon Press, 1973.

Heen, Erik M., and Philip D. W. Krey, eds. *Hebrews.* Ancient Christian Commentary on Scripture 10. Downers Grove, IL: InterVarsity Press, 2005.

Hurst, L. D. *The Epistle to the Hebrews: Its Background of Thought.* SNTSMS 65. Cambridge: Cambridge University Press, 1990.

Johnson, Luke Timothy. *Hebrews: A Commentary.* New Testament Library. Louisville: Westminster John Knox Press, 2006.

Käsemann, Ernst. *The Wandering People of God: An Investigation of the Letter to the Hebrews.* Trans. Roy A. Harrisville and Irving L. Sandberg. Minneapolis: Augsburg, 1984.

Koester, Craig R. *Hebrews: A New Translation with Introduction and Commentary.* Anchor Bible. New York: Doubleday, 2001.

Lane, William L. *A Call to Commitment.* Peabody, MA: Hendrickson, 1985.

Luther, Martin. *Nachschriften der Vorlesungen über Römerbrief, Galaterbrief und Hebräerbrief* in *D. Martin Luther's Werke: Kritische Gesamtausgabe* 57. Weimar: Herman Böhlaus Nachfolger, 1939.

Moffatt, James. *A Critical and Exegetical Commentary on the Epistle to the Hebrews.* International Critical Commentary. 1924. Repr. Edinburgh: T & T Clark, 1979.

O'Regan, Cyril. *Theology and the Spaces of Apocalyptic.* Milwaukee: Marquette University Press, 2009.

Peterson, David. *Hebrews and Perfection: An Examination of the Concept of Perfection in the "Epistle to the Hebrews."* SNTSMS 47. Cambridge: Cambridge University Press, 1982.

Schenck, Kenneth. *Cosmology and Eschatology in Hebrews: The Settings of the Sacrifice*. SNTSMS 143. Cambridge: Cambridge University Press, 2007.

———. *Understanding the Book of Hebrews: The Story Behind the Sermon*. Louisville: Westminster John Knox Press, 2003.

Thompson, James W. *Hebrews*. Paideia Commentaries on the New Testament. Grand Rapids: Baker Academic, 2008.

Vanhoye, Albert. *Structure and Message of the Epistle to the Hebrews.* Trans. James Swetnam, S.J. Rome: Editrice Pontificio Istituto Biblico, 1989.

Index of Ancient Sources

Old Testament

Apocrypha

WISDOM

PSEUDEPIGRAPHA

Greek and Latin Works

Index of Subjects